Cornered

Dr. Richard J. Sharpe
As I Knew Him

Linda DeFruscio

Twilight Times Books
Kingsport Tennessee

Cornered: Dr. Richard J. Sharpe As I Knew Him

Twilight Times Books
Kingsport TN 37664
http://twilighttimesbooks.com/

First Edition, January 2015

Library of Congress Control Number: 2014957681

ISBN: 978-1-60619-103-3

Credits
  Author photo by Mark Karlsberg, Studio Eleven, Inc.
  Cover artwork by Maureen Precopio
  Photos of younger Richard Sharpe by Linda DeFruscio.
  Photo of Richard Sharpe medical school graduation (1993) by FayFoto Boston
  Photo of Richard Sharpe in prison (2002) by Michael Fein.

Printed in the United States of America.

Disclaimer

The author has recreated events, locales and conversations from her memories of them, from her personal journals, and from the many stories that appeared in newspapers and on TV in conjunction with Richard Sharpe's crime, incarceration, and, ultimately, his death. The author also obtained information directly from her interactions with Richard Sharpe. In order to safeguard the privacy of the various people who walked in and out of Richard Sharpe's life, the author has changed names and in some cases identifying characteristics such as occupation and location of residence. Although the author has made every effort to ensure that the information in this book is correct, the author does not assume and hereby disclaims any liability to any party for any loss, damage, or disruption caused by errors or omissions, whether such errors or omissions result from negligence, accident, or any other cause.

Dedication

To my husband, Greg, for his patience, love, and the understanding he displayed in allowing me the space I needed, initially to maintain my friendship with Richard Sharpe, and later, to collect my thoughts and notes and begin the long process of writing my story. Greg endured prison visits and body searches in order to be at my side when I needed him, and he remains compassionate towards Richard's circumstances.

To my mother, Jean, who taught me not to be judgmental and who tolerated my questions and permitted me to write about her mental illness in the hope that her part in my story would be helpful to other people suffering psychological disorders.

Foreword

From the moment Dr. Richard Sharpe came into Linda DeFruscio's office for electrology treatment, Linda was captivated by his genius, his ambition, and his business acumen. Motivated by their mutual dedication to helping clients/patients and her personal desire to create a successful electrology and laser hair removal practice, Linda became entangled in his orbit.

Looking back over a decade after this once brilliant, highly successful doctor's life spiraled downward, ultimately leading to his killing his wife, Linda attempts to reconcile her enduring connection with Sharpe. Cornered makes us all question what we would do in this same moral dilemma. Would we stay loyal to our mentor and friend? Or, would we abandon him in his darkest hour?

Linda's life comes full circle in her story, from being a child visiting her own father in prison to being an adult visiting Dr. Sharpe in prison. She shares never-before-published revealing details—garnered from their conversations and from his letters to her from prison—about his early history, family life and more. Her portrayal of him in her book is necessarily complicated. Yet she is able to shift our view from the one-dimensional portrait presented by the media—of Dr. Richard Sharpe as cross-dressing wife killer—to a more intricate portrait that reveals him as an ambitious and disciplined student who worked his way through college and medical school, a successful dermatologist dedicated to curing his patients' cancers, a loving father and husband, and finally, a man whose untreated mental illness set him off on a downward trajectory that led to his family's destruction and his eventual imprisonment and death.

Linda's story of Dr. Richard Sharpe is framed within her own account of being swept up in the current leading to her own successful business, and the price she ultimately paid—emotionally, financially and professionally—for both her ambition and her loyalty. Linda, however, did not allow the various misfortunes that came her way, via her connection with Sharpe, to break her. She learned as a child that there is strength to be gained in life lessons, and this, in addition to her shining example of steadfast compassion—not only for Dr. Sharpe but for all people in pain—is one of the great values of the book.

I have known and worked with Linda DeFruscio for over twenty-five years. Though Linda's office is located in the greater Boston area, many of her clients are people from within the transgender community throughout

New England and beyond. And as I am a licensed clinical social worker specializing in gender identity issues, based in the same region but also seeing clients from around the country, Linda and I have had many mutual clients. Because of Linda's own personal history, which she generously describes in *Cornered*, I can think of no one who was better suited to befriend Richard Sharpe, and certainly there is no one else who could have given us the insights we find in her book about his descent into madness. Linda is a fastidious observer, a woman driven by an immense curiosity, and blessed with heart to match.

—Diane Ellaborn

Diane Ellaborn, LICSW, is a Gender Specialist, in full-time private practice in Framingham, MA, with over thirty-five years post Masters experience as a psychotherapist. She is a NASW Board Certified Diplomate in Clinical Social Work, a member of the World Professional Association for Transgender Health (WPATH), and clinical consultant to the International Foundation for Gender Education (IFGE). She has presented and provided trainings on gender conditions and treatment nationally and internationally and has also appeared on local and national television.

Acknowledgements

Special thanks to the many people who read and offered heartfelt encouragement and crucial advice on earlier versions of the manuscript, including Joseph A. Russo, MD, Lisa Robinson Schoeller, Melissa Robinson Schoeller, Silka Rothschild, Emily Walsh, and Diane Ellaborn, LICSW. Thanks to Joan Schweighardt for sharing her knowledge of the craft.

Preface

*W*HEN IT IS MY TURN, *I* ENTER THE OFFICE AND FILL OUT THE PAPERWORK. *I* PLACE *my purse and jewelry in a locker and prepare to go through screening and security. I am dressed appropriately, in a blouse, pocket-less slacks and a pair of canvas flats. Other visitors may be turned away for wearing tube tops, tank tops, halter tops, muscle shirts, farmers jeans, fatigues, above-knee skirts, slit skirts, wrap-around skirts, sweatshirts, sweatpants, windbreakers, pants with elastic waistbands, or clothing that is too baggy or too tight, but not me. I already know the drill. I'm not wearing a headband or barrettes. My zippers are plastic and my bra is a sports bra that doesn't have an under-wire cup or a back-of-the-bra latch that is likely to set off security apparatuses.*

When the first gate opens, I walk though, then stop and wait for the second gate to open. Then the third. Then the fourth. As each gate closes behind me, it makes a clucking noise, a solid thud, the sound of dense impenetrable metals coupling.

As I walk down the long hall I listen to the sound of my footsteps on the concrete floor. I am not skipping, but all at once I can imagine the sound of someone skipping, the echo it makes in the corridor, and then I can imagine skipping myself. I am not holding anyone's hand, but then I feel my hand in hers.

I am skipping and holding her hand and it is 1960 all over again. I want to go faster, but Mother wants to go as slowly as possible, or so it seems to me. I am trying to pull ahead and she is trying to hold me back. I am wearing a dress, as I always do on Sundays. I am thinking, Daddy, Daddy, Daddy, Daddy. It is taking forever, with all these doors and hallways, but in a short time I will be on his lap, in his arms. He will be tickling me, hugging me, holding me to his chest like I am the most precious thing in the world. I will be laughing. She won't say much, because they are divorced now and everything that needed to be said has already, but she will watch our display of love with a smile and a soft heart.

In the final hallway, as we wait for the last gate to open, I look up at the man three stories above us in the tower. He is looking down at us, his little head, which is all you can see, backlit by the sun. Behind his head, over one shoulder, is some kind of a rod, the barrel of a gun. His job is to make sure we are all standing where we are supposed to stand, inside the yellow lines. He never smiles. Other people might think he is scary up there, but I have seen him so many times before that I am never scared. I already know that he's not going to shoot. Not today. Not at us. Daddy, Daddy, Daddy, Daddy…. Daddy is in the cage, we say at home. We don't say jail or prison.

The last gate opens and in we go, to the visitors room. There are picnic tables there. We sit and wait and watch the door that the guards are standing around. When he sees us, his face will light up. It always does. I write him letters, telling him how much I miss and love him. I draw pictures for him with crayons on construction paper. I remind him to say his prayers so that he can get out soon. I even write letters to the prison, telling them he needs to come home. My mother says I would be less cranky if he were out; taking care of me, controlling my behavior, would be easier for her—even though he won't be living in the apartment with us anymore once he is out. Sometimes I visit him with Grandma. She cries the whole time because she can't stand to see her son in the cage. He doesn't tickle me as much when I come with her, because it wouldn't seem right for us to be laughing and carrying on while she is crying into her palms.

The last door opens and I step in, alone, and find a place to sit. Almost forty years have passed. This is a different prison than the one where I visited my dad. We don't touch the inmates here; we don't kiss their cheeks or sit on their laps. We must look at them through a thick glass. If we want to talk, we must pick up the phone. If we want to offer a gesture of comfort, we must add our smudge print to those already there.

Chapter One – Hair, Pseudonyms and Transgender Lives

MY MOTHER WAS AN ELECTROLOGIST TOO. BEFORE SHE GOT INTO THE FIELD, SHE worked in a factory, welding small parts for airplanes. She was good at working with small things; she was good with her hands. She liked electrolysis even more than airplane parts because along with the intricate hand work and exacting eye focus came people, different people with different personalities. When I got out of high school in 1972, she took me into her office (which was in our home) and did my eyebrows. She explained the process to me as she worked. I went into a dental studies program that same year, offered by Northeastern and Tufts, and after a year and a half I received a Dental Assistant certification. Thereafter I was accepted into a dental hygiene program, but at a school in Connecticut. (The ones in Massachusetts could only put me on a waiting list.) Instead of leaving my family to live out of state, I decided to follow in my mother's footsteps and go to school for electrololgy, and cosmetology too. While I was a student, I worked as a dental assistant (as well as a McDonald's counter person and a housecleaner) to pay my bills. I graduated from Eleanor Roberts School of Electrology in Boston in 1975.

In school, people came in off the street to get inexpensive treatments from the students. One day Bart Fish came in, our neighbor from near our home, and I worked on him. He told me that sometimes my mother worked on him too. Small world. I didn't know. Bart was married and had three kids, one still at home. He confided that he was a cross-dresser, which was why he didn't want facial hair (and probably why I hadn't known my mother was working on him). By the time he came to me, I was a licensed master barber as well as an electrologist. I worked on Bart's beard and also cut his hair and shaved him. I even practiced a few perms on him. On one occasion, his daughter freaked out. She said I'd sent him home looking like a poodle. She didn't mind the cross-dressing, because he did that elsewhere, in a different state; it was a separate segment of his life. But she couldn't endure seeing him every night at the dinner table looking like a priss. She made such a fuss that I went over one evening and cut off his curls.

My mother, I would come to realize, knew lots of cross-dressers, because they made up a good percentage of her clientele. But she had never talked to me about them. It was Bart who helped me to understand that some people just weren't totally comfortable with the gender they'd been born with; or they weren't comfortable all the time. He was lucky, he said. His wife accepted him as he was. He was her best friend and she didn't want to lose him just because he felt the need to alter his gender presentation now and then. Bart's job as a bra and underwear salesman provided him with the opportunity to travel to different cities, destinations where he could cross-dress without worrying about who found out. He had a friend in Manhattan, and she was okay with his cross-dressing too. He said to me once, "Cross-dressers will be some of your best clients. Don't be afraid of them. There's nothing to be afraid of. We're all just people."

Once the cat was out of the bag, my mother and I began to spend social time with Bart and his wife, chatting over lemonade on their porch or in our house. One day Bart offered to take me to an IFGE—International Foundation for Gender Education—meeting so I could learn a little more. His friend Merissa Lynn had founded the organization, in Waltham, Massachusetts. She wanted to help me to find clients. I told her I liked to write and she suggested I write an article about electrolysis for the IFGE magazine. She and Bart introduced me to other people.

Over time, Bart became my mentor and confidante. When Mom retired, he encouraged me to start my own business. Even though I was still very young, Bart and his wife were certain I would achieve success. I would inherit Mom's clients, and there would be some IFGE people too. To me, the transgender people were just regular people (perhaps a little more empathetic and more educated than other people I knew) who were conflicted about their gender identification. They lived, they died, and in between they worried about high blood pressure and paying their taxes like anyone else. My acceptance of them was automatic; after my conversations with Bart, I never gave it a second thought. As for Bart, he was a second father to me, my own father being away much of the time.

So I did it. I started my own business. At first I worked in the house, in the room that had been my mother's office. Then, with Bart's encouragement, I opened my office in Newton, and before I knew it I had a thriving practice. I liked being an electrologist. I liked the process. Each hair I removed gave me a surprise. One might have a big juicy black bulb at the end, and one might not. Analyzing each hair provided a clue as to what was going on under the skin. Also, I liked the people. They weren't all transgenders either; a lot of my clients were straight men with ingrown hairs or just too much hair, or straight women who needed work on their upper lips, chins, legs, or underarms. Some wanted eyebrow shaping. Sometimes pregnancy produces unwanted hairs in unexpected places. Electrolysis is a safe way to deal with it. Menopause can create hair havoc too. All kinds of people seek to control their hair growth.

Being an electrologist is not so different from being a psychiatrist...or a bartender. If a client comes in for hundreds of hours, and you are working together in a small quiet room, eventually they will open up and tell you about their life. I've had many a patient cry and admit they need to work on a particular issue. I always respond, "I'm not a therapist. I'm not allowed to tell you what to do. But I can give you my opinion." That always turns out to be what they wanted anyway, more or less.

I've done my share of venting too. Once, on the way into work, a crazy driver came within an inch of taking me out on the highway. I was really shaken up. I remember how happy I was when I got to the office and realized that my first patient was someone who would want to know every detail of the almost accident. The transgenders were always the most interesting to tell your troubles to, because they are really part female and part male. If you tell them a relationship problem, for instance, they will be able to help you to look at it from both perspectives. Talking to transgender clients is as comfortable—and as comforting—as talking to my mom or best girlfriends. In fact, I count a few transgenders among my best girlfriends.

Besides my work, I continued to write skin care articles for Merissa. One day I was even contacted by the famous—well, famous to those of us who work in skin care—Dr. Peter Chives, who asked me to write an article for the *Annals of Dermatology*, of which he served as editor-in-chief. Dr. Chives was the author of more than a dozen books, one of which was in its sixth edition and had been translated into several foreign languages. He was also the author of over three-hundred scientific publications. I was thrilled when he contacted me and said he considered me to be outstanding in my field and wanted me to review a textbook that had been written by one of his colleagues. I accepted of course. But while I had written lots of magazine articles, I'd never written a book review on a technical book, and I had no idea how to go about it. As it happened, one of my patients, a professional writer, volunteered to give me some tips. I submitted the final piece on time and the issue appeared at the end of 1991.

೮೨೮೮

When Chris Trembly first called me I was between patients and had the time to talk, which was good, because Mr. Trembly had some nice things to say. He'd read the article that I'd written for *Annals of Dermatology*. He liked it a lot; he thought I was a good writer. This was about the best compliment anyone could pay me. Chris Trembly said he liked to write too, but he didn't say what he wrote and I didn't ask. He'd called because he had ingrown hairs on his neck and he thought I would be the right person to remove them. We set up an appointment.

He came in a week later. He was a sweet, shy, soft-spoken, unassuming man. Dark eyes, longish dark hair. A combination of a young Mick Jagger and Keanu Reeves. Maybe 5'9, about 165 pounds. Mid to late thirties, which is to say about my age. He wore black pants and a white shirt and dark cranberry penny loafers with shiny pennies in the vamp inserts. I led him into the treatment room. I have a chart on the wall there featuring several graphics that define the electrolysis process. The first thing I do with a new patient is tell him or her how electrolysis works—a very fine probe inserted into a hair follicle on the surface of the skin, etc. I always enjoy this explanation. I use the chart as a prop.

Before I could get started, Chris Trembly told me, politely, that he didn't have time for the first-visit consultation that day. If I could just work on a few of his ingrowns.... He promised the next visit he would relish the opportunity to talk about the process. In spite of the fact that he was in a hurry, he was pleasant. When our eyes met, he looked right into mine. I had him get up on the table and I examined his ingrowns under the light and removed a few. We set up another appointment.

An ingrown hair can occur when a hair is shaved and it retreats below the skin surface, causing inflammation and irritation. There are ways to reduce the number of ingrown hairs, such as running one's razor under hot water for about thirty seconds. Shaving in one direction (the direction of the hair), and never using a blade more than three times, is also good. If you cheat, your skin will know. I was telling all this to Chris Trembly during our third session, because during the second session, as was the case with the first, he had to be somewhere and didn't have time for more than the removal of a few more ingrowns. I was happy to finally have the chance to impart my knowledge to him, to point to the illustrations on my trusty wall chart. He followed the movement of my finger diligently. Alternately, he looked into my eyes. His apparent interest in what I was saying stirred me to say more, to add more detail than usual. When I stopped to take a breath, he smiled a hesitant smile and said, "My name isn't really Chris Trembly."

I was taken aback not at all. There are those among my clients who prefer that I don't know their real names. Like Fred, for instance. In ten years I've never asked him for his real name and I never plan to. Fred adores his wife and his five kids. He has a nice home. He likes his life. When he first came to me, he said, "I don't want to change my life but I do want to be more of the real me. I want my hair thinned on my beard, knuckles and brows."

Over time Fred told me his story. He cross-dressed once a month, always in the daytime when he could fit his excursions into his work day. Generally he went to out-of-town malls or to hotels to have lunch alone or with transgender friends. Unlike my dear friend Bart, his wife knew nothing about it, and he had no intention of letting her find out—because he suspected she wouldn't approve. He knew he was right when she told him over dinner one night about the disgusting transsexuals she'd seen on some TV talk show. The last thing Fred wanted was for her to think of him that way and leave him. The second to last thing he wanted was to have to give up the one afternoon a month that he dressed as a woman. He came to me to find a compromise.

Money was no object for him, so we agreed that we would do very short sessions, removing only a few hairs at a time, several times a month. I said, "At this rate you'll be with me for a long time." "That's fine," he responded.

During each session I removed two or three hairs from under his nose, a few from his chin, his brows, his knuckles—so little that if anyone noticed at all, they would think he had scratched himself. While I worked, he liked to talk about politics. He had a government job, he said. During one appointment he told me a story about how he'd lost his purse while he was out. I said, "Oh my God, was your government ID in it?" No, he'd created a different ID for his excursions, for his alternate self; he even had a PO box just for his transgender mail. His interest in politics and his guile led me to suspect that he worked for an intelligence agency. But I never asked.

After eight or so years of ongoing appointments, we got to where he wanted to be; he was no longer "hairy." But he didn't look as though he'd had any hair removed either. We knew we had created a masterpiece when his wife said to him one day, "You know, now that you're getting older, your hair is thinning on your face. It looks great! You're more handsome than ever."

I saw him once with his wife, at my favorite luncheonette. He'd asked me years before never to say hello to him if I saw him outside of my office, and I'd never forgotten. So I turned away while I waited for my to-go order. I was about to pass their table on my way out the door when he said, "Nice day, huh?" I glanced at him. He was smiling. I glanced at her. She looked at me suspiciously. I said, "Yeah, it's beautiful," and hurried outside.

಄ೞ

I smiled at Chris Trembly when he said he wasn't Chris Trembly, and I went on talking about ingrown hairs. I was explaining that you could use a tablespoon of salt and warm water, mixed together on a piece of gauze, or even in your hand, as an exfoliant to heal any irritation...just like how ocean water works to heal the skin. But a few minutes later he interrupted my lecture again to say, "Did you know that an ophthalmologist from St. Louis, Missouri was the first person to use electrolysis on someone who had ingrown eyelashes in the year 1875?"

That stopped me cold. I stared at him. He smiled his sheepish smile. Then he pulled his wallet from his pocket and extracted two loose photos and handed them to me. The first was a picture of him wearing a lab coat over a dress shirt and tie, a stethoscope draped around his neck. The second appeared to be a photo of a woman, but I recognized instantly that it was him, in drag. I handed them back. "Are you a doctor?" I asked.

He nodded. I looked him over. As always, he was wearing a fresh white shirt and penny loafers, his signature ensemble. He said, "I'm a dermatologist. My name is Richard Sharpe."

Chapter Two – Don't You Love Her Madly...

MY OFFICE WAS ON THE SECOND FLOOR OF A BRICK BUILDING THAT TOOK UP about a third of the block on the main street running through town. There were several storefronts on the first floor. One of them, to the east and close to the corner, was occupied by my friend Ralph. He was renting the space to use as a beauty salon. At least once a week I would finish my work upstairs early and join him downstairs and take some of his customers if he was busy. It was fun to cut hair at Ralph's side.

One day while I was down there, a woman in her thirties came in for a cut and also to say that she wanted to learn the process so that she could do her kids' hair. She removed a book from the paper bag she was carrying and showed me the hair-styling instructional manual she'd bought. I told her, "I'm not allowed to teach you how to cut hair. I'm not an instructor." She said, "Well, can you at least tell me how to hold the scissors?" She sat down in the chair and I tied the plastic apron around her neck. I said, "Watch me in the mirror. I can give you some tips. I can't really instruct you. Anyway, you've got the book." We were both looking at each other in the mirror when a girl appeared behind us, sweeping up hair from the floor. "Hi, Stephanie," I said.

Stephanie was about sixteen, petite, with long, shiny, healthy-looking light brown hair, creamy skin, full lips and an unassuming aspect—especially for a kid as stunningly beautiful as she was. She worked in the salon a few days a week after school, answering the phones, sweeping, whatever had to be done. I turned around to look at her directly. "You *are* adorable," I said. I couldn't help myself. I hadn't realized she was in until she'd appeared in the mirror like a princess in a fairytale. "*Where* did you come from? What kind of parents do you have that could have made such a sweet and adorable kid?" I'd never had any children; if I had, I would have wanted a daughter just like her.

I embarrassed her a little, I could tell. She kept sweeping and answered me shyly. "My dad's a doctor and my mom's a nurse." She shrugged.

I turned back to the mirror and the woman waiting to get her hair cut. It figures, I thought to myself. The kid's got great parents who are really smart and who love her. How lucky can you get?

When I finished in the salon, I went home to my apartment. I had a roommate, Tommy. He worked nights, doing something with air-conditioning and heating, and as I worked days, we seldom saw each other. We both had the place to ourselves most of the time. It was a good deal...in the beginning.

When I first moved in with Tommy I had a boyfriend, Matthew. Matthew was from New Jersey and he was a full-blooded Italian, like me. He worked for a popular men's magazine in New York and did a lot of traveling for his job. He was in Boston frequently, and we enjoyed road races along the ocean (among other things). He generally ran a 10K and I ran a 5K. We'd meet at the end of a race to share oranges and gulp down water.

Even though we didn't see each other that often, we talked on the phone regularly, and after three years he asked me to marry him. But I already had my electrolysis practice going by then and I wasn't sure I wanted to give it up to move to New Jersey. I asked him to give me six months to figure out how to make that kind of a transition. Some people are good at picking up and changing locations. I'm not one of them. I was dragging my feet—and eventually I had to tell him that it was geographically undesirable to continue the relationship.

I broke up with Matthew over the phone. Coincidentally, Tommy happened to be home at the time. When he saw me crying, he sat beside me on the sofa and put his arm around me to comfort me while I told him my sad story.

He was friendly after that. He was a quiet guy and he was considerate regarding kitchen clean-up, sharing refrigerator shelf space and domestic chores. He was handsome. As far as I could tell, he didn't have a girlfriend, and I knew he wasn't sick because he gave blood on a regular basis at the blood bank. Slowly, over time, we became romantically attracted to each other.

I never went into his bedroom and he never came into mine. We got together in the common areas, basically in the living room. By avoiding each other's private space, we were tacitly agreeing that we would remain roommates first and foremost, lovers second—or so I believed. But the fact was that he was an excellent lover, and I enjoyed the time we spent together.

In the meantime, Rick Sharpe and I seemed to be on the way to becoming friends. We didn't talk much about our current personal situations. I probably mentioned that I had a roommate who was more than a friend, and he mentioned that he and his wife were working through some difficult times. That was about it. Mostly we talked about medicine, which he had a great love for. When we stayed on dermatology, I could follow along, but he was interested in every organ in the body, every system. He loved research.

He wanted to find a cure for cancer. A few years before he had co-founded a biotech company called Arcturus Pharmaceutical Corp for the purpose of creating products to treat skin cancer—as well as psoriasis and eczema and other disorders. He'd raised $9.5 million in venture capital to get the business going, and he'd had twenty-three scientists working there at one point. Eventually it went bust, as many biotech companies did during that period. But he remained passionate about the possibility of finding cures for killer diseases—maybe in part because his mother had died from breast cancer.

He'd even invented a software program to track women's mammogram appointments. He believed in this program wholeheartedly. He explained that many times and for a variety of reasons, a paper report will not reach a doctor's desk in a timely manner; or it will, but the doctor won't read it right away; or a woman who is told to come back for additional testing will put it off for a while. In any of these scenarios the consequences could be dire for the patient. They were for his mother. The piece of paper documenting the details of her malignancy got lost on a desk, and by the time it was found, her situation was irreversible. The tracking program guaranteed that reports were looked at and results were followed up on. No one believed in his program, until he presented it to the military. They were the first to license it from him.

More than anything, Rick Sharpe wanted to save lives, and he was devastated when he couldn't. He showed up at my office very upset one day because one of his patients, a twenty-nine-year-old mother, had come to him with an advanced melanoma on her face. He could see right away that she was too far gone and would die in a short time. The testing he did confirmed this prognosis. She had been to see another doctor and he had misdiagnosed her. I got so upset when he told me that I wanted to get that doctor's name and report him. But Rick wouldn't tell me. That wasn't the point, he said. Anyone could make a mistake. He didn't want to get anyone in trouble. The real culprit may have been the tanning beds she had frequented.

Rick had graduated from Harvard Medical School, where he'd also taught. Before he became a doctor he'd been an electrical engineer. His work in engineering allowed him to pay his tuition for med school; he worked the whole time he was in school. He was also a qualified pilot. He had an enormous amount of energy—both mental and physical. He moved fast. He talked fast. While I was working on him, he had to be still of course. But when we had finished and were just chatting, he hopped around, one foot to the other, like a revved-up kid. I noticed that he was clumsy; coming or going from the office he would bump into the wall or the door. He tripped once or twice.

The other subject we talked about was investments. I'd shared with him that things were tough for me as a kid and that I was hoping to make my own way in the world. I wanted a house one day, a beautiful house with gardens and trees, close to the ocean. That was my dream. My mother and stepfather had a house near the ocean for a short time, beginning in 1962. I was just a kid then and I didn't remember too much about it, but I had memorized the smell of the air, the comforting sound of the surf. There was a carriage house behind the main house, and I'd longed to move my dolls in and make it my own. But my stepfather began collecting pigeons and keeping them in there, and that was the end of that. I remembered my sister and I digging for periwinkle clams and her throwing jellyfish at me, my mother's white '62 Corvair, and how her cigarette smoke would curl back and saturate the back seat, even when she had the window open. I wanted to get into the stock market and make some real money and live near the sea. But I was conservative by nature and I didn't know if I could bring myself to take the risk.

Rick asked me questions about my family, about growing up the way I did, with my father in jail most of the time. I could tell he really listened to my responses. I felt like he could see the real me, the scared kid I felt like half the time, and the self-made, self-assured woman that was the other half. Our conversations were never very long because I had other patients waiting and he had hospital rounds to make. But they were never lacking either; we liked each other.

One day he came in and told me he had the perfect stock for me to start up with—Upjohn, the pharmaceutical company. He asked me if I'd heard anything about them, because by then I was paying attention to what companies were doing and how their stock prices were being affected by their activities. I said I'd heard that UpJohn was about to be bought out. "I knew it! I knew it!" he exclaimed. He said he was going to buy a lot of UpJohn stock, right away, and that I should too.

I didn't have much money to work with, but I called Fidelity, the company that had arranged my 401K, and told them I wanted to buy $1000 worth of Upjohn. I took a deep breath. This would be my first real venture into the stock market. I would never have taken the leap, but I trusted that Rick understood my financial circumstances and wouldn't steer me into a situation he wasn't fairly certain about. Two weeks later, Rick called me at work and told me to sell. I had been watching Upjohn and I knew it was still going up. Maybe he was wrong, I thought. Maybe I should hang onto it awhile longer. I called Fidelity, but not the same day that Rick called me. The stock had already begun to decline. Still, I doubled my money. I was happy.

I didn't see Rick for a few weeks; this was a busy time for him and between his dermatology practice and his hospital rounds, he couldn't always make his appointments. Then one late afternoon, on a day when he didn't have an appointment, he showed up just as I was getting ready to leave for home.

Rick Sharpe didn't have one of those broad ear-to-ear grins. His smile was always tentative, even a bit awkward, as if he was afraid to really indulge in happiness. I suspect he felt he didn't deserve it. But on this occasion, he was beaming. He asked if I was done with work for the day, and when I said I was, he insisted I come down to the street because he had something important to show me.

I hesitated. I had never spent a minute with him outside the office. As far as I knew, he was still a married man. I had rules about married men. I had rules about a lot of things. But how could it hurt to go outside and see what all the commotion was about?

The first thing I saw when we got to the street was a brand new shiny Porsche. Black on black. I looked at Rick, and his expression told me that it was his. He said, "I bought it with the Upjohn money. I put in twenty and sold for sixty. I made $40,000. Come and take a ride with me."

I stared at the car and said nothing. He was talking about how we could swing by his house in Gloucester. He had mentioned the house before. He and his wife had married very young, right out of high school. For years, they'd had nothing, and then, once she was working and he was out of medical school, things improved substantially and they were able to buy the Gloucester house. He said it was beautiful, not far from the sea.

I still didn't answer. He seemed to know why I was hesitating. "Carmen's in Cambridge," he said. "She's staying in the condo and I'm staying at the house. She wants a divorce. We can drive over so you can see how the car runs and see the house and then we can drive right back. I have late rounds at the hospital, so I have to come right back."

I had never been in a Porsche before. It was a beautiful late summer afternoon. A light breeze was blowing, lifting my hair off my neck and shoulders. The imploring look he was giving me confirmed that he really wanted my company. Again, he looked like a kid. "Sure," I said, finally, "I'll take a ride with you." He opened the passenger door so I could slide in.

He talked about the car—a 1992 911 Carrera RS 3.6 Coup—as we drove out of town, how well it handled with its high compression cylinder head, timing systems, torque, brakes, shocks.... I tried to pay attention but I was more interested in the feel of the thing; we rode along so smoothly we could have been on a cloud. But then we got out onto the highway and he said, "Watch this," and the next thing I knew my heart was in my throat because he had the pedal all the way down to the floor and we were no longer floating but flying.

He glanced at me, and when he saw my expression, he laughed. It may have been the first time I saw him laugh full out like that. He was telling me about how balanced the car was, how this model was made for ease of handling, for people who really knew how to drive. I could hardly hear him over the sound of my heart beating so close to my brain.

If possible, we went faster yet. I was totally freaked out, certain we were going to die. I could tell he had control, that he was in fact a good driver, but how could that matter in such heavy traffic? We wove from lane to lane, like downhill skiers. Eventually the traffic thinned and we didn't need to weave any longer, but we were still flying. His cell phone rang. Then his pager went off. I screamed, "Answer your pager! Answer your phone!" because I imagined that answering one or the other would force him to slow down. "It could be a patient," I cried. What I was really thinking was that it could be his wife, that she would unwittingly save our lives. He did answer the phone, but it wasn't her and he didn't slow down. He answered some questions that seemed to be about one of his patients and put the phone back in its holder on the dash. He continued to speed. At one point, going around a bend, I grabbed his leg and tried to pull his foot up from the pedal. I shouted, "You have to stop! You can't do this."

"My reflexes are excellent," he responded, and he laughed some more.

We turned off the highway just as the sun began to set and proceeded along on country roads, full of twists and turns. He slowed down, but not nearly enough to suit the terrain—or me. Yes, his reflexes were excellent, and the car obeyed his every little wrist flick as if it were a dog whose sole purpose was to do its master's bidding. He was a great driver; it was a great car. But I was upset. I was mad. We were speeding and it was wrong.

I sat in a huff, certain we would never reach our destination alive. He giggled; he tried to nudge me into a better mood. I told myself that I must remember the roads, the rights and lefts we were taking, in case I had to find my own way home. I had no idea where we were. There were few houses, but lots of trees. I had heard plenty of stories about deer appearing in the road in rural communities like this. We passed a large marshy area. The trees became taller beyond it. I reminded myself that he was a doctor, a graduate of Harvard Medical School, a professor, a researcher who wanted cancer eliminated in his lifetime. I took a deep breath and tried to relax. Finally we pulled into a driveway and he turned off the ignition. The curtain of silence that descended seemed profound after our joyride.

The house was magnificent, a large, stately light-colored colonial with a two-story two-car garage, on a cul-de-sac. A room connected the house and the garage. Beyond the house were oak and maple trees, beyond them, a forest. There were gardens everywhere, bird houses, a pond....

We went in the side door and he switched on a light. The rooms were large and empty. I followed him down a wide hallway and past the front door and the winding staircase opposite it. Rick explained that his wife had all the furniture moved to the Cambridge condo.

There was one lamp in the living room. He turned it on and it produced just enough illumination for us to be able to see. On the floor in the corner was a stereo set and a pile of CDs. Rick found what he was looking for and popped it into the CD player. A second later the unmistakable voice of Jim Morrison shot through the speakers—*Don't ya love her madly Don't ya need her badly Don't ya love her ways Tell me what you say...*—and Rick immediately began dancing.

He danced like a crazy person, a lunatic, without any rhythm. He looked more like an uncoordinated acrobat than a dancer, flying across the room, sliding on the wood floor, jumping, twirling, leaping, almost manic. *Don't ya love her madly Wanna be her daddy Don't ya love her face Don't ya love her as she's walkin' out the door Like she did one thousand times before....*

I stared at him in wonder. He *was* a child. He was a free spirit. In my heart I forgave him for the scary car ride. In an effort to improve my mood, I began to dance too, conservatively, standing in one spot, small movements of my hips and arms, feet going nowhere. He was too busy skipping back and forth across the room to notice. I believe he forgot I was there.

I migrated toward the fireplace mantel to see whose picture had remained there in an otherwise empty room. I thought it would be his wife, Carmen. But it was a girl, a teenager. I picked it up and looked more closely. It looked just like Stephanie, the adorable girl from my friend Ralph's hair salon. I glanced at Rick, still skipping and hopping with Morrison and his band. He seemed too young to have a daughter Stephanie's age. He saw me holding the picture and yelled over the music, "That's my daughter," as he flapped by.

"Wait a minute," I cried. "I love this girl! She works with me at the hair salon!"

He didn't answer. The music was too loud and he was dancing at the other end of the room now.

I stood there saying, "Wow, I can't believe this is your daughter." I remembered asking her who her parents were, and now I knew. Somehow knowing Stephanie was his daughter made me feel safer. Suddenly I felt destined to know him better...and her. Maybe the entire family.

Rick announced cheerfully that there was a Jacuzzi in the other room and asked if I wanted to go in it. He had to shout because the CD was still playing. I said I didn't really want to and I didn't have a bathing suit anyway. He said we could go in in our underwear. I followed him into a room off the kitchen. He approached the hot tub and turned on the jets. Quickly and unselfconsciously, he stripped down to his underpants and climbed in. The room was dark; I couldn't really see him in there, just his outline. He said to me, "Come on, come on, I won't bother you."

I wanted to go in. Something about the music and the house and the ride in the Porsche had ignited my sense of adventure. I was excited. I felt called upon to step outside myself. "I can just go in with my bra and underpants?" I asked.

He said, "Yes, that's fine. I'm not going to bother you."

I went to the darkest corner of the room and quickly removed my blouse and slacks. It occurred to me that if he and his wife divorced, I could wind up in a relationship with

him. I couldn't help but say to myself that it would be "interesting" if I were to marry a doctor. Those of my family members who made an honest living were all service people, albeit skilled service people, and they had married other service people.

I eased into the hot tub. Now Jim Morrison was singing, *Come on, come on, come on, come on, Now touch me, baby, Can't you see that I am not afraid?* Before I had time to wonder whether those words might be an omen of things to come, Rick swam over and pushed his whole body against me—just plowed into me—and tried to plant a big kiss on my face. I pushed him away. I said, "Get away from me. Go figure out your marriage. Family is important. Even broken families. I know; I came from one."

He laughed, as if to prove he'd only been joking. He moved to the other side of the tub and amused himself by clapping water between his hands. He was getting water all over the place. It was flying out of the tub and onto the floor. He didn't seem to care.

He didn't come near me again, which was for the best. In spite of the thoughts I'd had, in spite of my confusion, my reaction, which had been instinctive, felt like it had been the right one.

I suggested we get out of the tub. While I was dressing he excused himself and I could hear him speaking on the phone in another part of the house. He was calmer when he returned. He said he'd called Carmen, to remind her to walk the dog, and also spoke to Stephanie, to remind her about a school project she was supposed to be working on.

On the way home he drove the speed limit and we chatted about my allergies. People think I'm being a hypochondriac when I say I can't be around cats or certain kinds of candles or in certain chemically-infused environments. But Rick was really listening, nodding. He recommended a medication, and when I said I was already taking it, he got quiet and pondered. Awhile later he made another recommendation, and I agreed to try it. Then he told me about one of his patients, a woman he was treating for lichen planopilaris, a lichen-like rash that appears out of nowhere, from no known cause. He said the woman had noticed it early, and as a result, the intralesional and topical steroids he was using to treat it appeared to be working.

Things were back to normal. Except for the fact that I was not removing ingrown hairs from his neck, we could have been having a session in my office.

Chapter Three – A Free Cut and a Split Lip

IN THE END I LIKED RICK SHARPE MORE RATHER THAN LESS AFTER OUR TRIP TO Gloucester. I wasn't impressed by the drive of course, but I liked that I had glimpsed the free spirit in him at the house, and I wondered how often he allowed it to escape. I was glad we were friends. When he mentioned, during one of our sessions a week or so later, that he needed a haircut but had been too busy to schedule one, I invited him to stop by my apartment so I could cut his hair for him. I gave him the address.

He showed up that evening. He was in between hospital rounds, so I tried to be as quick as possible. I tucked his collar down and spritzed his hair with water, then threw a towel over him and began to cut his hair in the kitchen. When we were done he asked if he could run the water from the faucet in the tub over his neck to get the loose hairs off before he went back to work. I pointed him to the bathroom. I told him to take his white dress shirt off and shake it out in the tub too, because there were hairs on the back of it.

I usually didn't wake up when Tommy came home, unless we'd planned that I would wait up for him, which we had not. But he was making a lot of noise in the kitchen, slamming the refrigerator and cabinet doors, and my sleep was disturbed. I got up to see what was going on and he immediately pointed out that there were black hairs in the tub and demanded to know to whom they belonged. I explained that a doctor who was a friend of mine had dropped by for a haircut. He asked me if I'd had sex with him. I was astonished. "Of course not," I said. I don't like trouble; even if I had wanted to have sex with Rick Sharpe, I would never have let it happen in the apartment.

I volunteered to clean the hair out of the tub right away, but that wasn't good enough for my possessive roommate. He continued to yell, and when I ignored him, he began to throw things around in the kitchen: small things, refrigerator magnets, pot holders, dish towels, etc. I stood leaning against the counter with my arms folded and watched him calmly. After a while, when he'd settled down, I said, "You know what? You're crazy. I gave the guy a haircut. I give you haircuts. I give a lot of people haircuts." I should have packed my things right then, but ultimately he apologized and I let it go.

A few weeks later I informed Tommy that I would be going to New York City for a big skin care conference over the weekend. He asked if my doctor friend was going to be there. I said yes, I supposed he was, that probably every dermatologist in our corner of the country would be there. But I added that I was traveling and rooming with my colleague Marilyn, and that with so many speakers and guests expected, it wouldn't be surprising if I didn't even run into Dr. Sharpe. I could tell by his expression that he remained suspicious. I resented feeling that I had to explain anything to him.

In fact, I did see Rick at the conference. We ran into each other in the hallway of the hotel that most of the attendants from Boston were staying in and agreed to have a bite to eat together. But first he had to call his daughter, Stephanie, about something. I walked to his room with him and waited out in the hall to give him privacy while he made his call. It occurred to me that if anything was going to happen between us, this would be the place. We were alone, for the moment at least; we were in a different city, a different state. I had seen his house; it was empty; I knew he and his wife were not living together. The timing was excellent.... But nothing else was. He emerged from his room and we went down to the lobby to join the others at the buffet.

We had taken Marilyn's car to the train station. Tommy was home when she dropped me off. I said hello and headed into my bedroom to change out of my conference clothes and into sweatpants and a T-shirt. I left my bedroom door open and could hear him out in the kitchen talking to himself, saying, "Something happened in New York; I know something happened in New York." Then he yelled in to me, asking if I had seen the doctor and if I'd cheated on him. This made me laugh; since I had no commitment to Tommy other than to have my share of the rent money each month, I couldn't have "cheated" on him even if I'd had a fling with Rick Sharpe. I called back that I'd seen Rick and nothing happened. But he must have heard in my voice how exasperated I was, because as I came around the corner from my bedroom and stepped into kitchen, he threw a sixteen-ounce can of WD 40—and it split open my upper lip.

On the way to the hospital he swore he'd been throwing the can at the refrigerator, that he couldn't have known I was about to emerge in the kitchen at just that moment. My lip was throbbing; the towel I held over it was already soaked in blood. I was in too much pain to pay much attention to anything he said. When we got to the hospital the doctor who examined me said they would need to call in a plastic surgeon, that's how bad the gash was. The nurse who accompanied him kept giving Tommy the evil eye. I could tell she thought my injury was the result of foul play. Later, when a police officer showed up, I surmised she'd called him. The officer asked Tommy to step outside so we could talk privately.

Tommy claimed he had a gun collection. He'd told me once he kept his guns under the bed. He might have. Sometimes I caught a glimpse of his room when the door swung open; it was always messy, anything might have been in there. The rest of the apartment was always neat. I never gave the possibility of him having guns much thought either way. A lot of people I knew went to firing ranges or practiced skeet shooting out in the country. But I realized now that if I said Tommy had purposely thrown a can at me, there was a good chance the police would check the apartment and find his guns. That scenario could end badly for him, and if it ended badly for him, it could be even worse for me. If I had learned one thing from my father, it was that snitches always get theirs in the end. Anyway, it *was* possible that it had been an accident.

I was bandaged now, but I spoke the words as clearly as possible. "It was an accident," I said. The police officer eyed me skeptically for a moment. I believe he had come in hoping to be able to make an arrest. Finally he went away. Then Tommy was back beside me, saying how terrible he felt, going on and on about how he'd never purposely hurt me. Twelve stitches were required to sew me back together.

The young couple who lived above Tommy and me had a new baby. Lucky for me—if not for the parents—its nonstop colicky crying began right around this time. I told Tommy I couldn't stand it, that it was driving me crazy; I was going to have to find a new place to live. I was getting to know him pretty well now, and what I knew was that he was not the kind of guy you could just tell straight out that you were leaving. I said I was going to check out a place down the street, and once I'd settled he could come by and visit. I got my stuff out when he wasn't around and bought some extra locks for my new door. To his credit he never tried to contact me.

Chapter Four – Pizza and Éclairs

ONE AFTERNOON RICK CALLED ME AT THE OFFICE TO ASK IF I WANTED TO HAVE an early dinner with him before I went home. I said I already had plans with some friends, Cecil and George, my neighbors down the street. I'd met Cecil at the health club I went to. I'd made cheesecake brownies the night before. Cecil, George and I were going to indulge in pizza and brownies at their apartment. Rick asked if he could tag along, and I couldn't see any reason why he shouldn't.

Since he didn't know where Cecil and George lived, I suggested he pick me up at the office and we drive there together. We picked up the pizzas on the way. Then we sat in their living room, making small talk and eating. Rick ate a whole large cheese and pepperoni pizza by himself. It was sort of astonishing. He was a small-framed man. I don't know where he put it.

No sooner had he gobbled down the pizza than he got to his feet and announced that he had to go. He hadn't even had time to eat his brownie. I wrapped it for him to take on the road. As for me, I wasn't going anywhere. I was still eating. Cecil would drive me back to my car later. When he'd gone, my friends said that he was nice, a good conversationalist, but they asked if he was always in that much of a hurry. I thought about it. He was; he was always in a hurry. They asked me about his personal situation, with his wife. I said I really didn't know. I only knew that they were living apart and that the prospect of divorce had been laid out on the table by one party or the other. Or at least that was what Rick had told me.

Two mornings after the pizza gathering Rick surprised me by calling me from the psychiatric ward at Cambridge City Hospital and telling me he'd vomited all night after our pizza dinner. He spoke quickly, giving me too much information in too short a time and no chance to digest it or ask questions. He needed me to come and get him. He'd had a horrible night, he said. After he left Cecil and George's apartment, he headed back to Gloucester, but he had to pull the car over continuously to vomit. He never got sick; he didn't understand it. When he got home, he had diarrhea too. He'd seen Stephanie earlier in the day, at Carmen's condo in Cambridge, and they'd both eaten éclairs that they'd found out on the counter. He had no idea how long the éclairs had been there. Ironically, knowing that I was a big fan of éclairs, Rick had once warned me about leaving them sit around too long—because they could carry salmonella.

Rick had a project he needed to work on that night, some research that he was doing with Dr. Chives, the famed dermatologist I'd written the article for. He sat down at his desk, thinking it would help if he were able to distract himself. But he kept throwing up and couldn't stay focused. It was terrible for him to be so sick and so alone, he said. It was almost dark out by then, but the street lights weren't on yet. Everything looked so gloomy. Suddenly he felt an overwhelming urge to go to Carmen, for comfort. She was a nurse. She knew how to care for people.

He got back in the car and drove all the way to the condo, and as he had a key, he let himself in—and, he said, he found Carmen in the living room with Clark, an assistant RN from the hospital where she worked. They were half naked. Carmen pulled her clothes on and Clark shuffled away to pull his on in privacy. Then he ran out the door while Rick and Carmen were still regarding each other. Once they were alone they started screaming at each other, with her saying he had no right to be there and him trying to get across that he was terribly sick, maybe even dying.

Maybe they wore themselves out screaming, because somehow he managed to stay the night, and in the morning the three of them, Rick, Carmen and Stephanie, sat down to have breakfast together, almost like a normal family. But while they were eating, the arguing flared up again, and Carmen, who was feeling sick now too, accused him of putting poison in her orange juice. Rick was still sick himself. He accused her of poisoning the brownie— my brownie!—that he'd brought along with him. Apparently he'd had a bite of it with some water and had promptly thrown up again. When he tried to reach for her, she grabbed his hand and bit his thumb. He lunged at her; she lunged at him. He held a fork up to defend himself and it scratched her forehead. She ran to the phone and dialed Pauline Feldman, his psychiatrist. Pauline, who'd been treating him with antidepressants, agreed to come to the condo right away. When she arrived, Rick said, Pauline found him saturated in vomit and in a state of despair. She said, "Come on, let's take you in to the hospital."

This was what he told me. I suspected that some of it was true but I also believed that there were parts that he was leaving out.

My first thought was that he'd probably thrown up from eating so much pizza. My second thought was that these were crazy paranoid people and I didn't need to be involved. I had just gotten away from a crazy paranoid person. But Rick was begging me; he needed a ride back to the condo to get his car, and I didn't feel right letting him down either. I said I would be there as soon as I could. Then I called another friend of mine, Bill, and asked him if he would ride over with me. I thought that would be a better idea than going alone.

As it turned out, Bill and I sat in the waiting room for a very long time. After about two hours, a door opened and Rick was rolled out on a gurney, yelling loud enough for the whole hospital to hear, "I know my rights! I know about patient rights." Then he disappeared into another room and the door shut behind him and his caretaker.

Bill and I just looked at each other. "That was him," I said. We sat another two hours, four hours in all, before we saw Rick again. This time he was dressed and on foot, but he still looked delirious, and he was ghostly pale. He walked over to us and announced that Carmen was on her way to pick him up and that he regretted that we'd had to wait so long for nothing. I threw my hands up and told Bill I would drive him home. What else could I do?

The article that appeared in the *Herald* about the incident the following day baffled me even further. It said what he'd said, that both he and Carmen had accused the other of poisoning, that food samples that had been sent out for analyses all returned negative results; no one had tried to poison anyone. But during the course of their fight, the *Herald* reported, Rick had stabbed Carmen in the head with the fork. It didn't say anything about the fact that she had agreed to pick him up the next day.

I was curious to see what Rick would say about the incident when I saw him again, but I didn't see him. He canceled the electrolysis appointment that had been scheduled and didn't make another one. Nor did he call to see how I was doing or to suggest a stock purchase. Basically, he removed himself from my life.

I figured it was for the best.

Chapter Five — Family Roundup

MY MOTHER HAD HER FIRST ELECTRIC SHOCK TREATMENT WHEN SHE WAS twenty-one. She was nervous to begin with, but somehow she managed to hold it together the first time my father went to jail during their marriage. It was the second imprisonment that sent her over the edge, and according to him, she was never the same after that. She got to the point where she would fall apart over the littlest things and wind up back in the hospital.

She was seventeen and Dad was thirty-three when they married. He'd already had a whole life before her, but she said she didn't care; she was crazy about him. They had a few good years—during which time I was conceived (on her eighteenth birthday, in the back of his 1954 black and white Oldsmobile Super 88)—before his first arrest. When he got out they had a few more years together. Then he got arrested again. Since he would be gone for a while this time, my Uncle Felix stopped by one day to drop off a box that my father had asked Felix to keep for him. My mother opened it and found it full of love letters written to my father by his first wife, Agatha. They were gorgeously written letters, pure poetry, all in chronological order in their envelopes. Mom's heart was broken after that. She just couldn't get Agatha's words out of her mind.

I was three when she divorced him. Back then you could do that; having a spouse in jail was considered a legitimate reason for an automatic divorce.

My father's name was Hugh, and his best friend from childhood was Al. After divorcing Hugh, my mother married Al. He too had had a whole other life; he'd been married to another woman, Erma. Al and Erma ran a restaurant together—a five-hundred-seat establishment in downtown Boston. Business was good. They were good. But Al wanted to have a baby, and Erma couldn't conceive. So, after ten years of marriage, he decided to leave her and go to my mom. He went directly, more or less, from one to the other. It was okay by my mom. She was the kind of woman who needed a man in her life. I guess a lot of women did back then.

Erma was shocked that Al could just walk out like that, leaving her and the business, and one day she showed up at the tenement apartment we were renting in Brookline Village. My mother answered the door. She was very pregnant at the time. I guess that said it all. Erma freaked out, yelling and crying, but eventually she saw the futility of standing there on the stoop as if events could be reversed, and she retreated. The baby, Harriet, was born not much after that. She was two-and-a-half-years younger than me.

Al had been in prison too, but only once and only for one year. He said it was enough for him; he didn't intend to make the same mistake twice. But what he really meant was that he didn't intend to get caught twice. He held down real jobs, but he still did some thieving on the side. He couldn't help himself. He enjoyed it, and he was good at it. He could walk into a building dressed as a maintenance man, go up to a wall, remove a high-value painting, and walk right back out and no one would lift an eyebrow. I guess anyone paying attention assumed the painting was going somewhere to get cleaned, or re-hung elsewhere. Once he took his old boots off in the car and went into Filene's in his stocking feet and came out shortly thereafter wearing a new pair of boots.

Al loved my father and promised him that he would take good care of me. But Harriet was his of course, and while I can't say that he was much nicer to her than he was to me, he had a soft spot for her. He was stricter with me, and seldom affectionate. I didn't mind the lack of affection because I got plenty of love from my dad—albeit during prison visits. What I minded was the lack of authenticity. I wasn't the real child in this new family scenario.

The threat of an orphanage hung over me for years. Al didn't bring it up often, but then he didn't have to. I heard him mumble it a few times under his breath, and in my mind it became a fact of life, a distinct possibility given our lifestyle. My mother was always sick, and when she was away, it seemed conceivable that she might not come back, that she could be restricted to a facility for who knew how long. I worried that they could both leave, she to be hospitalized and he to take up with yet another woman. They had their moments of happiness, but they fought a lot too. She didn't give him as much attention as he would have liked. Sometimes when they fought he threatened to burn down the house.

We had an aunt and uncle who took us in one time—I was eight and Harriet was almost six—for about four months when my mother was hospitalized with one of her more serious breakdowns. But it was a hardship for everyone. They had three kids of their own to feed and care for. During the time we stayed with them, my uncle, who drove a diaper delivery truck, would drive us to our school in Brookline every day. Except for the fact that the dirty diapers from his pickup the previous day had had the entire night to fester, we enjoyed riding with him, bouncing along in the front seat and listening to WBZ on the radio. But in the afternoons we had to find our own way back, taking the T from Brookline to Boston and then taking the bus to Everett. Staying with them was a good short-term solution. There was no solution I could see that would provide for the long term if things really fell apart.

I did my part to ensure stability, which is to say, I became a near perfect child. I kissed Al's ass when my mother wasn't around. I changed his sheets. I did his laundry. I made his dinner if he had to be out. The way I saw it, the better my behavior, the less chance of finding myself in an orphanage one day. The feeling persisted even when I got older. My reluctance to go to dental hygiene school out of state was surely rooted in my fear that if I wasn't there to keep our fragile family unit together, it would disintegrate altogether.

In the end, our family held together for twenty-two years. Mother returned from each of her periods of hospitalization and Al never did leave for another woman (until years later after my mother divorced him), and he never did burn down the house. In fact I learned a lot from him over time. For one thing, I learned to cook. After giving up his own restaurant, the one he'd had with Erma, he went on to work for other restaurants, as a chef. He could cook anything. Harriet and I especially loved his potato pancakes, served up with applesauce and sour cream. He didn't really instruct me, but I picked up a lot just by watching.

But more importantly, I learned—again, by example—to hang tough, to not let myself crack up like my mother did when things went wrong, even though I knew I had the genes for it. I was grateful to him for that, and I was grateful for the fact that he provided for the roof over my head. Without him, who knows what would have become of me?

My father, Hugh, got into the food business too when he got out of jail, stocking groceries on shelves in a friend's Brookline food market. He was forty-three at the time. He married again as well, an eighteen-year-old named Camille. They'd actually met four years earlier, when Camille was only fourteen. She was living on welfare back then, in a shack with floors so crooked even the rats had trouble scurrying back and forth. She took a bus to Walpole regularly to visit him in prison.

Their marriage didn't make sense to me. I didn't know why he would want to marry someone so unpolished and so young. I didn't know why she would want to marry someone who was her father's age, and just out of prison. I guess she figured an older man would have the power—and eventually the money—to save her. And maybe he had the need to feel like a savior. Maybe I was just jealous that his new circumstances would take him yet further away from me…and dash my lifelong dream that one day my biological parents might reunite.

I was fourteen when Belle was born to Camille and Hugh. Belle was beautiful, with silky blond hair and blue eyes. Three years later they had Henry, who was also beautiful, though I believed my Dad was too old to still be having more kids.

He'd had his share of them over the years. He had the dubious distinction of having been *asked* to perform stud services for a few people. Before he met my mother, a couple who had been his neighbors in the Boston area asked him to intervene because the husband had concluded he was sterile. The couple had two girls, but I don't know whether they were twins or my dad helped out twice. It wasn't something he was prone to talk about. Then, during the time he was married to Camille, he had an affair with a woman named Cecily whom he'd met at the racetrack. She had a son who supposedly grew up to be a doctor. Who knows how many more half siblings I had? My father's hazel eyes, dark hair and money (there were times he *did* have it; such is the life of a thief) charmed the ladies no end.

I spent every Sunday with Hugh and Camille and Belle, and, when he came along, Henry. When we were younger, that made Harriet very jealous. She seemed to think I was getting something she had been denied. But the truth was, I was no more the real kid at Hugh and Camille's than I was at my mother and Al's. I got my love back in those days, as many kids do, away from my family.

I met Darren in junior high school and had a fifteen-year relationship with him. Like Matthew, the guy from New Jersey who came after him, Darren was a full-blooded Italian. (My parents always hoped that I would marry an Italian and keep the ethnicity thing going.) I cared about Darren so much that I actually spent six months traveling with him in his truck, the bed of which contained a mattress and his motorcycle. We camped our way west and stayed with some friends of his in California for three months and then camped our way east again. Darren loved California so much that he decided he wanted to live there. He asked me to forgive him for some cheating he'd done in the past and to marry him and go back with him to live on the west coast. I didn't want to hold him back from the life he envisioned, but I didn't see how I could live that far away from my crazy family either.

I was in my late twenties when Belle, then fourteen, became anorexic. It didn't surprise me. I think she felt like she had no control over her life, and what she put into her body was at least something she could be in charge of. Belle was the caretaker in their family, the one who was always having to pick up the pieces, simply because she was the only one capable of it. My father was still stealing. Camille was going back to school to learn to cut hair, but she was also finding time to have an over-the-top social life—hard drinking and partying. And Henry was still a kid. There was a lot of tension, a lot of arguing. Belle kept the peace—but then she threw it up.

For three years we took turns dragging her back and forth to the children's hospital. But then their insurance company said they'd reached the limit that they were entitled to for Belle's disorder. She couldn't go back anymore.

Belle wrote a note before killing herself at the age of seventeen. Basically it said, Please take good care of Henry, and take care of the dog. I guess what she was really saying was, I can't be responsible for anyone anymore. I'm too young for so much responsibility. I've had it.

The gun she used to blow her brains out belonged to my father. He'd showed me the place where he kept it once, in a hole cut into the wall in the basement, near the furnace room. I remembered my mother telling me once that when she was married to him he kept two small pistols in his socks, in the top drawer of his dresser. I said, "Why would you want to have a gun in the house?" He said it was for protection. "If you ever need it," he said, "now you know where it is."

I only saw the hole, not the gun itself. It was dark in the corner where he'd cut into the Sheetrock, and the gun must have been sitting on a spacer between the studs, deeper into the hole. He kept a framed picture, some sort of nature scene, hanging over where he'd sawed the door in the Sheetrock, so no one would suspect. But he must have made the mistake of showing Belle at some point too.

Even though my father's criminal expertise consisted primarily of B & E (breaking and entering), the police immediately considered him a person of interest. It was a good thing Belle had left the note behind. That got him off the hook. Henry, second in line for questioning, was off the hook too. *Take care of Henry and take care of the dog.*

None of my father's fingerprints were found on the gun—only Belle's. My father said that only proved it wasn't his gun. He said she must have got it from her boyfriend's house or from another friend's. I could have told the police that my father always wore gloves when he handled guns.

Henry loved Belle so much that he began to talk about killing himself too, so that he could be with her. It got so bad that the Department of Social Services had to get involved. They took him away for a short time and offered him counseling, and they brought him back again when my father, who was also a mess, was in better shape.

As for Camille, she never drank another drop of alcohol again after Belle died. She gave up her social life too. She even divorced my father. Belle's death turned Camille's life around completely. Eventually she married a man her own age and continued working in a hair salon. Henry lived with her for a while, until he got a job bagging groceries and was able to get his own place, very close to Camille's, making it easy for her to keep tabs on him.

Hugh never married again after Camille left him. In the beginning he had Henry with him, and then, after his father who lived in Palm Beach died, Hugh's mother, my grandmother, came to stay with him too. The three were living together in a one-bedroom apartment. It was then that Hugh was arrested for the last time for a B & E. He swore he didn't do it, and in fact the police report said that a guy with sideburns in his early thirties had been seen leaving the scene of the crime. My father was sixty-three by then. But a navy blue '83 Cadillac had been spotted in front of the house that was robbed, and my father owned just such a vehicle.

After his arrest Grandma was shipped back to Florida, and that was when Camille took Henry to live with her. Dad got three to five years for that caper, but he was paroled after a little more than a year. The parole board commissioners said his behavior had been good, and the evidence for the crime had never been solid in the first place. Supposedly the robber had taken some $25,000 worth of jewelry. The police had searched my father's car and apartment and never found any jewelry at all. But when I went over to clean the place out so that the apartment could be rented to someone else, I found his mask and gloves.

As for Al, after my mother divorced him, he married Phoebe, who was one of my electrolysis patients and also one of my best friends. In fact, he'd met Phoebe at my place one day when we were sitting at my kitchen table eating crab sandwiches. Phoebe was divorced, with three grown kids. She was engaged to marry again, but she broke it off to go out with Al and married him instead. At their wedding, Al wore the wedding ring from his marriage to my mother—and Phoebe, unbeknownst to her, wore my mother's old ring. Before their divorce, my mother accidentally dropped her ring down the kitchen sink drain. She thought it was gone for good and forgot about it. But Al took the drain pipe apart when she wasn't around and retrieved it. My sister Harriet noticed it on Phoebe's hand at the wedding reception and began to say, "Isn't that...?" Al kicked her under the table. Al and Phoebe enjoyed a twenty-year marriage.

You might think that with having both a father and a stepfather who liked to steal that I might be prone to the sticky-finger syndrome myself. In fact, I only stole one thing in all my life. When I was twelve or so, Harriet and I went to Filene's basement in downtown Boston and I stole a pair of nylons. We were going to a wedding and I needed them. Harriet took a pair too. We ran into a friend of ours in the store, and when we took out the nylons to show her, a store detective saw us and brought us to a back room. He scared the bloody pants off us. "Shall I call your daddy?" he asked, looking at me. "He's in jail," I said. "Shall I call your mommy?" he asked. Harriet and I looked at each other. "She's in the hospital." The detective shrugged. He said, "Then who am I supposed to call?" I stepped forward and said he should call Harriet's dad, my stepdad. If my mother had been home, we would have been grounded for months. But Al would just tell us not to do it again.

We paid for the stockings, but then we had no money to get home on the trolley. Luckily the conductor took pity on us—two young girls in tears and looking like they'd just escaped an earthquake or a crashed plane—and gave us free transfers. The store detective did call Al too. As soon as we walked in the house, he said, "You two were stealing? Don't do that again."

As I got older I lost my patience with people who felt the need to take what wasn't theirs. Once I mentioned to my mother that I had seen a gorgeous suede jacket, again in Filene's, and that I was planning to save up and buy it for myself. My stepfather must have heard me, or she told him, because when I opened my Christmas package a month later, there it was, the jacket I'd described. I wore it for about a year (I guess I was in denial) before I got up the nerve to ask Al how he'd paid for it. I wasn't afraid to ask him; I was just afraid of how he would answer. He said, "I didn't pay for it." Even though I loved it more than anything, I went to the Salvation Army the next day and handed it over.

Chapter Six – Looking For Love

WINTER PASSED AND THEN SPRING AND RICK SHARPE DID NOT CONTACT ME. I heard through the industry grapevine that he was seeing an electrologist with an office close to his home in Gloucester. It made me sàd to think of him out there alone, in that big house, without any furniture. Ralph had closed his beauty shop by then, so I didn't see Stephanie anymore either. I had my stock market conversations these days with my tennis partner, Stu. Rick and Stu had never met, but once Rick called when Stu was picking me up to go to the courts, and I put Stu on the phone to say hello. They wound up having a long conversation about Vestar and some other stocks. Stu and I liked to talk about Rick's UpJohn investment, how he made so much money in one fell swoop. He was our inspiration, and we imagined that one day we would invest with that kind of gusto ourselves.

One day in the summer Stu and I decided to take a ride to the Gloucester house. I wanted to see it in the daylight. I remembered the exit because it was the same one that went to the beach. But I didn't know if I would be able to recall the roads that came after the exit. It was a bright, sunny day, though, and Stu was up for a ride to that part of the world—whether we found the place or not. We planned to get sandwiches and drive to Wingaersheek Beach afterwards and watch the sailboats tack back and forth.

We made a few wrong turns, but eventually we found the place. I asked Stu to park in front of the house next door, so we wouldn't be noticed. The property looked different in the daylight. If anything, it was even more beautiful. The lawn was plush and green, and the flowers in the gardens were all in bloom. Hosta plants hugged the front perimeter of the frog pond and the foundation of the house. There was a well-shaped, mature peach tree I hadn't noticed before, laden with beautiful golden fruit. I didn't see the Porsche; it could have been in the garage.

It had never been our intention to barge in, but now that we were actually there, I felt an overwhelming desire to speak to Rick, to ask him what I had done to make him decide to turn down the friendship I had offered. I said to Stu, "Do you feel like going up to the door and seeing if he's there?" I told him to say we happened to be in the neighborhood, on our way to the beach. Then if Rick wanted to say hello, he could come out to the car.

Stu was wearing a funny lopsided smile when he came strolling back to the car, alone, a few minutes later. He opened the door and climbed in. He said, "I hate to tell you this, but his wife is there, and she's out to here!" He stretched his arms out in front of him, past the steering wheel, to suggest a very pregnant woman.

Then it all made sense to me. He hadn't thrown my friendship back in my face after all. He'd just been busy making it up with Carmen. Very busy. I smiled. I thought of my mother, hugely pregnant with Harriet, opening the door to find Erma on her stoop. "What did you say to her?" I asked.

"I said I was a friend of Rick's and just happened to be in the neighborhood. She was really nice. She said he was out at a nursing home, checking the moles on old people. She said to come on in, that he would be home in a little while and they were going to be having a party, for a cousin of hers. She wanted me to join them. I said, No thanks, just tell him Stu said hi."

Stu and I stared at each other. Rick's happiness made me just a little bit sad. I was happy for him of course, but I was sad that a chapter had closed in my life. Still, I was glad we'd come. "If you want something done, do it yourself" is probably the motto that best defines me. I looked around. Rick could be pulling up at any moment. "Let's get out of here," I said, and we took off for Wingaersheek.

Chapter Seven – The Laser Changed Everything

PEOPLE, EVEN PEOPLE IN THE INDUSTRY, WILL TELL YOU THAT THE FIRST LASER FOR hair removal got its start in the late 1990s. In fact, the technology was actually invented in the late sixties. Dermatologists used the first models to remove lesions from the skin, but they noted that in so doing, hair was also removed, as well as tattoos. The early models that were ultimately adapted specifically for hair removal back then were deemed unsafe, and the Food and Drug Administration shut them down. Models that were presented in the seventies and eighties also had problems and didn't stay long on the market. In 1995, there came a laser that got the FDA's blessing—initially. But while it was safer than other models, it still wasn't safe enough, so the FDA shut it down yet again. Then, finally, in 1997, the FDA gave the okay to a model that was easy to use, had an epidermal cooling system, and had far less potential for side effects. But the price of these new (Class IV) lasers— between $80,000 and $100,000—made them prohibitive for most skin care professionals.

The big difference between electrolysis hair removal and hair removal with lasers was that the laser could treat multiple hair follicles at a time, resulting in less appointments and faster results. But laser hair removal wasn't for everyone. First of all, there was no telling whether the hair was gone forever. Secondly, there could be some blistering. For someone like Fred, my long-time client who didn't want his wife—or anyone else—to ever suspect that we were slowly but surely removing hairs from his face and knuckles, laser hair removal would not have been an option.

Another problem was that the laser worked best on people with coarse dark hair and lighter skin—which leaves out big segments of the population. Because the light energy from the laser is absorbed by the pigment melanin and then transformed into heat energy to disable the follicle, in people with darker skin color, and thus more melanin, the skin can compete with the hair follicle for the light energy, which can damage the skin. The darker the skin color, the more risk for burning, infection, and even skin discoloration. That said, there were still plenty of people out there in the world who were going to absolutely love the laser. And there was one genius out there who saw the immense potential in the technology from the get-go and went all out to harness it—and that of course was Dr. Richard J. Sharpe.

Rick started calling me again and talking to me about lasers. Even if I couldn't afford one, he said, I had to have some access to one, because otherwise my patients who wanted to at least give it a try would go elsewhere, and my business would fail. He was as certain that the laser was going to be the next big thing as he had once been about UpJohn stock.

Still, I didn't take his warnings seriously at first. I had forgotten all about him in all this time, some five years by then, and I was not interested in either him or the laser. His phone calls were only annoying to me. I kept thinking, You treated me like junk; you never even called to see if I was dead or alive—and now you suddenly care whether my business is a success? But as I sat there each day, in my quiet office with my epilator, pulling out my patients' unwanted hairs one by one by one, I had a lot of time to think. And eventually I concluded that if I was going to be a smart businesswoman, I was going to have to at least consider the laser. The next time Rick called I said I was open to discussion.

The first laser Rick bought weighed in at a hefty three-hundred pounds. He hired piano movers to haul it around. He'd waited until the end of the year, when manufacturers were ready to give discounts in order to move stock, to make the purchase, and he'd charged the entire amount—$62,000—to his American Express.

Rick had a plan; he would use the laser himself on his patients in his Gloucester office a couple of days a week, and on the other days, he would have it delivered to the offices of people like me who couldn't afford lasers of their own. We would give him a percentage of the money we earned.

He was like a mad scientist during this time. He still had his regular dermatology patients plus his rounds at the local hospitals and nursing homes, and he'd also begun doing liposuction procedures. Taking on the laser work would require a huge commitment of energy and time. But he wasn't about to let the opportunity pass him by. In order to ensure that he—and the rest of us—had enough business to make moving the monster laser from one place to another viable, he was setting up a computer system whereby he would have multiple websites for different areas of the region—all pointing business his way. For instance, if you searched for "laser hair removal Boston," you would be taken directly to his site. Likewise for locations in the rest of Massachusetts, and in Maine, Rhode Island, New Hampshire, Vermont and Connecticut. In fact, anywhere in New England, if you wanted to know about laser hair removal—and other related services—you were going to get Dr. Richard J. Sharpe, who could then redirect you to one of the eighteen affiliate offices—of which mine was one—that agreed to work with him. Optimizing websites with the proper search words, linking pages to each other, fixing back links and working to improve search engine rankings was practically a full-time job in itself.

In order to support the colossal Internet system he was creating, Rick brought twelve computers into his house, which was the headquarters for the online component of his consortium. The electrical wiring and cables he had installed to sustain the computers would have been sufficient to support the needs of the Boston Hynes Convention Center. He was constantly on the phone—with one of us, with a domain hosting service, or with other website designers—making it all happen. He bought up domain names as fast as if they were highly discounted gold nuggets, and he created meta tags using every possible keyword. He even used words that seemingly had nothing to do with lasers or hair removal. For instance, he included "Hyaluronic Acid," which I always thought was a molecule in the natural jelly that keeps our joints lubricated. Rick said it was more than that, that there were inhabitants in a village outside Tokyo with high levels of hyaluronic acid in their diets, which was keeping them from aging at a normal rate. I still didn't know what that had to do with lasers, but that was Rick, always a step ahead of everyone else. I think he hoped to target another group of potential clients. Maybe it included other doctors, scientists, chemists and researchers. Carmen didn't understand what he was doing either, he lamented once to me. She was always standing behind him, watching him optimize web pages and talk on the phone at the same time. "She probably thinks I'm cheating on her or looking at porn," he chuckled.

I went to Rick's dermatology office for laser hair removal training sessions. The first time I came by Stephanie was there and he demonstrated on her leg. Then he disappeared into his own office and left me to practice on Stephanie on my own. She caught me up on things going on in her life. She was about to graduate from college, and she now had not one but two much younger siblings: Leo, who Carmen had been pregnant with the day I stopped by with Stu, and Judy, who was still a toddler.

Stephanie looked great, as beautiful as ever, and she was just as sweet. I said to her, "You should learn the laser and work with your father. You could make lot of money." She said that she had a full-time job lined up with Xerox, selling copiers and office machines. In fact, a month or so later she came up to my office and tried to get me to buy a new copy machine. In the end she did do some work with a few of the laser affiliates.

Before I left that day, Rick called me into his office to meet one of his patients. When I opened the door I was shocked to see a chipmunk sitting on the patient table. Well, really it wasn't a chipmunk; it was a woman with very swollen cheeks, further accentuated by her incredibly ebullient smile. I turned to Rick for an explanation. He laughed and said that he'd taken some of her own fat and transferred it into her face. When the swelling went down, she would look ten years younger. "Her own fat?" I gasped. I knew about fat transfers but had never heard of anyone doing it to their face before. The woman rubbed her backside and said, "My butt is sore, but I'll never miss the extra fat there."

Rick's life was not the only one that had changed utterly in the years since I had last seen him. I had met Gary, a kind, creative and good-looking military man originally from Texas. Gary had been married to a woman from South Carolina and they had two sons. He was with the Coast Guard at the time and he was transferred to Massachusetts. His wife moved up with him, but she didn't like New England, and I guess there were other problems too. When her grandmother back in South Carolina got sick, she packed up the kids and as much stuff as she could fit in the family van and told Gary she'd be back in a few weeks. She never returned. He'd been devastated.

They divorced and eventually we got together through a dating service, and we just hit it off. I knew what I was looking for in a mate—someone good-looking and smart, and maybe with military experience. I believed military men had better manners and were more respectful, and I liked the grooming and polished appearance and solid education components. Another plus would be if he played tennis, which Gary did. I remember asking Bart Fish once, "How do I find the right man?" He said, "Who do you admire of the men you know?" I'd always admired my cousin who served in the Air Force and later worked as a commercial pilot. "There's your answer," Bart Fish said.

When Gary's older son, Toby, was ready for high school, he informed us that he wanted to live with us in Massachusetts. Having never had a child before, I was nervous about what it would be like to be a stepmom. I put together a two-page document asking him to define his objectives. Was he interested in sports? Which ones? What were his academic goals? Was there a religion he was interested in practicing?

It took six months, but eventually he answered all my questions and put his signature on it. In the meantime I sold my condo and bought a three-bedroom house in Newton. Then Toby moved in and we were three. Later Gary and I decided to open our house to international exchange students. We made a room for Toby in the finished basement and took in three more kids, each for various periods of time. When each of them moved on, another moved in to take his place. The house was not that big, but we made it work. I was still hoping that one day I would have enough money to buy a big house, the kind that could accommodate any number of people that I might want to invite into my life—and now I was thinking that my dream house was likely to happen sooner rather than later, because of the laser. I had become a believer too.

I got thirty-eight percent of the money brought in by the laser and Rick got the rest. In the beginning, my office got the laser every other Saturday. I would set up all my laser patients for the same day. The minute the work day ended, the piano movers were there to pick the laser up and move it to the next location. Rick had been right; the laser was exceedingly popular. Almost everyone wanted to give it a try. And because Rick's complex innovative Internet marketing network was so successful, more and more new clients were coming my way. In a very short time, two days a month with the laser was not enough. So Rick arranged to leave it with me for two consecutive days, four to six times a month. But still it wasn't enough, and the other seventeen laser leasers must have had the same complaint, because before long Rick announced that he'd bought two more lasers—a portable Diode and a second Gentle Lase.

Carmen, who had given up nursing to take care of their young children, got involved. She became Rick's office manager. A great deal of work was coming in. Thanks to his perseverance and his 800 number, the business phones in their home office were ringing off the hook. Lasers were being shuffled from one location to another. New patients were being allocated, depending on whose office they were closest to and which of the affiliates had the most time available. None of us had any extra time, but somehow we fit them in. Suddenly we were all making a fortune—at least on the days when we had the laser.

Due to the nature of the business—the stigma that goes along with hair removal, for people keeping secrets from spouses and those keeping secrets generally—a lot of people paid in cash. We were told to put the money into an envelope with all the receipts and give it to the movers when they came to pick up the laser. Then the movers would deliver it to Carmen and she would figure out who was owed what and we would get a check a little later.

For my employees and me, this method was a little nerve-wracking. At first it was always the same three moving men who showed up, in Rick's beat-up turquoise late '80s Ford Econoline van with its handicap extension ramp, to get the laser. But now that there was so much shuffling going on, sometimes one or two or even all three of the men would be new faces. At the end of one particularly busy day when we had taken in more cash than usual, I asked my associate, Reena, to run to the bank, deposit all the cash and stick a check for the amount into the envelope with the paperwork that went to Carmen. The next day I came into the office to find Reena in tears. Carmen, she said, had called and screamed at her. "What did you do with all that cash?" she'd yelled. "Don't ever do that again. That's not how I want it done."

I felt worse than Reena, who had only been following my directions. By now I'd met Carmen a few times and I really liked her and I wanted badly for her to like me, for us to be friends. I called her immediately and apologized. I tried to explain why I'd made the decision to deposit the cash and I suggested that it might be safer if she picked up the money herself. Phones were ringing crazily in the background during our conversation. Because of all the commotion, we didn't really make any headway and I resolved to go back to putting the cash in an envelope and hoping for the best. Later, I mentioned the incident to Rick and he said he would discuss it with Carmen. "You did the right thing," he said. But either he never discussed it with her or it was a battle he'd lost, because we didn't hear anything more about it.

A few times Gary and I joined the Sharpes and their various colleagues and friends at their house in Gloucester for social gatherings. The house was as lively on those occasions as it was on workdays when the phones were ringing off their hooks and the computers were buzzing with queries from potential new clients.

Carmen was a gracious hostess, and everyone loved her. Half the neighborhood would always be there, and always some of her neighbors would float from person to person introducing themselves and telling stories about how Carmen had brought meals over when they were sick, or how she had offered to take care of their kids when they had to be away, or how she had given her time and money to some community benefit or event. They said she tipped the trash man; she tipped the window washers. One day she noticed that one of the workers at the house had a cracked windshield on his car. When she asked why he was driving around like that, he said his insurance company wouldn't cover it and he didn't have the cash to fix it. Immediately she said, "I'll get that fixed for you," and she did. There was no end to her good deeds and generosity. Even the neighborhood dogs were ardent fans and knew that they would get TLC and a food treat if they sat outside the front door or the slider in the back and barked.

People mentioned Rick's generosity too—especially in conjunction with Carmen's. One of the neighbors had had a lighting strike on her house, and while the insurance company paid for the repairs from the fire damage, she'd lost all her linens and kitchen items. Rick and Carmen had a huge party for her, and attendees brought bridal-shower-type gifts, quickly outfitting her with everything she would need to recover from her household loses. But a few neighbors grumbled that Rick drove too fast on the country roads that wound through the quiet neighborhood. And at least one of the neighbors disapproved of the fact that he delighted in getting his young children—and their young children too—to crouch down with him on the lawn and observe the movement of the snakes that slithered through the gardens and the turtles and frogs that lived in the pond in front of the house. In fact, the Sharpe children knew all about snakes and turtles and even kept some as pets. Rick took them to the pet shop regularly. It was one of the activities that he most enjoyed doing with them.

Mostly when people talked about Richard Sharpe, they talked about how smart he was, how his mind was always working at full speed. People who had known the Sharpes for a long time liked to talk about how he and Carmen had had it so rough when they were kids, how they had to struggle to pay the bills and put themselves through school, and all the time while taking care of a baby who they had refused to give up for adoption even though everyone tried to convince them it would be for the best. They liked to comment on how great it was that after all their years of poverty and hard work, things were finally paying off. They were right about that. All eighteen laser leasers were raking it in, so Rick and Carmen had to be making a fortune, more money than they'd ever dreamed of.

Carmen sent me an invitation to Stephanie's college graduation party, and she followed it up with a phone call to make sure I was coming. She said it would be very special for Stephanie to have me there. On the day of the party I found myself alone with Carmen in the kitchen and I asked her why she'd waited so long to get pregnant again. She and Rick were still in high school when Stephanie was conceived.

I was hoping for a little girl talk, something to get Carmen to warm up to me. People were gathered in the dining room and the room where the

Jacuzzi had once been (which was now a sunroom) and out on the deck and on the lawn below us. I could see her two little ones from the window, running in circles with some of the other smaller children, chasing an adorable golden retriever puppy that belonged to one of the neighbors. They were all laughing, squealing with joy. Carmen was looking for something in the refrigerator. She answered me very matter-of-factly, without turning. She said she'd been unable to conceive for a while, that she'd had to have a hysterosalpingogram, a procedure that flushes out the tubes. Afterwards she got pregnant easily.

When she withdrew from the refrigerator, with a bowl of fruit salad, she was wearing her impish smile. She seemed always to be smiling. It was part of her charm. Her hair was cut short around her cherubic face and her teeth were movie-star white. She seemed so capable. It was impossible not to admire her. Her twinkling eyes darted from me to a plate of cookies on the table. I could see her mind was not on the conversation I was trying to have with her. I said, "Do you mind if I get some cheese?" She said, "No, go ahead; help yourself." I hesitated. I felt shy about going into someone else's refrigerator and rifling around. But then she put down the container of fruit and went back into the refrigerator and retrieved the cheese platter. She handed it to me. "Here you go, dear," she said, and, still smiling, she picked up the fruit bowl and cookie platter and hurried outside to her other guests.

Just before Christmas of 1998, Carmen came to my office with a huge, beautifully-wrapped fruit- and cheese-laden gift basket. She also had another package, a festive holiday gift sack filled with an abundance of colorful tissue paper, for me. I would have opened it then and there, but she was in a hurry. She said she was playing Santa, making deliveries to all eighteen offices in just one day. I thanked her for her and Rick's generosity and wished her a beautiful holiday. Then, as she was turning to leave, I remembered the transgender conference coming up in January and I called out excitedly, "Carmen, we need to talk about the conference!" I expected her to be excited too, but she only waved her arm at me in a manner that made me think that the mention of the conference was annoying to her. "We have to have the lasers there," I insisted, hoping to bring home the relevance. "Are you angry about something?" I asked. Now I was on her heels, following her to the door.

"No, no, it's nothing," she said. She opened the door and went out without looking back.

The First Event transgender conference is an annual January function that attracts all kinds of people: physicians, educators, students, transgenders, cross-dressers, transsexuals, transvestites, gays, significant others.... Its purpose is educational, offering workshops and presentations delivered by everyone from psychotherapists to reassignment surgeons to poets and artists. But of course it is also a great way to have fun and make new friends. For years transgender people got virtually no support from the society at large. Now that was changing and conferences like the one coming up in Boston were highly anticipated and well attended throughout the country.

For those of us in the business world who had transgender clients, the conference was a great opportunity to answer questions from potential new clients. Electrologists always had booths at the conference. So did hair stylists, wig makers, makeup artists, clothing manufacturers, book publishers, jewelers, and many others. Of course we had to have a booth there, and we had to have one of the lasers. All eighteen of us—and Rick—had the laser work down pat now, and we were ready to take on even more business.

I sat for a while staring at the door through which Carmen had disappeared. Eventually I opened the bag she had given me. The vase inside was beautiful, dark blue porcelain with specs of other colors. Handmade. She had to have bought it at a gallery or studio. It was not the kind of thing you find in a department store. Towards the end of the day I made calls to some of my seventeen counterparts, to wish them a happy holiday. While I had them on the phone, I asked them if Carmen had stopped by and what she'd given them. Everyone I spoke to reported that they'd received a candle.

Chapter Eight – Clothes Make the Man (or Woman)

IN JANUARY RICK SAID THAT YES OF COURSE WE WERE GETTING A BOOTH AT THE transgender conference, a big one. He and Carmen were already working on the details for the display staging to announce the launch of "LaseHair," the umbrella for our alliance. Under that umbrella fell all the other things that the eighteen of us were doing collectively—such as power peels and Botox and collagen work—and the dermatology and liposuction. Rick wanted each of us to spend at least some time during the four-day conference manning the booth. The cost for the booth and the signage was substantial; everyone needed to participate in the effort to bring in enough new business to justify the expense.

The first day of the conference, Carmen was there with some of the others setting up. After the setup, she sat down to have coffee with Gina (who was the first transgender in the Commonwealth of Massachusetts to win custody of her children over her former wife). But she left long before the doors opened to the public. I was one of the early arrivals, along with two of my laser-leasing colleagues, Mike and Norma, who both worked in the same office. We were all impressed with the job that Carmen had done on the booth. It was much bigger than most of its neighbors, in a great location where you couldn't miss it in the conference hall. Its back wall featured a dark blue chintz curtain on which an electric blue banner had been affixed with the alliance name and phone number and of course the name of our fearless leader and medical director, Dr. Richard J. Sharpe. Tacked to the curtain all around the banner were smaller off-white banners, each listing one of the many undertakings that our alliance could accomplish to enrich one's aesthetic life: Laser Hair Removal, Electrolysis, Botox, Power Peels, Liposuction, Hair-loss & Propecia, Collagen & Fat Transfer....

As soon as the doors opened, attendees started pouring in. It was fun to look at the people and guess which ones were sporting a different gender than the one they'd been born with. Having so many transgenders and transgender supporters all together in one big ballroom made for a very festive environment. Here at last was a place where people could be themselves without censure. Everyone seemed to be in a good mood. Everyone who came by our booth was friendly. Some people were downright giddy.

When Rick arrived, an even-more-cheerful-than-usual Norma asked him if he wanted to borrow one of her dresses. Because she planned to stay overnight for a few of the days of the conference, she had a room upstairs in the hotel where the event was being held. She said he could buy a wig from one of the vendors. "It will be good for business," she pleaded. "And besides, you'll probably look better than half these guys here."

Rick looked at the faces of those of us who were already there at the booth. Then he turned to look out at the jubilant crowd milling their way down our aisle. It was obvious that Norma's idea had captured his imagination. "I can't," he said finally. "I don't have that much time." He explained that he had set up a laser at the office of Gail Sweetwater, an electrologist in Somerville. He'd promised to hurry back to teach her how to operate it. Then afterwards he had a liposuction in Hamilton, and a few dermatology patients to see in Gloucester. Then he would return to the conference again. Carmen had reserved a room for him so that he'd be able to take a rest if he needed one.

But Norma wouldn't take no for an answer. "Come on, Rick," she urged. "It'll be so much fun."

He sighed. "Okay," he said finally. "But only for a few hours."

I caught my breathe when Rick and Norma emerged from the elevator sometime later. I could just see them moving through the crowd. Rick kept his eyes downcast and his shoulders slightly forward, like a shy debutante about to meet a room full of people.

Some cross-dressers are six feet tall and have wide masculine shoulders and you can tell from a mile away, no matter what they are wearing. Others are more petite and it takes a moment or two to be certain, even for someone as experienced as me. Rick was one of the latter types. He looked almost beautiful. The wig he and Norma had chosen featured long dark shiny straight hair with longish, wispy bangs. The dress was a mock two-piece, a silk chiffon with a flowered bodice—gold on black—with a black calf-length skirt, size 8. It fit him perfectly. He was wearing makeup too, mascara and eyeliner and lipstick. Norma had applied it sparingly, just the way she'd done her own. Norma had loaned him a simple necklace, a faux diamond in a plain setting on a gold chain. The only thing that gave him away was his shoes; he was still wearing the same worn cranberry penny loafers that he wore all the time. I had seen him plenty of times sitting with one leg crossed over one knee and the sole of his shoe exposed—or with both feet up on the desk relaxing. Those penny loafers were so old they had holes in the bottom. But once he was behind the booth with the rest of us, his feet were not exposed.

I had never seen Rick dressed before—at least not in the flesh. I knew he dressed on Halloween because he had mentioned that a few times. He and Carmen would dress as sisters. Once, on the day he'd first told me his real name, he had shown me a snapshot that a friend had taken of him at someone's house party years ago. He was not the type to go to clubs and I would have been shocked if anyone tried to tell me he'd ever had a homosexual encounter. Rick Sharpe liked women. Anyone with eyes could see that he was madly in love with his wife.

I couldn't get over seeing him dressed. I kept sneaking looks at him. His smile was just as tentative—maybe even more tentative—than it was when he was his regular male self. I had to wonder whether he was ever one-hundred percent comfortable in his own body. I recalled the day he got his Porsche, and how he had joyfully skipped across the room to his Doors music. It made me feel sad to know that he was keeping so much of his true self under lock and key.

For the short time he was with us that day, he seemed to enjoy interacting with the conference attendees, and the people were very comfortable with him. We took pictures of him, alone and with the rest of us. He stood in the middle for one of the group photos that I took, and the first thing I noticed when I looked into the viewfinder was how timid his smile was compared to those of Norma and Ida, the electrologists standing on either side of him. Both women were all teeth and gums.

Finally we let him go up and change so he could leave for his appointments. But later we got a call from Cheryl, one of Rick's medical assistants, who had gone to Gail's Somerville office to teach her how to do power peels. She was still there when Rick arrived. She said she opened the door for him and she knew right away that something was different. Then she figured it out. She said, "Rick, do you know you're wearing mascara?" In his haste, he had forgotten to remove it. We all had a good laugh over that.

Chapter Nine – The Collapse of the Kingdom

RICK AND I WORKED ON A CLIENT NEWSLETTER TOGETHER, SOMETHING THAT would really describe the scope of our services. We were happy with the way it came out. I didn't quite understand why we were still trying to enlarge the alliance though; we all had more work than we could possibly do. How much more could we grow? Rick said that as long as there were independent professionals out there who might want to join us, there was no end to our growth potential.

With all the money they were bringing in, Carmen thought it might be time to move to a newer house. Rick seemed to be okay with that, as long as the house hunting process didn't interfere with his work. He was so busy now, working probably seventy hours a week, maybe more, and he had a lot on his mind. He was still spending a lot of his time on the phones and with the computer, embellishing our marketing machine. And then there was his medical work, and his research, and a skin product that he had recently developed, something to get rid of acne. (At the time, the preferred acne deterrent was Accutane, which required regular blood tests to determine whether it was having adverse effects on one's liver. The alternative that Rick created, called Alpha Hydroxy Gold, had no effect on the liver and yet did the job of getting rid of blemishes on the skin. Patients loved it.) And there were the canisters.

The lasers used a coolant that came in a canister. The canisters were expensive and Rick and the rest of us were going through them quickly because of our workload. In addition to everything else, Rick had a degree from years back in automotive studies. He knew that he could have canisters manufactured for pennies, and he could buy the coolant—which was the same as that used in cars—by the gallon and fill the canisters himself. But the company that made the canisters found out about his plans and threatened to sue him.

Rick didn't think their argument would hold up in court, but it was one more thing to think about, one more thing to keep him tossing and turning at night. And as if that was not enough, he had two liposuction patients threatening to sue him. One was upset because Rick had not removed enough fat from her body. He believed that it was unsafe to take more than five liters, and he stuck to that and all his patients understood that. So again, it was not a claim that was likely to hold up in court, but in the meantime, it was there, hanging over his head. In the second liposuction case, the patient didn't have the patience to stay on the table for as long as it was taking (patients getting lipo don't always need general anesthesia, just a local where the small tube enters the skin) and opted to leave before Rick was done. Not surprisingly, she wasn't happy with the end result either.

The amount of energy that he was expending during this time was mind-boggling. Watching him—on those occasions when I visited his Gloucester office—was like watching a video on fast forward. He was up, down, coming, going.... He talked fast. Our conversations were unsettling sometimes because I could not keep up with him; I could not gather my thoughts and put together an intelligent response in same instant in which I knew he was awaiting it. His dark eyes seemed to drill into mine, expecting something I couldn't produce. I only hoped that he wouldn't max out and fall apart, that it wouldn't all get to be too much for him. I voiced my concern once, and he said he was almost there, almost where he wanted to be. He just needed to build his kingdom a little larger—make it just a little more secure—and then he was going to kick back and relax and enjoy his time with his family.

He came so close to reaching his goal.

It was Norma, the same woman who had dressed Rick at the transgender conference, who discovered the house—a mansion located on a quiet street in Wenham, about twelve miles from Gloucester, and that much closer to the highway to Boston. The house was still in the process of being built when it went on the market. Something had happened with the previous owners—divorce, possibly—and they had changed their minds about going forward.

Carmen immediately saw the benefits of buying an incomplete house. The frame was there, the electrical and plumbing were in; it was eighty percent finished. What was lacking were fixtures, appliances, cabinets, textures, colors...the things that make a house a home. For someone as creative and design-oriented as she was, it was a dream come true. Even though she was incredibly busy herself, with the two younger children and the LaseHair office management, she wanted to take on this additional responsibility; she wanted it badly.

Rick was happy in the Gloucester house. He loved the marsh down the road, a constant source of snakes and frogs for him and kids. He loved that the ocean was so nearby. The Gloucester house was on a cul de sac. It was quiet. They could let the dogs—they had two at the time, a blind chocolate lab and a Lhasa Apso—roam freely.

Carmen argued that the Wenham house was in a better school district. She was right about that. And they could easily afford it. She would oversee its completion herself, so he wouldn't have that additional burden. Bruce, Rick's brother, who worked in construction, could come up from Connecticut and advise her. There was a man who had come to paint the Gloucester house the year before, Art; Carmen thought he could help with the painting at Wenham and a lot of the other finish work. In the end, there was nothing for Rick to do but sign the paperwork and apply for the construction loan. Once the construction was complete, they would sell the house in Gloucester and move to Wenham.

Anyway, that was the plan.

I can't say exactly what happened between the time they first saw the house in Wenham in November of 1999 and Carmen's death only months later in July of 2000. Virtually all of my conversations with Rick during that period were about business. Even so, with there being eighteen offices of people who were in touch with Rick and, to a lesser degree, with one another, on a regular basis, we were able to piece together a story, albeit mostly from Rick's point of view and without the details that would become clear later, at the trial. Here is what we *believed* to be true:

In December, Rick's sense of anxiety—over his workload, the canister lawsuit, the lipo lawsuits, etc.— got worse. He realized he was working too hard, and what for? As a result of his business ventures and his proficiency in the stock market, he and Carmen (still in their early forties) had amassed over five million dollars. Eighty percent of their wealth had come to them in the previous five years. One day just before Christmas they went for a family walk in the woods behind the house in Gloucester. They discovered a pond that was covered with leaves and brush. Rick and Carmen worked with the kids to clear the brush away. Beneath it was a layer of ice. The kids didn't have their skates with them, but they began skating back and forth in their shoes, having a great time. Rick and Carmen settled themselves on a downed tree to watch. They were happy; it was a good time to break the news. Rick explained to Carmen that he was going to cut back to working only two days a week. He was burning out. He was having anxiety attacks. He couldn't do it anymore. He planned to give up the liposuction, the ClickMed—a software program he'd developed for doctors—and some other aspects of his work. They discussed the possibility of taking a vacation, but he knew that would only be a Band-Aid on a festering wound.

In January they closed on the Wenham house. At first the deed was in both their names, but because the canister and the lipo lawsuits were still up in the air, the estate planner Rick hired suggested they put the house, and virtually all their other assets, into Carmen's name alone for now. While they were at it, Rick transferred funds into trust accounts for the two smaller kids. He also began working out the logistics for a trust account for Stephanie. In short, he divested himself of practically everything.

Rick had always made an effort to keep fit physically. But now that he was determined to scale back, he was going to the gym after work a couple of days a week, to do aerobics. Sometimes he was the only man in the group, but he didn't care. He believed aerobics was one of the best forms of exercise and he enjoyed it. He also hired a personal trainer, Hazel, to work with him on weight training. By late February things were coming along. He was exercising more and putting together a plan to bring in other people at the management level so that he could work less. But one day at work he didn't feel that well, and he decided to skip his aerobics class that afternoon and go home.

Rick found Judy and Leo in the sunroom. Judy was coloring. He sat down beside her and started coloring too. But Leo tried to pull the coloring book away from them, a sign that he felt neglected. So Rick left off coloring and forced himself to chase him around for a while. He tickled him when he caught him. When Carmen came into the room, Rick explained that he'd skipped the gym because he felt so bad. He didn't think he could eat any dinner. Carmen suggested he go up to their bedroom and rest. After she and the kids ate, she would bring them up to say goodnight before she put them to bed.

He slept for a while. But Carmen didn't come up with the kids. Generally he and Carmen took turns reading to the kids on their bed before sending them off to their own rooms. Rick went downstairs to see what was going on. Carmen was watching CNN. The kids were playing. It looked like everyone was staying up later than usual. She said she'd be up in a little while.

Rick went back to bed and fell sound asleep. Sometime later he awoke and wondered why Carmen had still not come up with the kids. He went downstairs, but no one was home. He thought they must have run to the store for something. He went upstairs again and listened for their return. After a while he began to grow anxious. It was getting late and still the house remained quiet. He went downstairs once more and called Carmen on her cell phone. She didn't answer. It occurred to him to call the police but he didn't know what to tell them. He had no idea what was going on. He spent the rest of the night torturing himself with the possibilities.

Carmen called in the morning and announced that she wanted a divorce. Rick couldn't believe what he was hearing. According to him, it had come out of nowhere. He asked where she was and she refused to tell him. He said that not telling him where his kids were constituted kidnapping and he would call the police. She said if he called the police, he would sorely regret it.

Rick called Ann Marie, a business lawyer he knew, to talk about his options. Stephanie was living in the apartment above the garage at the Gloucester house at the time. He talked to her too, but she said she had no better idea of what was going on than he did. He called Carmen again, and she answered. He gave her an ultimatum: either she agreed to tell him what was going on, or he would call the police and charge her with kidnapping. She agreed to meet with him on neutral territory, at Ann Marie's office.

Carmen brought Leo and Judy to the meeting. They seemed confused and unsure how to greet their father. As for Carmen, she refused to make eye contact with him. Rick suggested they see a marriage counselor but she said it was too late for that. Finally she agreed to come to Ann Marie's office again the following day, without the kids, so that they could make sense of the situation.

The first thing he asked her during the second visit was whether there was another man. She said there was not. Between his attempt to scale down his business and Carmen's sudden abandonment, the laser business was falling to shambles. The whole time they were in Ann Marie's office his beeper was going off. The affiliates had questions—about scheduling, about late payments, about problems with the lasers. These complications were par for the course, but usually Rick was at the office to deal with them, and Carmen was available to make sure the lasers arrived at the various locations on schedule. While they were standing there, one of the affiliates called to say she hadn't received her laser that day—and she had patients coming in all afternoon! She was in a panic. "Come on," Carmen said, "let's go deliver the laser to her."

They drove to the office. The undelivered laser was sitting in the company's blue van. Carmen got behind the wheel and they took off to deliver it. While they were driving along, Rick mentioned that he'd decided to put the Cambridge condo, which they'd been renting out for some years, in

Stephanie's name. The little kids had the trust funds, but Stephanie's fund was still incomplete. He wanted her to have the condo in the meantime.

The days passed. Rick lost thirty pounds. He cried all the time. His life had been pulled out from under him. Carmen was staying in a hotel with the kids until the Wenham house was deemed habitable. She told Rick that he was forbidden to come by for any reason. She would bring the kids to him on the days when he could see them. She'd hired a very aggressive lawyer, Wyler Grange, to work with her to draw up divorce papers.

Rick called me during this time and asked me to come to his Hamilton office and help him. He said there was plenty of space and I could do electrolysis and laser on some of his dermatology patients who wanted it. I could only come on my days off; I had my own business to run. He had other people helping out as well. Without Carmen to manage, and with Rick tense and distracted, the general atmosphere in his office was one of apprehension.

Although Carmen had said that there was no other man, Rick heard through the grapevine that there was. Work was still being done on the house so his kids were exposed to a lot of men, but there was one they knew better than the rest—Art—and his name came up a lot when they were visiting Rick. Art, a painter, was the one Carmen had hired to be the contractor for the finishing work in Wenham. Rick knew the rumor was true when he stopped into Dunkin Donuts in Wenham one morning and overhead the construction people in line in front of him laughing about their boss, who was "porking the rich bitch."

Carmen and Rick had been married twenty-seven years. He was devastated. He tried to talk to her, but she got a restraining order. Even though he had cut back substantially, he was still working, still seeing patients, still going on…because he still had some hope. But then everything came to a standstill—which seems inevitable in retrospect.

Rick was upstairs one night in the Gloucester house, working on one of the lasers—the portable Diode, which had two separate parts. It wasn't running properly. It was burning people. It needed to be recalibrated. He had taken it apart and decided to carry it downstairs—one piece at a time—where he had more tools. Each piece was heavy, about eighty pounds. The staircase was what is known as a "bridal staircase," which is to say that it is neither straight nor spiral. A bridal staircase features a graceful curve—easy to forget about if you are carrying something heavy and bulky in front of you, if you are clumsy. He was still at the top of the staircase when he fell.

He tumbled all the way to the bottom and spilled out onto the black and white ceramic tile floor in the foyer. The laser fell on top of him.

He lost consciousness for an indeterminate amount of time. When he came to, he took painkillers and crawled into bed. But when he awoke the next morning he felt worse. Much worse. He went to the hospital and the doctor who saw him determined that he was post-concussive and had a fractured pelvis and a fractured tailbone. He stayed in the hospital for several days.

ঙ০৩

One of my epilators was at Rick's Hamilton office, where I had been using it on the days I'd been there to help out. I hadn't been to his office in several weeks, since his accident. No one had. I needed to get my epilator back, to have it as backup in case anything happened to the one I used in Newton.

I called Rick at home one day and asked if I could come by to pick it up. He said, "No, don't take it back, leave it where it is." I told him, "It's nothing personal, but I want it back." He acquiesced. He wasn't able to meet me at the Hamilton office because of his condition, but he said I could stop at the house and get the office key. The front door would be unlocked and I should let myself in.

Gary knew I was nervous about meeting with Rick and volunteered to drive over with me. On the way, I shared my last memory of working with Rick. I had been in one room using my epilator to do electrolysis on patients while he had been preparing for a liposuction consultation. I happened to be out in the hallway when his lipo patient arrived. This woman was as thin as a rail; "skinny" would have been an understatement. As soon as Rick was available, I asked him what fat he planned to extract from her. He said she had a little extra padding on the inside of her knees, like a bunion that sticks out on some people's feet. "What!" I exclaimed. "You're going to lipo the knees on a woman who probably doesn't weigh a hundred pounds? Doesn't she need that fat to make her joints work?" He almost laughed. He said, "Linda, it bothers her. It's an elective cosmetic procedure. This is the way of the future. You're going to see more and more people taking advantage of technology to change the way they look." I remembered at the time thinking it was good to hear him talking about the future, that maybe he had some hope that his life would improve.

I asked Gary to wait in the car. I knocked on the door to let Rick know I was there and went in. I had come to associate the Gloucester house with

Carmen and the kids, with the neighbors coming and going, friends, family, cars, noise, food. It was shocking now to find the place as quiet as a tomb and all but empty, just as it had been the first time I'd been there. I walked through the rooms, aware of the echo of my footsteps, and found Rick in the living room, sitting diagonally, like a plank leaning across a straight chair, in the corner by the picture window. His weight was all on one hip, so as to keep from irritating either his pelvis or his tailbone. His crutches were leaning against the wall. When he turned from the window to look at me, I knew I was looking at misery personified.

To cover up my shock, I said the first thing that occurred to me. "What are you doing here sitting all alone in the corner of the room like this?" All I could think was, This isn't him. This can't be him.

He whispered, "I can't move. Everything hurts."

I saw the key ring on the window sill and took it. There were quite a few keys on it. I could already imagine myself standing out in front of his office trying one key after another until I got it right. But I didn't want to ask. I wanted to get my epilator and go home.

"Don't leave me, Linda," he pleaded. "I'll be back to work in a few months. Everything will be the way it was."

We looked at each other. I said, "Rick, do you want to work at getting your wife back? What about some therapy?" There had to be something he could do. In my view, he had let his business consume him. He hadn't given Carmen enough of his time and attention.

He was trembling now. His voice broke. "I really love Carmen," he cried, "and I need my family back."

It wasn't going to happen; I knew that then. My intuition had kicked in and briefed me. But I said, "Yeah, I know you do. Maybe you should try to work on your relationship."

"I'm not giving up," he reaffirmed. "I love my wife and children. Please, will you come back and work with me?"

I said, "Sure, when you get it together and feel better, I'll come back to your office."

That was in mid-April. I didn't see him again for a long time.

Chapter Ten – Calm Before the Storm

EVEN THOUGH SHE HAD A RESTRAINING ORDER AGAINST HIM, CARMEN DID LET Rick back into her life—for almost a week—just before the shooting. I didn't talk to him all that much during this period of time, but he was in touch with our other associates and they were in touch with me. We were all worried about him, so it was natural that we would share whatever knowledge we had about his activities. And share we did. The following account is based on the truth *as Rick perceived it*, what he said to various associates and what he would later say to me, after it was all over.

Rick was getting around by then, but he was still in great physical pain. As for the mental anguish, it was incalculable. Carmen filed divorce papers, which included allegations of abuse and mention of his cross-dressing incidents. According to Rick, they had fought like cats and dogs when they were younger, the both of them throwing things on occasion, but her accusations were full of hyperbole. As for the cross-dressing, she had known about it from the time they were teenagers. She had loved him in spite of it. Her decision to bring it up now could only be, he believed, because she saw that it was an effective weapon; to use it as such was the equivalent, in his mind at least, of sticking a knife in his back.

It's easy for a man of medicine to self medicate. In addition to the medications that had been prescribed for him after his fall, Rick added Zanaflex (a muscle relaxer that includes hallucinations among its possible side effects), Ultram (a pain killer which can also cause hallucinations), Klonopin (for panic attacks), Celexa (an antidepressant which includes suicidal thoughts among its possible side effects), Amitriptyline (another antidepressant, which can cause memory impairment and confusion),...and plenty of wine.

Rick moved what was left of his business into his house. He hired a man by the name of Niles Petersburg to help run LaseHair. Niles could do the laser troubleshooting as well as the scheduling and the financial stuff that had been Carmen's domain. Niles had work in Florida as well, so he was continuously flying back and forth. When he was working for Rick, he stayed at the Gloucester house, which made it seem less lonely. There were a few other people still working with Rick too, and they came to the house daily. Milly, who had been his secretary, was one of them. She was still living in her boyfriend's house, but they were considering splitting up, and she was glad when Rick told her she could stay at the Gloucester house too when she needed time away from the boyfriend. In spite of the people surrounding him, Rick remained profoundly depressed.

He had hired a divorce lawyer, Helen Thomason, to make sure he had regular visitations with Leo and Judy. Thomason was able to negotiate with Carmen's lawyer, Wyler Grange, for some hours each Monday, Wednesday, Friday and every other weekend. Because of the restraining order, he could not go pick up the kids himself. He had to wait for them to be delivered. Just as well. With all the meds he was taking, this once-confident driver could not risk driving more than a few miles if he didn't have to.

On Saturday evening the weekend before Easter of 2000, Rick was happy not to be alone. Norma and Mike, the affiliate electrologists, were there and so was Milly. Mike had made something on the outdoor grill and the four had just sat down to eat when the phone rang. It was Carmen. Rick had seen her earlier in the day when she'd picked up the kids and she'd been very cold. Now, to his surprise, she was warmer. She said she wanted to talk to him. He explained that he was just sitting down with some people to eat. It was 8:00 p.m. and she had a sitter only until eleven. She asked him how long it would take to get rid of his company. Desperate to learn what Carmen wanted to discuss, he said he could have them out in a half hour.

Everyone was gone by the time Carmen called back at nine. She was in her car, on her cell; she came right over. By redistributing what little furniture was left in the house, Rick now had a sofa and a chair in the living room, and they sat in there. They began to talk about their relationship—so many good times and so many bad times over the years. He cried, remembering. Eventually Carmen got off the chair and came to the sofa to comfort him. She began to kiss him. One thing led to another and soon they were making love.

Later he asked her about the painter, Art. This time she didn't deny it. She said she had been confused, that Rick hadn't been paying any attention to her; the painter had. Rick just listened. He didn't want to rock the boat now that he was back in it. She had to leave, because of the sitter, but she said she would come back for him in the morning, that they would go to the Wenham house together. Rick said he wasn't sure that was a good idea, that he would have to think about it. She countered that there was nothing to think about; she would be there at eight.

Sure enough she was there first thing, with Leo and Judy in tow. She looked at what he had packed and announced that it wasn't enough. She ran down to the kitchen for trash bags and helped him pack up more of his clothes. She drove her family back to Wenham.

This was Rick's first opportunity to tour the house since Carmen had begun to work on it. The four of them went from room to room taking in the design motifs that Carmen had implemented. Later he and the kids went into the wooded lot across the street and found a pond. Eventually they located a small snake. The kids ran back to the house and returned with a box and they made a nice home for the creature. Hours later Judy got upset when Rick said it was time to let the snake go. He explained that the snake had to go home, that his family was waiting for him.

That night, according to Rick, he and Carmen made love again—desperately, the way they had in high school, the way it had been over the years when he'd return from a business trip that had separated them for several days. They couldn't get enough of each other. She apologized for seeing Art. She said she wanted a reconciliation. Rick was thrilled. He called his lawyer first thing in the morning and left a message saying he didn't need her services anymore. Carmen tried Grange but wasn't able to reach him.

Leo wanted to go skateboarding that afternoon. There was a school in Gloucester that had skateboard ramps, so they drove over. It was chilly; Rick and Carmen sat in the car and watched the kids play. When an ice cream vendor appeared in the parking lot, Rick jumped out of the car and bought everyone ice cream. The kids went back to the ramps, then Rick and Carmen ate their cones while listening to oldies on the car radio. They were happy, at peace together. He asked Carmen if she'd gotten through to Grange yet. She hadn't.

They only had one altercation the entire weekend, and it was over quickly. He asked her that evening how the stocks were doing now that the accounts had been transferred into her name. She told him to look for himself and handed him the most recent portfolio. He was stunned to see that the reports were from Fleet Bank. They had always had their stocks with Fidelity. But even more stunning were the final month-end tallies. In the short time she'd been handling the account, it had fallen by almost fifty percent. He asked her what was going on. She explained that Grange knew someone at Fleet who was supposed to be very smart and he'd suggested she switch. Rick held up the documents. "Grange's person couldn't have been that smart!" he exclaimed.

He could have said more. But he swallowed it, he said. They had just gotten back together after a long and—for him—sickening separation.

On Monday he had to get back to the Gloucester house. Niles Petersburg was coming over; he had things to go over with him. Carmen dropped him off in the morning. In the afternoon he called to say that if he was going to stay in Wenham he was going to need at least one of his computers. Most of his computers were desktop models. Carmen didn't want the new house looking like an office. She suggested he get a new model laptop. He immediately called Dell and ordered one. Later, after she had picked him up and brought him back to Wenham, they laughed to think that now that they didn't have to pay a fortune to divorce lawyers they could easily afford the new computer. But when he asked her if she had gotten through to Grange yet, she said no, not yet.

On Tuesday Carmen dropped him off in Gloucester for work again, but she was too busy to pick him up later in the day. Rick asked Milly if she would drive him to Wenham. Carmen had dinner almost ready when he walked in. But she didn't say much during the meal, and when he asked her again if she'd gotten through to Grange, it didn't surprise him too much when she said no. He stayed over that night and decided the next day that he didn't need to go back to Gloucester to work. Instead they took the kids to the toy store—because Leo wanted a new card for his Pokemon game. After the purchase, Rick assumed they would all go back to Wenham, but when Carmen drove past the exit, he realized she was taking him back to Gloucester.

When they arrived she told the kids to stay in the yard and she and Rick went into the house. As soon as they'd closed the door behind them, she admitted that she'd made a mistake; she didn't want a reconciliation after all. It was over. Rick began to tremble and then to cry. He begged and pleaded. He said the least she could do is agree to counseling. She was running out of patience. She threw the phonebook at him and said, "Fine. Find a counselor, but do it right away."

He made a few calls and found a therapist in Beverly who was willing to see them on short notice, within a few days. As Carmen was turning to leave, he asked if she could at least drive him back to Wenham to get his things. She said she couldn't. As he had his medications there, and other essential belongings, he got in his own car and followed her back. When they arrived, she said, "Go in and get your stuff," and she and the kids waited in the car until he came back down with his things. (Later Grange would send a letter to Rick's lawyer saying that his following her back to the house that afternoon constituted stalking.)

On the day of their meeting with the counselor, Carmen picked him up. As they were both hungry and had enough time before their appointment, they stopped at a Burger King. Carmen said he was too skinny and needed to eat. He agreed with her assessment. It was the most civil exchange they had that day. He left the counselor's office with no more hope for saving their marriage than he'd had going in.

Milly was at the Gloucester house working when Carmen dropped Rick off. Given her own relationship problems, she was not adverse to Rick's idea that she stop working and have a beer with him. In fact, they drank all the rest of the day and all that evening. And that night they slept upstairs, together, bonded by heartbreak.

The weeks passed. The combination of painkillers, antidepressants, booze, utter hopelessness and more free time than he'd had since high school accentuated Richard Sharpe's dark side. He found he liked to torture himself. He and Milly drove by the Wenham house one evening. His intention was to see if Art was there, to confront him. There was still a restraining order against him. He shouldn't even have been in the neighborhood.

While Milly waited in the car, he went around the house to the window that looked into the den and watched his family for about ten minutes. The kids were on the floor, playing a board game in front of the TV, and Carmen and Art, according to Rick, were spread out on the couch. Though fully dressed, Art, Rick said, had his hands everywhere and was pressing his pelvis into hers. In the end, Rick turned from the scene, went back to the car and he and Milly drove off.

But the scene stayed with him.

On Thursday, July 9, Rick had dinner with Milly, Stephanie and Niles Petersburg. Niles stayed over that night. When Rick awoke in the morning, he heard Niles moving around downstairs and came down to join him. The two men had coffee at the table in the dining room while discussing some problems concerning the business. There was a time when Rick made all his business decisions quickly and with confidence, based on a combination of intuition and his uncanny abundance of knowledge. These days he was a basket case. He couldn't get over the smallest of business hurdles without Niles Petersburg at his side.

While they were talking, the front door opened and Leo and Judy came running in. Rick was surprised. Carmen wasn't supposed to drop off the kids until about noon. Leaving Niles to sort through the rest of his notes alone, Rick got up from the table and rushed to greet his children. They immediately went into the sunroom to check on the pets in the mini reptile zoo, the snakes and the iguana. Niles Petersburg finished his business and left.

Cindy, friend to Leo and Judy (and sister to Geri, a little girl on whom Rick had once performed emergency plastic surgery after she'd fallen and gashed her face open), came by to hang out with the Sharpe children. Around noon the kids and Rick took a vote about where to go for lunch, and McDonalds won. During their time there, food got stuck in Leo's retainer and Rick had to help him to remove it. Later they stopped at the pet store to buy food for the pets. The kids made an earnest attempt to get Rick to buy yet another reptile but he refused. They were back at the house feeding the animals when Britta, Cindy's mom, called to see if Cindy was still there. Rick said they were having fun, that either he would drive her home a little later or Carmen would when she came to get Leo and Judy.

Shortly thereafter Carmen arrived. Rick believed the kids wanted to stay but Carmen told them to get in the car. This weekend it was Carmen's turn to have them, but Rick asked if she could let them come by for three or four hours on Saturday or Sunday. She said she didn't know; she'd think about it. She might be going out and getting a sitter. He said it was crazy to get a sitter when he was available.

He called her later to find out if she'd decided about letting him have the kids for any time over the weekend, but she didn't pick up her phone. Pepper and Mike, two of the laser affiliates, had been working at his house along with Milly. After Pepper and Mike left, Rick asked Milly if she'd wanted to get something to eat. While she was getting ready, he called his brother Harry. Harry was building a new server for LaseHair and Rick wanted to see how it was coming along. When he got off with him, he tried Carmen again, but she still wasn't answering.

He and Milly went down the street to the Blackburn Tavern. There was a band there and it was loud and crowded. Milly, who knew a lot of people in town, walked around, saying hello. Rick sat at the table in the corner sipping red wine and feeling sorry for himself. He kept thinking that he must find a way to get back to his family; he *must* find a way home.

The forecast that night was for rain. Milly knew that Hector, her ex-boy-friend, would not be home and she wanted to stop at his place to close the windows. She and Rick were in the black Pathfinder Rick owned in addi-tion to his old Porsche. She was driving. She wanted Rick to come in with her, Rick would say later, because there was a desk there that belonged to her and she thought they might be able to use it at his house. While he had picked up a few pieces of furniture here and there to replace what Carmen had taken to Wenham, the house was still pretty much empty.

Hector was a welder. Rick had met him a time or two. The cottage he lived in was cluttered but Rick noticed the gun rack on the wall in the living room right away. Milly led him to the desk she'd been talking about. It was old and bulky. He didn't really want it. He told Milly he'd wait in the Pathfinder for her while she finished what she had to do. On the way out he stopped at the gun rack and removed one of the guns, a rifle, and a box of bullets. The box was light. There might have been three or four bullets moving around in it. He was thinking that he had to get home, that if Art the painter was still there, he had to confront him. He put the gun and the box in the back of the SUV and waited in the passenger seat for Milly to come back out.

That might have been where it ended; Rick might have gone to sleep and come to his senses in the morning. But when they got back to his house, Rick realized that he'd lost his beeper. It had fallen off the clip on his belt. Thinking he might have left it in her ex-boyfriend's cottage, Milly became upset. She decided to take her own car and go back to look for it. If she didn't find it, she'd try the tavern. Rick was tired. He was used to getting up early and going to bed early. He sat down and listened to music for a while, but he kept thinking about how he had to find his way back to his family. Finally he went out to his SUV and drove to Wenham.

Rick pulled up in front of the house. If there were other cars in the driveway he didn't notice, or so he would later say. He had the one thing on his mind, that he had to find a way home. Once, years ago, a guy he'd gone to see in Texas about business had showed him how to fire a gun. Other than that, he had no experience with firearms. He'd never had an interest. He'd never wanted a gun in the house because of the kids. But now he was drunk, medicated, crazed. It was about midnight. He wanted to talk to his wife; he wanted his family back. He had to convince her.

The door was unlocked, so he opened it. There were people in the house. A woman was right there in the foyer. Rick said he wanted to talk to Carmen but Carmen was already moving toward the door. She was waving a document, the restraining order probably, saying something about calling the police. Then there was a loud noise, a flash of yellow light. The door slamming closed. Rick fled.

At some point his head cleared enough for him to notice the gun and the box on the passenger seat. He had to get them away from him. He opened the passenger window and threw them out. He kept on driving. When he reached Burlington, Massachusetts, he pulled off the road and went to sleep. When he awoke in the morning he turned on the radio. It was then he heard that Carmen Sharpe had been shot dead the night before. He felt sick, wretched, despondent, shattered. He had only wanted to find a way back to his family. He stopped for gas. He bought a six pack of beer, a bottle of Gatorade and rope. He didn't stop again until he was in New Hampshire. Using his own name, he checked into a rustic motel. The manager of the motel, who had heard the news, called the local police.

The SWAT team had to evacuate the other guests into the torrential downpour before they could throw the tear gas canisters into Rick's room. He came out immediately. They put him on the ground, cuffed him and took him away.

Chapter Eleven – Immediate Aftermath

I LEARNED ABOUT THE SHOOTING THE SAME WAY EVERYONE ELSE DID—FROM RADIO and TV news. There were approximately thirty hours between the time of the tragedy and the time of Rick's arrest, so there was plenty of opportunity for the media to create sidebars to fill in any gaps. They had the chance to find former patients who were willing to say that there had always been something strange about Dr. Richard Sharpe, that he lacked a bedside manner, and that yes, come to think of it, he *had* asked them to remove *all* of their clothing, even when the mole they had come in about was in full view on their face or their hand or their arm. In fact, this is standard procedure for dermatologists, because moles can be anywhere there is skin, including places that patients don't think to look, such as the back or between the toes or even between the buttocks.

During the thirty-hour manhunt, the Gloucester police dispatcher informed officers searching for Rick that he might be dressed as a woman. Apparently they had talked to Carmen's divorce attorney and made that assumption based on the fact that Rick had dressed at conferences and at a party or two over the years. Not surprisingly, the officer who oversaw Rick's arrest at the Tuftonborough Police Department in New Hampshire agreed that he did seem to be developing breasts. The newspapers jumped on this information, and there was not one headline ever after, locally or nationally, that didn't identify him as "the cross-dressing dermatologist," or "the gender bender doctor" or some other tag that meant the same thing. The few available photos of him in women's clothes were quickly located and tossed out into the fray. The media went after them like guppies to food flakes.

In short, the media got the chance to sensationalize the story by focusing on his cross-dressing—and by extension, they assaulted all cross-dressers and transgender people. They used "cross-dresser" as an adjective to mean "sick" or "bizarre." They used it to imply that the potential to commit murder had always been dormant in him, simply because he *was* a cross-dresser.

I am not making a judgment here about what Rick Sharpe did. Nor am I making a judgment about whether or not it was an accident—or whether or not he was insane when he did it. I am simply saying that constantly identifying him as a criminal and as a cross-dresser is to infer that all cross-dressers have the potential to be criminals. That, I know, is not right. I wasn't the only one who thought so either. The International Foundation of Gender Education and GLAD (Gay & Lesbian Advocates & Defenders) issued statements to that effect, saying that Richard Sharpe's gender identity was in no way relevant to the case. Other organizations issued statements too. But the media could not be made to relinquish their hyperbolic statements.

Rick was transferred from Tuftonborough, New Hampshire to Essex County House of Corrections in Middleton, Massachusetts. Having failed to hang himself in his room at Pine Lodge, he was considered to be at high risk for suicide, so Essex had him transferred to Bridgewater, a state mental health facility for the criminally insane. Bridgewater treated him and released him to MCI-Walpole, a maximum security prison in Cedar Junction, to await his trial.

I woke up one morning a week or so after the tragedy and found that my beautiful long brown hair had turned a silvery gray.

Chapter Twelve – Loyalty

OVER THE NEXT SEVERAL MONTHS I WRAPPED MYSELF IN A PROTECTIVE COCOON as much as possible. I went to work each day, came home at night, had dinner with Gary and whatever exchange students we had at the house (Gary's son Toby had started college by then) and accepted the good wishes of family and friends who understood how I was feeling.

I was in shock; I found myself wondering if I had ever seen any sign that Rick was capable of murder. The last time I saw him, the night I went to get my epilator, he had been sad, broken even—but not angry. I tried not to think or talk about what had happened, but there were times it was impossible. For one thing, there was an uproar in my office with patients wanting to know if the Dr. Sharpe in the news was the same one mentioned in the 1998 newsletter they'd received from me. (Some of these people would never return for services, even though they were meant to be long-term.)

Rick Sharpe had been my friend. He had been a mentor to me. He had taught me how to make money, how to succeed in the business world. I had always liked him. I had always admired his mind, his ability to follow an idea to its logical conclusion—like a champion chess player. I had especially admired his noble goals, his desire to find a cure for cancer, to get women to have the tests they needed to avoid ovarian and breast cancers. Now I was being forced to acknowledge that he was capable of killing someone— someone he loved more than life itself. I couldn't reconcile the facts with my admiration for the man.

In the meantime, life went on.

Over time I spoke to all of the other laser affiliates. In order to continue to do laser hair removal, we hoped to find a new medical director, a doctor who could sign off for us. It wasn't essential to have a sign-off doctor, but it was "recommended" in the Commonwealth of Massachusetts, and we wanted to do things by the book. We found two who were willing to help, Drs. Chives and Souza. But we had no idea how long we would be able to continue to use Rick's lasers. The two working ones had been out when the tragedy occurred, so we went on using them—until we got a letter from the lawyers representing Carmen's family asking us to desist. As I had patients who were in the middle of their treatments, I met with the two sign-off doctors and both agreed that I could use the lasers at their offices on specified days. My laser patients would have to meet me at these alternate locations. It was confusing. But it was better than losing my laser business altogether.

Each of the affiliates found their own way of dealing with the loss of the lasers. Some went back to straight electrolysis…or whatever they had been doing before. Some made fallback arrangements that had nothing to do with skin care or hair removal. The woman who had been my associate was so upset that she couldn't stay with me any longer. She gave up her business completely. Her husband was a pharmacist, and she decided to go to work for him.

Milly Thieman called me one night when I was really too tired to have a weighty conversation about anything, let alone Rick Sharpe. She said she felt terrible about the gun. She said she didn't know that he had taken it from her ex-boyfriend's house; she had no way to know he'd put it in the back of the car. Now she was afraid that if she made any attempt to visit Rick, people would think that she *had* known; they would think that she had somehow allowed the tragedy to happen. She begged me to contact him. She had been writing to him and could confirm that he was needing very badly to have contact with the outside world. He was sinking into a black hole, and her letters alone were not going to pull him out.

I spoke to Stephanie once during this time. She called the office during business hours. I believe she was still in a state of shock. She seemed confused and distrustful during the few minutes we spoke. Who could blame her? Calls were still coming in on Rick's 800 number, she said. She wanted nothing to do with them. What she wanted to know was whether she could have them routed to my office. Thinking this would ensure continued LaseHair business, I said yes right away. Later I received a call from the lawyers representing the family. They had decided that I should pay a percentage of the business brought in by the 800 numbers to an account set up for the family. I agreed.

Dealing with the calls coming in on the 800 number, however, turned out to be a headache of limitless proportions. Rachael, my secretary, could barely keep up with them. Our phones rang all day long nonstop. And only a small percentage of calls represented new business. Some of the calls were from people who wanted Botox or liposuction, and we had to tell them that LaseHair was no longer providing those services. Some people wanted Alpha Hydroxy Gold, the skin product Rick had invented. Others were desperate for the software he had created, and I had no idea how to get it to them. Other calls were from people insisting we make good on their contracts. As part of his marketing strategy, Rick had put out offers whereby patients could get three laser treatments for the price of two if they signed up—and paid up—at the time of the offer. Those people were upset now. They either wanted the treatments they were due or they wanted their money back. All I wanted was peace. I agreed to give them the treatments they had been promised. Fran, one of the affiliates who worked out of the Winchester office, was the only one who offered to help me work my way through the freebies.

Other people called just to grumble. They had trusted the doctor. How could he have done such a thing? What kind of a maniac was he? And what about the cross-dressing? What was that about? Their calls were even more distressing than the people wanting their freebie treatments. Some of the callers attacked me in a very direct way. They had received the newsletter that Rick and I had created together. In their minds, the document might as well have been a marriage certificate. I was guilty by association, and availing themselves of my services in the future was the last thing they could imagine. At the end of the day I could only be glad that life had toughened me up in such a way that I was able to withstand so much abuse…and that I had Gary to go home to.

I made no attempt to contact Rick. Frankly, I was depressed and I had no desire to talk to anyone except Gary and my closest friends and family. I was overwhelmed by the confusion that had been left in the wake of Rick's colossal blunder. But Milly called again and again, begging me to reconsider. She said Rick had put me on his list of people he wanted to be able to call. Now the prison needed me to confirm that I was okay about being on the list.

I knew from my father that prison calls are monitored, even taped. In a high profile case like Rick's, which hadn't yet gone to trial, there would definitely be people listening and recording. Even though my stomach was doing flips and I was having trouble breathing, I reminded myself to say very little the first time he called me.

To say that he was depressed would be a gross understatement. I asked him how he was and he said he cried every day, every night, that all he wanted was to go back in time and change things. He said he would write, and I thought that would be a better idea—though I knew his letters would probably be photocopied. I told him I would pray for him and he said he would pray too.

At work I ran out of the acne product—Alpha Hydroxy Gold—that Rick
had invented. Because it worked so well, anyone who'd ever bought it once
wanted to buy it again. The formula had been on his computers, but all
twelve of them had been confiscated. I called some of the other affiliates to
see if anyone else knew the formula. No one did.

The next time Rick called I was glad to have something to ask him about
other than his life at the prison. It wasn't that I didn't care about his wellbeing—or lack thereof; it was just that any conversation about where he was
made me think about what he had done to get there, and I was uncomfortable with that line of thought. So I asked him instead about the ingredients
that went into Alpha Hydroxy Gold. Without his computers, and as befud-
dled as he was—he sounded like an old man on the phone—he couldn't
remember the formula either. But there was a woman, Skye, a friend of his
from med school, who was a chemist, and he thought she might be able to
recreate the product if she were sent a sample. She had been writing to him
since his incarceration and he felt certain she would be willing to help out.
As it happened, I had just a little of the product left in my own personal
bottle, so she would have something to analyze.

Rick suggested that we call the new product, once Skye had recreated
it, Alpha Hydroxy Platinum, so that no one would sue us for the rights to
the product under the old name. This led to a brief digression in which he
told me tearfully about his many attempts to reach Stephanie by letter and
phone, and how she would not respond to him. I waited patiently for him
to come back to the matter at hand, and eventually he did. He was poor
now; any money that remained in his name would go to his lawyers. If I
was able to work with Skye to recreate the product and it could continue
to be sold nationwide via the 800 number and the LaseHair website, then
some percentage of the profits could be put aside for him. That seemed
reasonable enough since it was his formula. We also talked about ClickMed,
his women's health tracking software. I had received a call from a military
office asking for an update of the software. There was no way Rick could
update software from a prison cell. Apparently they were not aware that
the Dr. Richard J. Sharpe who had created the program was the same one
who had killed his wife. Rick asked if I could send him some pocket money
for canteen, so that he could buy coffee, pencils, soap…small luxuries. I said
I would.

Although it seemed like a good idea to replicate the acne product, after
I got off the phone with Rick I put it out of my mind. Frankly, I didn't

feel like expending the energy to get it going. But then Skye, who lived in Pennsylvania, contacted me. She was very excited about the chance to get involved. Rick had told her, and me, that the product worked well for animals too. It made their coats shiny and got rid of psoriasis and lesions on their bodies. He suggested to Skye that she make gallons and gallons of the stuff. Some could be used as part of the Alpha Hydroxy line and the rest could have some additional ingredients added to make the cat and dog version.

Skye had a daughter named Patricia, who lived in Arizona. Back when Skye was going to Harvard with Rick, Patricia had babysat for Stephanie. She knew the family fairly well—though she hadn't been around when the younger kids came along. Patricia also wanted to be involved in Alpha Hydroxy. She was willing to do the shipping and the paperwork and help with web design. Skye and Patricia had the idea to take the product on the Home Shopping Network (and make a fortune, they hoped). Patricia had been corresponding with Rick regarding suggestions on how best to advertise it. She was already looking into ordering bottles, creating labels, etc. All they needed was a sample of the formula to get things going.

This arrangement—a collection of workers taking their orders from Rick, even a remote Rick—offered me the first hope I'd felt in weeks. It wasn't just the hope of making lots of money again either. It was about camaraderie, about the excitement of working with other people to get something out there on the market and watch it grow to become successful. And maybe too, seeing that Skye and Patricia still believed that Rick Sharpe was a worthwhile human being made it easier for me to allow myself to believe that. I wanted to; I wanted it badly. As upset as I was with him, in my heart he was still my friend. I just needed to be able to justify my feelings.

ဢဢ

When I was six years old, I had a friend named Suzie. Suzie lived in the projects across the street from the apartment complex where I lived. We would meet at the park down the street daily with our baby dolls in their doll carriages. We fussed over our dolls, making sure they were tucked in tight in their blankets when the weather was cold, that the carriage hoods were up to keep the wind out. I loved Suzie. She was my best friend.

Suzie had never been to my house before, and one day I decided to bring her home for dinner. I had been to her apartment plenty of times. Her mother was white and her father was black, making them the first mixed-raced couple I had ever encountered. Her father was a lawyer. I didn't know what a lawyer was back then, but I knew it was something important, like being a doctor. The night I invited her for supper, we went to her place first to get permission and then we went to mine.

The entrance to all the apartments in our building was through a huge wooden security door. I could hardly reach up high enough to get the key into the lock. The two of us had to pull the door together to get it to open, and it took some maneuvering to get our baby dolls safely through in their carriages. Then we had to go up a steep flight of stairs, maybe twenty steps in all. Finally we got to my door.

The first thing I saw as the door opened was my stepfather, Al, sitting in the living room reading the paper. He stared at us for a second. Then his expression shifted from curiosity to fury, and all at once he flew out of his chair, screaming that there was no way a black person was coming into our house—only he didn't say "black person." He ran at us. Not knowing which carriage was mine and which was hers, he threw them both down the stairs and our babies went flying. He slammed the door behind him.

We were both crying hysterically as we ran down to the front entrance. We retrieved our dolls and carriages and got the big heavy door open again. I held it while Suzie dragged both carriages outside. Somehow I managed to leave my finger behind when the door slammed close. I broke my finger and lost a nail.

But I didn't lose a friend. In fact, my stepfather's awful prejudice made me swear to welcome people who were different from me into my life from then on—and that has come to pass.

But what was interesting to me now, what I kept coming back to, is that while I hated how Al had treated Suzie, I surprised myself by realizing, over the weeks that followed, that I didn't hate him. I still loved him. He was the one who took care of me. He was there. He was raising me. When my real father, Hugh, got out of jail, he married Camille and had more kids, yes, but he never settled down. There were lots of nights when he was out thieving. Al didn't go out at night. He might have been yelling and screaming, but he was there.

Interestingly enough, Al had no prejudices against cross-dressers or transgender people. Bart Fish, our neighbor, had saved him from that. He liked Bart; he even helped Bart with his lawn work. Maybe if he had gotten to know a person of color earlier in his life, he wouldn't have been the way he was.

Chapter Thirteen – The Magic Formula

WE WENT FORWARD WITH THE PLAN, SKYE AND PATRICIA AND I. I SENT A POR-
tion of what was left in my personal bottle of Alpha Hydroxy Gold
to Skye and very soon she had recreated it and I received the first shipment
of the new bottles—Alpha Hydroxy Platinum. (We hadn't begun work yet
on the animal skin care product, but Patricia, who had horses and cats and
dogs, was looking forward to it.) Just as fast as the product came in, I sold
it to my regular clients and people calling on the phone. Everyone loved it,
and it smelled good too. We made the product available to the other former
affiliates, and some took advantage of it.

We had barely begun our new enterprise, however, when I received a call
from Patricia saying that there had been a terrible accident at her mother's
chemical plant, and that she had to shut down her entire operation post-
haste. Apparently she was anticipating lawsuits and headaches of her own,
so she could no longer be involved with the product through her company,
even if the plant did reopen eventually. Rick suggested that she try to create Alpha Hydroxy from home, and she did that for a short time. But her
kitchen was not conducive to that kind of work. When Rick had made
the formula at home—in the apartment over the garage that later became
Stephanie's—he'd had an industrial eye station there, which looked something like a water fountain. If you got any chemical in your eye, you could
rush over, stick your head in the eye station and wash it out right away. At
some point Skye told Rick, Patricia and me that she was done with Alpha
Hydroxy for good. I asked her for the formula but she refused to give it to
me.

But I was hot on the idea now, and so was Rick. I think focusing on something outside of the prison gave him a *raison d'etre*, and while he was still
just as tearful and despondent on the phone when we spoke of other matters, when we talked about Alpha Hydroxy Platinum, he came to life again
a bit. I would not say that he showed enthusiasm; it was more of an urgency.
Knowing there was at least that to talk about made it easier for me to pick
up the phone when the caller ID confirmed it was him on the line.

Since Skye no longer wanted to be involved at any level (she became
depressed after the accident at her chemical plant, and who can blame her?),
I took what little product I had left from Rick's original formula and sent
it to a compounding company. The chemist, whose name was Dennis, did
the best he could, but when he sent back the sample he had created for my

approval, I couldn't help but notice that it had a terrible smell. I called him and said, "This won't do. The clients are used to something that smells good. Can't you put in some perfume?" I could almost see his puzzled expression over the phone.

Dennis tried again, and this time with some success. It still didn't smell great, but it didn't smell awful either. I bought a batch from him, just enough to sell to my regular clients until I could determine how they liked it. They came back in the weeks that followed and said it was good; they wanted more. So I went back to Dennis to order a second batch, but this time he gave me some story about not being able to get selenium, one of the key ingredients. Without selenium, he said, he couldn't make the product. He was vague when I asked *why* he couldn't get selenium, and I hung up the phone thinking there must be some kind of a shortage of the mineral.

I called Ralph, the pharmacist who was the husband of my former affiliate, and asked him what the story was with the selenium deficit. He laughed; he said selenium was available everywhere. We discussed what Dennis had said and concluded that maybe Dennis just wanted out because the deal I had cut with him wasn't lucrative enough. Or maybe he thought he would be crossing a line with some of the other ingredients.

After all my efforts to date, I thought it might be worth one more try. I could offer Dennis more money, or money based on sales if he preferred— something to make his staying in the game worthwhile. But this time he admitted that it was not about money. He said that the rules had changed: there were two ingredients that were FDA approved but they weren't approved to be mixed together. If it could be ordered via a prescription written out by a doctor, that would be different. Then he could make it. I don't know why he didn't tell me this before. I could only think that he was paranoid by nature. I knew doctors who would sign off on the product. But now I suspected that even once I made arrangements with them, Dennis would find other reasons not to be involved.

One of my friends, Estelle, was a Boston internist. I mentioned my dilemma to her and she told me about a great compounder she knew, a man named Craig who worked in Rhode Island. He did a lot of compounding for animal products, but also for people. I called him, and he seemed very nice over the phone and agreed to work with me. In the meantime, I contacted Marta Raymond, one of Boston's and New York's top dermatologists and a friend of mine for many years. Marta house-sat for me a few times back when she was still in college. We had always stayed in touch. Marta used the formula regularly and loved it. She agreed to write the prescriptions I needed. Then I called back Dennis to ask him for the formula—he was only too happy to give it to me—and Craig began making Alpha Hydroxy Platinum. His version smelled good too.

But when I first told Rick that I had finally succeeded in finding someone to create the product, he insisted that I have Craig work on a version for animals too. That I didn't want to do. There are only so many hours in a day. While I already had clients for the acne product and could justify all the trouble I'd been through, I didn't have any clients for the animal product. Rick insisted that we could generate them, that he could create instructions on setting up an appropriate website for the product from his prison cell and that Patricia and I could work together to implement it. Using the magic traffic-producing strategies that he had used for the LaseHair site (which eventually disappeared from lack of updating), we could ensure that anyone who was concerned about their pets' skin health would find their way to us.

While at first I had used the making of Alpha Hydroxy Platinum as a technique for guiding Rick away from his own personal trials and tribulations, now I asked about his troubles to divert him from his nagging about the product. It was easy enough to sidetrack him. Even when he was obnoxiously arguing in favor of his ideas, his misery was just below the surface. He was working with a defense team now, Ben Falcon Sr. and his daughter, Joan. He talked to them daily about what he had done, going over the details again and again of the weeks leading up to the event. Then he dreamed them again at night. Now that he had a legal team, he had filed a request with the court asking that he be allowed to have contact with his children; in the meantime, Stephanie had filed a six-page affidavit describing his abusive behavior throughout her life, and saying that her mother's decision to leave Rick was at least in part so that Leo would never learn that his father had been a cross-dresser. Except for the few conversations with me, and his letters to Milly, Patricia, Skye and a few others who remained loyal to him, he lived his mistakes and their consequences over and over again. Despite my promise to myself that I would not feel pity for him, I did. I couldn't help it.

Chapter Fourteen – Visitors

JUST AS OUR CONVERSATIONS COULD RUN THE GAMUT FROM WHAT HE HAD DONE to how to build traffic to a product or service website, his letters were also a mixed bag. Generally he didn't say too much about individual inmates, but he wrote frequently that he had to be alert constantly because some prisoners could turn violent without provocation. Some of the rougher men were willing to protect him because he was smart and could help them with letter writing or other logistical problems. You had to be able to make a deal. You had to have something ready to offer at all times, even if it was only a cup of coffee. My father hung out with gangsters in prison; they liked him because he could tell a joke, make them laugh. He liked them because they could provide some measure of safety. If not for them, he'd often said, he wouldn't have survived.

Except for the ongoing eruptions of barbarity, prison life was mostly mental torture with one day's activities being exactly the same as the next. They had Rick on all kinds of medications, the combination of which led to some disturbing side effects. But he was afraid to go off of any one of them because he didn't want to find out how bad he really was. At certain times of the day, he said, he felt like jumping out of his skin. At night he had panic attacks, sometimes all night long. He found himself always waiting for morning, when his anxiety from the night before would begin to subside. He said he didn't think he could make it from one day to the next without his connections to those of us on the outside. Almost every letter, whether it was a ten-page tutorial on how to create meta tags on websites or a half page note just to say hello, ended with extreme gratitude for my friendship. In return, I sent blank greeting cards with short notes to say he was in my prayers.

Rick remained obsessed with getting in touch with Stephanie. He told me he wrote to her to tell her he loved her and to ask her to forgive him for not giving her enough time and attention when she was growing up. He asked me if I thought she would write back, and I said it was possible, though I didn't think she would. How would I know what she was thinking? In one long letter to me he detailed the story of Stephanie's conception and birth. He and Carmen had started having sex a month or two after they met, in high school. By September of 1972 they were finding ways to be together virtually every day. They had become addicted to each other's bodies, Rick said. They had sex in his car, out on the football field in the dark, at Carmen's various babysitting jobs, even at Carmen's house, with her parents just in the next room…. They used condoms, but a few times they got carried away and passion overcame good judgment.

Except for the last paragraph of his letter, in which Rick apologized for rambling and then spent a few sentences thanking me for my friendship, Rick could have been writing a diary entry; his narrative was that detailed and personal. It was clear that he couldn't stop thinking about the past. It had to be a safer place for him than the present or the future.

The letter about Stephanie's conception was the last I heard from him for quite some time. No letters and no calls. But then I heard from Milly, who said that he'd been put in the "hole," in solitary confinement. Later, when he got out, we learned that Stephanie had called the prison to complain about his many attempts to contact her. She said she feared for her life. His period of isolation was his punishment, and to ensure he didn't try to contact her again.

Rick's time in the hole must have been traumatic, because the next few times he called he said almost nothing and I had to do all the talking. He reminded me of my mother after her shock treatments, when she would be confused and aloof. Just before he'd gone into isolation, his best friend Glenn's sister, Jill, had died unexpectedly, and when Rick felt ready to write to me again, his first letter was about Glenn and Jill and their father. It made me wonder if he had spent the entire two weeks in the hole (twenty-three hours a day of confinement with one hour when he was allowed out) thinking about Jill's death.

The best part of Rick's youth, his letter said, was hanging out with Glenn and Jill. They all had go-carts, and they would ride them back and forth for hours on the street. When they got older, they would listen to loud rock music in Glenn and Jill's basement. Their father, who was an electrician and a building contractor, liked electronics and had a high-priced, high-powered stereo system.

Once, before Rick started dating Carmen, he went to a school dance alone. He had a girlfriend at the time, but her parents wouldn't let her attend. He was feeling gloomy and lonely and awkward standing there by himself when Jill appeared out of nowhere and asked him to dance. They were slow dancing, talking about school and other kids, when Jill's boyfriend, who was called Spinner, materialized and immediately put Rick in a headlock and said he wanted Rick outside because he was going to kick his ass. Jill intervened, and in the end the three of them wound up out in

Spinner's car drinking beers from a cooler. Rick never went to another dance alone after that. If Carmen couldn't go, he stayed home too.

Rick mentioned in his letter that Jill and Glenn's dad was in his mid-seventies now and had diabetes and high blood pressure. He had also lost his vision in one eye, Rick thought because of stress. I had to shake my head. Others might describe people in terms of their hair color or weight or height or some aspect of their personality. Not Rick Sharpe. He described everyone in terms of their health.

I received several more letters detailing Rick's young adulthood. He didn't say much about his home life as a child, but he had said enough in conversations over the years so that I already knew that his father was abusive and he had not been happy at home. In one letter he mentioned his cat, Blackie. His father accidentally ran him over and the vet wanted to put him to sleep. But Rick had a tantrum in the vet's office and his mother agreed to let him try to nurse the cat back to health. Blackie may have been his first patient, he said. Blackie had lost an eye and had a few fractures, but he managed to live a while longer. He slept in Rick's bed, curled up in front of his face. Now Rick lamented that he couldn't have a cat or dog in prison. What a difference it would have made in his depressed state. At the end of the letter he switched gears and wrote, "If Carmen really planned to kick me out of her life, why would she buy a million-dollar house with a three-car garage for just her and the kids?" Even after everything that had happened, he still refused to believe that Carmen had simply stopped loving him.

Eventually his period of reminiscence passed and he reverted back to his efforts to try to live some part of his life on the outside even though he was physically behind bars. Now he was on a kick to provide Patricia with the support she would need to be able to sell cryogen for laser canisters and aluminum oxide for microdermabrasion work through websites. He felt this could be extremely profitable. He also wanted her to learn how to use the laser herself. He got it in his head that she should fly from Arizona—where she lived on a horse ranch—to Massachusetts and stay at the Gloucester house for a month or two. It was currently on the market, but it would remain his until the family's civil suit against him was settled. Of course he wanted me to be the one to tutor Patricia on the laser. I didn't have the time or the inclination.

Rick had two older brothers, Bruce and Harry—both of whom lived in Connecticut where Rick had grown up—and a sister, Patsy, who lived in Florida. I knew of them from Rick's chronicle letters and maybe from a mention or two before his incarceration, but I had never given them much thought. Now Bruce, the younger of the brothers (Patsy was the youngest of the siblings), contacted me and asked me if I would accompany him to the prison to visit Rick. I could hear in his voice that he was nervous, that it wasn't so much that he wanted to meet me as that he didn't want to go into the facility alone.

This I understood, even though my experience of prison had been different. Since Rick's incarceration the subject of prison visits came up frequently among people I knew—even among those who had never met Rick—and the consensus seemed to be that going into a jail was a "very scary" thing that most people didn't have the spine for. Many people can't even bring themselves to go into a nursing home. For me prison excursions were tedious and time-consuming (not the actual visits but the getting in and out through security) and nerve-wracking and even humiliating (depending on the attitude of the guards). But I couldn't really say that I was *afraid* to go into a prison. I told Bruce I would go with him. On the morning of the day of our visit, I showered with perfumed soap just so that if I *did* feel any anxiety, I could breathe in the soft aroma and calm myself.

We met at my office. Bruce was smallish, maybe even shorter than Rick, but handsome and with beautiful thick dark hair. We shook hands and then hugged before taking off in my car. The ride would have been about forty-five minutes but I managed to get lost. We chatted while we drove along to Walpole, but I could tell that he was very nervous.

We followed the protocol—giving up our possessions at the lockers in the front office and going through the various gates one at a time—and finally arrived at the visitation room. It was divided into two sections—one for visitors and one for inmates—by a partition and a wall of glass. A guard showed us where to sit, and after a while Rick was led in wearing his orange uniform. The sun coming through one of the windows on our side of the room cast its light all along the glass, creating layered reflections and blinding glares, and making it very difficult to see the inmates.

I almost didn't recognize Rick. He had lost a lot of weight. He looked like a Halloween prop, a skeleton in a baggy orange jumpsuit. His hair was long, unkempt and greasy. His expression was hang dog. He looked much older than he had only months before. It was weird to see someone I had worked side by side with lowering himself to sit at the counter on the other side of the glass. There were tears pooling in his eyes. He smiled, sort of, and picked up the phone. Bruce picked up the phone on our side. "Sorry to see you in this situation," he whispered. Rick nodded and bent his head to hide the next wave of tears. When Bruce passed the phone to me, I said pretty much the same thing but in different words.

Mostly, Bruce and I looked at him. There wasn't a whole lot to say. It was awkward anyway speaking into the phone, especially since we knew the calls were likely to be recorded. Rick didn't speak much either. In fact, he seemed to be in a state of shock. He just stared at us; it was almost as if he was trying to memorize every feature of our faces so that he could take the images back with him, into his cell. Sometimes Bruce and I looked at each other. When it was time to go, we put our hands up on the glass, and Rick lifted his hand and spread his fingers over ours, first Bruce's and then mine. We told him he had our support, because that is what you say to inmates when you visit them. That is all they really want to hear. And in that moment, by saying the words, it became true for me. I had accepted some of the responsibility for the wellbeing of Richard J. Sharpe—and naturally some of the burden.

Chapter Fifteen – URLs and 9-11

I STARTED TO BECOME FRIENDLY WITH HARRY, RICK'S OLDER BROTHER, ABOUT THIS time. We began to talk over the phone about the Internet business Rick had generated for LaseHair. Harry, a computer expert himself, thought it might make sense for us not to take over the LaseHair or ClickMed websites, which were part of Rick's estate, but instead the various "concealed" satellite sites for which they were umbrellas. Rick wanted this too, I knew, because he thought it might enable us to help offset some of his legal fees, but it sounded suspect to me. Besides, there were so many ancillary websites, so many different URLs that fed into the main ones. I didn't even understand what a URL was at this time. I didn't understand what would be required of me and if it would even be legal. Harry stressed that the upkeep of the sites, which he seemed to think I could handle, was crucial to maintaining a high ranking on the web, that Rick's domain names had been leased annually, but they would all expire at different times. I remained hesitant while he worked tirelessly to optimize the websites and get them ready. He even bought software to help make the changes. But in the end it didn't matter. Even Harry could not manage the upkeep of a system as complex as the one Rick had concocted. The system quickly fell apart. I was glad it hadn't been necessary for me to get involved.

Around this time Bruce, who had been staying in touch with me by phone since our prison visit, got the idea (no doubt also from Rick) that he could buy a laser and rent it to me the same way that Rick had rented out his back before things fell apart. In this way he would be able to pay the monthly payment and still make a profit, most of which he could hold aside to help with his brother's legal expenses. And I would have a laser without having to come up with the large deposit myself. I liked Bruce and the plan seemed to make good sense. Certainly it was better than having my clients continue to travel to other locations so that I could work on them.

Rick's trial was coming up, though no one knew for sure what the exact date was yet. Rick's lawyers had agreed that he would plead insanity. Based on what I'd heard about the events leading up to the shooting, this made sense to me. I didn't get much of a chance to discuss the news with Rick himself though, because he got put back into the hole not long after my visit. This time it was because another inmate was insisting that Rick had offered him a million dollars to help him escape. The guy was almost ready for parole, so maybe he thought by incriminating Rick, who was not well liked in the prison—probably because he was a doctor, certainly because he was a wife-killer, maybe because of the cross-dressing stuff too—he could better assure his own liberty. Or maybe Rick had in fact talked to him about escape, though why he would want to try such a thing when his trial was just around the corner was beyond me. To make matters worse, in a separate incident two men who had been sought after for who knows what crime were captured in a motel room where they had placed a newspaper clipping with a picture of Rick into the frame of the mirror. What that had to do with Rick, no one knew, but his stay in isolation was extended as a precaution against a possible escape attempt.

When he finally got out of the hole, he was broken again, barely able to speak on the phone and not up to writing any letters. While he had been away from his cell, someone—either the guards or other inmates—had ransacked his few possessions, taking his letters, photographs of his kids (which I assume either Bruce or Rick's lawyers had sent to him) and whatever reading material he had. He was devastated over the loss of the photos, but there was nothing he could do about it. Eventually he called me to ask if I would send him a magazine or two, something scientific. But rather than mailing it to his attention, he gave me the name of an inmate who had befriended him and who was not detested the way Rick was. The other inmate would give the magazines to him when they arrived. As I found out from a call to the prison, the magazines had to be sent directly from the publisher's distributor.

This time Rick bounced back from his malaise more quickly than when he had gone into isolation the first time. In a matter of weeks I was receiving letters from him again informing me that Patricia would soon be arriving in Massachusetts and asking me to train her to use the laser. Patricia's task while staying at his house was to remove his medical instruments, which he said had a collective value of over $50,000, and also all the laser canisters that he had stored in his garage. He wanted her to bring everything to my house for temporary storage! I didn't have the space. Even if I did, it didn't seem like a good idea to have any of his possessions there, especially with the exchange students living with Gary and me. Again, he had asked me to do more than I was willing. To his credit, he never got upset when I told him no; he seemed to understand that I could only go so far. But that didn't stop him from trying to convince me otherwise...sometimes relentlessly.

He still held out hope that Harry and I would take over the LaseHair satellite sites, but when we finally got him to understand that we weren't willing (or even able) to do so, he came up with another idea. Forget about salvaging the sites from the old system and build an entirely new Internet presence called Web Health Alliance. It would be vague enough to have the capacity to serve as an umbrella for all kinds of health-related websites. We could even branch out into medical areas we had no knowledge of, collecting new clients for other healthcare professionals, who would be happy to pay us a percentage for our business-generating services. Since Harry was not interested in building a site from scratch, Rick suggested that Patricia work with me on this new project. "We will dominate the web," Rick said on one of his better days.

To this purpose, he began to send extensive instructions, pages and pages of them, written as fast as he could think, by the look of his chicken scratch, on how to go about building the new site and all the tributaries that would be needed to support it. "There are many search engines, but only about ten to fifteen are used by ninety-five percent of web surfers. Search engines are programs that reside on big computers that can be thought of as electronic librarians for the Internet. When you ask a search engine for a result, you are asking it NOT to go out on the Internet to search but instead to search its electronic card catalog. In order to get your website (URL) into various search engine card catalogues, you must submit it to the search engine. You can do this directly to each search engine or you can use a program which submits your URL (site) to many search engines at one time," Rick wrote, but that was only the introduction. It got worse thereafter. I could not make heads or tails of his instructions. I simply was not savvy regarding computer matters. In frustration, he started sending his letters to Gary, who in fact *was* computer savvy. But the system that Rick was describing was so elaborate and complex that even Gary could not follow it. You would have had to be a computer hacker to comprehend Rick's instructions.

Gary remained good natured, and although Rick and his calls and letters were taking up more and more of my time, he did try to do what Rick wanted. I think too he didn't want to admit that he was just a little bewildered by his assignment. As a matter of self-esteem, he would likely have burrowed through and made it happen, but in the end it was just too time-consuming for a man who worked long days to begin with. It was not as if he could just pick up the phone and call Rick when obstacles arose.

On top of all that, it was getting expensive. We purchased over thirty URLs to get us started and set them up per Rick's instructions. The strategy had all to do with wording, and word groups. Rick was still insisting that Patricia would be able to sell the pet allergy product, easily, once we got things up and running. We caved and bought up URLs for that too. When it became clear that Gary would not be able to do what needed to be done on the Internet, we hired another person, a transgender person, whom I' met some time ago. She *was* a professional computer geek, but even she was not able to follow Rick's instructions. Web Health Alliance seemed destined to remain a work in progress. Rick suggested that I pay Patricia to help, even if only twenty dollars per hour. Apparently she was flat broke and needed the money in order to put in the time. By now she had already made the trip from her home in Arizona to Rick's house in Gloucester, and she was busy moving his surgical equipment and his canisters to another location. Where exactly was something I didn't care to know, as long as they weren't coming to my house. One afternoon Patricia took the time from her long list of Rick-generated tasks to meet with me in Newton. She was a pleasant young woman, with reddish blonde hair and hazel eyes. But we didn't click. For whatever reason, we didn't quite trust each other. We avoided having a conversation about Rick's instructions for the Internet. I guess we both had our own reasons.

When my birthday rolled around in October, Rick sent me a home-made card with a picture of Sylvester the Cat, the lisping cartoon feline who spends his life pursuing Tweetie Pie, the famous cartoon canary. This Sylvester had fur missing from two of his legs and half of his tail. The caption read, "Maybe after my final laser treatment you won't be allergic to me." The reference was to the fact that I was allergic to cats—though Rick insisted I wouldn't be if I got involved in the making of the cat allergy product and then got myself a cat to bathe in it. The drawing, which was nicely done, had been accomplished by one of Rick's fellow inmates. The next letter I received from Rick suggested that Sylvester be scanned into my computer for future use on any websites or materials generated to sell the cat allergy product. His business mind just couldn't be turned off for long.

ಏಁಛ

Bart Fish, the cross-dressing neighbor who had become a father figure to me years earlier, had died back in the mid-nineties. He was in his seventies at the time and suffering from cancer, and I took it very hard. Sometimes I believed that God sent people like Bart into my life to keep me from bellyaching over the fact that my parents had been too preoccupied with their own agendas to give me much guidance—because Bart had been a treasure, and no sooner had he passed on than I met Oscar Henning, another older man who took me under his wing and became a mentor and confidante.

A younger man, Keith, worked out at the same health club as me at the time and we got to be friends. Oscar worked out there too and we saw him frequently and couldn't help but notice that Keith and Oscar had a lot of physical traits in common, even though Oscar was a much older man. They had virtually the same facial features and bone structure, the same forehead, the same torso, the same skinny legs, even the same eye color.... It was uncanny. One day they got to talking and discovered their families were from the same town outside of Boston. Then they got to listing the names of distant relatives, and sure enough they concluded that many of the same people were on both lists and that they were somehow related.

After that the three of us hung out together at the health club, but Oscar and I really hit it off. I admired the way he thought, his creativity, and the fact that he was a natural caregiver. Like Rick Sharpe, he had graduated from Harvard. He'd become a realtor, a loan consultant and also a used car salesman. He'd counseled me when I bought my first condo, before I bought my house. We swam together at the health club, but Oscar also had a pool at his house, and he invited me to swim there, to bring any friends I wanted. I got to know his wife and learned more about their lives. Maria had been a teacher, and years earlier she and Oscar had adopted one of her students, a girl who had lost both her parents. Maria suffered from MS, and while its progression was slow, Oscar did everything possible to make life easier for her. When the time came for me to turn in the junker car I was driving, Oscar arranged for me to buy Maria's car, a Buick Regal, for a marked-down price.

Now, years later, Oscar and Maria were, like so many older people, dividing their time between a home in Florida and their home in Massachusetts. Earlier in 2001, Oscar's mother had passed away, and in September he flew up from Florida to convince his sister, who had lived with their mother all her life, to give up the house and live with Maria and him. Unfortunately, his sister was a classic hoarder, and he knew it would be a serious mistake to leave her for long on her own.

I picked him up from his friend's house to drive him to rent a car. It was approximately 9:00 a.m. and the sky had a hue like I'd never seen before. We had the radio on, so we heard the news that a plane had crashed into one of the towers at the World Trade Center in New York. Even before we heard about the second crash, Oscar was convinced that it was a terrorist attack, that this event would mark the beginning of a whole new shift in the way the world worked.

Gary and I had our own problems to deal with after 9/11/2001. We had the kids to console, Gary's son and our exchange students (one of our long-term students returned to Japan at the request of her family, who felt she'd be safer there), and we ourselves were too stunned to think of much beyond our immediate needs. But I did receive phone calls and letters from Rick during that time confirming that he felt just as badly as the rest of us, and eventually I went to visit him, this time on my own. We spent the entire visit talking about the attack, and about other events in our lives that had brought us to our knees. Rick confided that he was devastated when Princess Diana died in 1997. We didn't discuss the fact that Rick himself was the author of an event that had brought people to their knees, but it was there, lying like an anaconda beneath the surface of everything we did say.

Chapter Sixteen – The Trial

A FEW WEEKS BEFORE RICK'S TRIAL, SKYE, PATRICIA'S MOTHER, DROVE SEVEN hours from Pennsylvania to visit with Rick, and to spend time with her daughter, who was still in Gloucester. She didn't get to see Rick as much as she intended. By then jury selection had begun and Rick was being taken each day to the courthouse to participate in the process. Early on there was an incident. According to the local papers, Ben Falcon Sr., Rick's lawyer, alleged that one of the guards had assaulted Rick, throwing him into a wall when he asked to use the phone. Falcon said that his client had suffered a concussion and that jury selection would have to be suspended until Rick was well enough to travel to court. The guard in question alleged that Rick had assaulted *him*. Who knows? Unless someone can (or is willing to attempt to) prove otherwise, the prison system is always right. Rick was hospitalized briefly—I glimpsed him on the news being loaded into an ambulance on a stretcher—for his injury and then placed back in the hole. He was also put on suicide watch.

Despite the setbacks, the trial began in late November of 2001. Those of us who knew Rick thought the insanity defense had the potential to be effective. Rick had snapped, we believed. But we would have to wait to see if the jury agreed. We knew only that many people had been excused from serving on the jury because they had admitted upfront that they had a prejudice against cross-dressers.

When I first read about the people being excused from their civic duty in the papers, I had a daydream wherein I got in front of all of them and told them about Eugene, a pilot who became Olivia the minute he landed on foreign soil. Eugene was a client of mine—and a friend. His wife knew about his occasional cross-dressing episodes and she didn't care as long as they took place infrequently and at enough of a distance so she would never have to hear about them from someone else. In fact, most of them took place in Japan, where he'd had a regular route. Eugene was very sexy, very good looking, the kind of ripped, broad-shouldered man women really like. And he liked women right back. But he also liked to be one now and then.

Eugene flew United for more than thirty-seven years before retiring to Boston's South Shore. Over the course of his career there were three times when he refused to fly. In all three instances, he had given the plane a final inspection and found something that displeased him, some small detail that he felt had the potential to cause a problem in the air. In the first instance, his two-hundred plus passengers were made to vacate too, until the problem could be resolved. In the second instance, another plane was made available. On the third occasion, the problem Eugene had detected was deemed insignificant, and when he continued to disagree with that assessment, another pilot was found to fly the aircraft. The flight went okay. But Eugene didn't care. He was not going to take a chance with the lives of all those people, not if there was even a glimmer of a possibility that something could go wrong. I wanted to say to those prejudiced jurors, Would you walk off a plane if you found out Eugene was flying it?

Another person I met was a cardiologist who performed lifesaving bypasses. She didn't talk a lot, so I didn't know much of her story. I only knew that she had once been a man and now she was a woman. I wondered how many of the people whose lives *she* had saved would have walked away from their operations if they had known she was transgendered. Then there's Alera. How many of the moms of the eight thousand babies delivered over the course of her thirty-five-year career would have walked out if they had known that Chip, as she was then called, a much celebrated ob/gyn, was waiting for retirement to become the person she had always known herself to be on the inside? She'd waited because she didn't want to be judged or lose her job. She had loved her work so much. She welcomed every baby into the world with an exuberance and joy that surely had some lasting effect on each of them.

I went only once to observe the trial in the courthouse in Lawrence, Massachusetts. All the other days I taped *Court TV* and replayed it in the evenings when I got home from work. This meant that in addition to the trial itself, I watched many hours of Nancy Grace and the other talking heads offering their views as the trial unfolded.

The first thing that struck me was the timing of the trial. Frankly, it couldn't have been worse. November 2001 was a time of fear and confusion for most Americans, and I guess a lot of other people around the world too. September 11, which saw the deaths of almost three thousand people, was only weeks behind us. Pilots were packing stun guns in their cockpits in case of new attacks. And an already shell-shocked New York was trying to recover from the crash of an American Airlines flight that killed some two hundred and sixty people when the jet snapped in two over Queens. We had just gone to war with Afghanistan, and President Bush was laying out plans to attack Iraq. New Anthrax scares were being reported daily. People everywhere were fighting mad—or scared to death. No one was in the mood to listen to a sob story about a history of abuse leading to insanity. Right from the start the talking heads declared that they didn't find Rick likeable in the least, that he wasn't just some nice guy who snapped. People hated him, the talking heads told their viewers and each another. They flashed his cross-dressing snapshots onto the screen every time they broke for commercials. It was interesting to note that during this time it was impossible to get a newspaper from any of the local stands; they were always sold out.

The problem with the insanity defense was that in order to reveal Rick's psychological defects, his lawyers would have to make the jury focus almost exclusively on the manifestations of those defects, which were acts that would not show him in the best light. Knowing about these acts would surely only make the jury like him less. The hope was that the final judgment would arise from a true and earnest evaluation of Rick's psyche...and not be a popularity contest.

The prosecution, in the meantime, would focus on Rick's intelligence and all of his many successes. It wouldn't make sense to argue outright that being intelligent and successful negates the possibility of being mentally ill—because most intelligent people know this is not true. But Ronald Latto, attorney for the state, would ensure that Rick's achievements were always front of mind, so that his misdeeds would look like manipulation of the worst kind rather than the acts of a man with a shattered psyche. His aim was to convince the jury that a calculating Richard J. Sharpe had killed his wife because she had refused to give him back the three million dollars that he had put in her name prior to their separation. "I didn't care about the money," Rick called out when Latto mentioned it in his opening remarks. The judge told Ben Falcon Sr. that one more outburst like that and his client would be removed from the courtroom.

Falcon's opening statements amounted to a list that included: an incident when Rick had thrown a clock against the wall, because Carmen had failed to wake him up on time; a time when Rick had attacked a DJ at a high school reunion, because the DJ was about to play a song that had once meant something to Carmen and another boy; a time when Rick had slapped Carmen in front of police; the fork incident, and so on. Except for the fork incident, I had not known about any of these, and I found it hard to imagine that Rick's dark side had always been that dark. The shooting, Falcon stated, was not an instance of temporary insanity. Rick's mental disorders had been ongoing since childhood. If the killing had been premeditated, then why was it that Rick had only sixty or seventy dollars in his pocket, requiring him to use a credit card when he fled to New Hampshire? While Falcon spoke, Rick sat with his head bent, picking at his forehead and then his neck and then his forehead again. On the TV screen his skin looked pasty. His hair was too long. His cheeks glistened with tears.

And so the trial began. Britta McMahn, Rick and Carmen's neighbor in Gloucester, the one whose daughter played with Leo and Judy, the one whose younger daughter Rick had performed plastic surgery on, described for the courtroom how the four of them, she and her husband Don and the Sharpes, had gone out to dinner once in 1995, and Rick had talked to Don about ClickMed, the software program he'd developed. Don worked in an Internet business and Rick wanted to get his advice. When Carmen put her two cents in, Rick promptly told her to shut up. He said she didn't know what she was talking about. Britta testified that she'd spent enough time at the house to know that this was not unusual behavior. She'd heard Rick tell Carmen that she was ugly, that she was gaining weight. In late February of 2000 Carmen told Britta that she was leaving. The Wenham house was not quite habitable yet, so she would have to stay someplace else in the meantime. She didn't tell Britta where she planned to go, but she asked her to watch the kids while she packed.

Britta talked to Rick on phone several times after Carmen left. She testified that often he wanted advice on how to get Carmen to come back, but he spoke about the money too, how angry he was because Carmen was refusing to give it back, and once Britta heard Rick tell Leo that his mother had stolen all his (Rick's, not Leo's) money. When she said this on the stand, Rick blurted out, "I seriously doubt that," and got himself in trouble with the judge once again.

Britta talked to Rick several times on the day of the shooting, because her daughter was there playing with Leo and Judy. Most of the conversations were about whether Britta should pick up Cindy or if Rick would bring her home and if so, at what time, etc. But during one conversation Rick asked Britta if she would try to facilitate a date for him with Carmen. Britta said there was no way, that Carmen had started a new life and he needed to move on as well. Rick then went into a tirade about the money and Wyler Grange, Carmen's divorce lawyer, and how none of this would have happened if Grange hadn't gotten involved.

When Falcon questioned Britta, she admitted that Rick told her often how much he loved Carmen, that it was clear to her that he simply could not accept the fact that she had left him.

Rick had said nothing but good things about Britta McMahn to me. He had led me to believe she was his friend, that she understood everything he was suffering through. It surprised me to see how reluctant she was to say anything positive about him.

Ruthy Marshall, the girlfriend of Vance Corrado, Carmen's brother, had been in the Wenham house when Carmen was shot. She described the event on the stand, and then Vance did as well. The Wenham house had been full of people on the night of July 14, 2000. Carmen, Vance and Ruthy had all returned from a harbor cruise. Ruthy had come up with her two-year-old daughter, so there were three little kids there, along with the college student babysitter who had come to take care of them. Just before Vance, Ruthy and Carmen's return, the two-year-old had poked the babysitter in the eye. Carmen had a look at it when they got back and decided the young woman needed to go to the hospital. Carmen and the sitter were just collecting their things when Rick pulled up in his SUV and parked some three hundred feet away, where the driveway met the road. When he opened the door and peeked in, he saw Vance's girlfriend in the foyer. He was just asking where Carmen was when she appeared, waving the restraining order and reminding him that he wasn't supposed to be there.

The next thing anyone knew, a gun was fired. One bullet entered Carmen Sharpe's chest and severed her spinal column.

The jurors already knew every detail of the shooting from the prosecutor's opening remarks, and so these initial testimonies served mostly to elicit emotion.

Hector Lepore, ex-boyfriend of Milly Thieman, was a different matter, and his testimony led to the only element of mystery regarding Carmen's death as far as I could tell. Hector and Milly had moved in together at his house on Washington Street in Gloucester in 1994, and they'd had a child. But the relationship came to an end in August of 1999 and he'd asked Milly to move out. Their son was four at that time. Since Milly had no place to go, she stuck around, sleeping in an upstairs bedroom, until late Spring of 2000, when she began staying, at least sometimes, with Rick. The boy stayed with his father. Hector dropped him off at Rick's house to see his mom on days when there was no school.

Hector had met Rick twice, both times when picking up his son. The last time had been only weeks before the shooting. Rick had told Hector that he needed some welding done, referring to some work on the lasers, but Hector said he didn't have the time. Then Rick mentioned to Hector that Milly had mentioned that he was a gun collector and might want to sell off one of his guns. Or at least that's what Hector testified. Rick told him he wanted a gun for home protection, because he kept money in the house. Hector said he wasn't planning on selling any of his guns.

The mystery was that the bullet that had been found in Carmen's body had been a .22. But Hector testified that the gun that Rick had ultimately taken from his house on the night of July 14, 2000 was a .30 caliber Weatherby. Interestingly enough, neither the prosecution nor the defense made too much of this enigma. The prosecution seemed to believe that Rick must have had two guns, and that he took the Weatherby along on July 14 so that the killing would look spontaneous rather than premeditated. The defense didn't come right out and say it at this point, but I believed that they thought Hector Lepore had only *said* the stolen gun was a Weatherby because it was a pricier weapon than whatever Rick had actually taken and would garner more on an insurance claim.

Between courtroom footage and commercials, one of the talking heads asked another, "If Sharpe already admitted he killed her, why isn't the defense objecting to all the testimony confirming the murder?" A good question, I thought. Another good point made by the same person was that both of Rick's outbursts had come when money had been mentioned. He was playing right into the hands of the prosecution—and making the jury dislike him even more.

Zack Daw was the boyfriend of Cheryl Rice, a woman who had worked for Rick for some time. Zack, who worked in plumbing and heating, had met Rick over the years, either picking up Cheryl from work or at LaseHair gatherings. He testified that Rick had offered him $500 to go into the motel room where Carmen stayed with Judy and Leo after leaving the Gloucester house while waiting for the Wenham house to be finished. Zack said that Rick wanted him to see if there were any documents of interest—bank statements, legal papers—lying around. Zack testified that he told Rick he wouldn't do it, but in fact, according to Rick, Zack did meet him in the parking lot of the train station just across the street from the motel. This was right after Rick had injured himself falling down the stairs with the laser. Rick had had to check himself out of the hospital in order to make the rendezvous, he'd said. While he and Zack were talking, Carmen left her motel room with the kids, and Rick got himself out of the car and hobbled over to the motel on his crutches, and as Carmen hadn't locked the door behind her, hobbled right in and had a look around.

Niles Petersburg, who Rick had hired to keep LaseHair running after his accident, testified that the company was on the verge of going under, that it needed cash. He also testified that Rick talked to him regularly about how upset he was about losing Carmen and the kids. Niles Petersburg knew all about Wyler Grange, and the contractor, Art, who Rick suspected was living with Carmen. Petersburg confirmed that Rick and his children interacted fantastically when Carmen would allow Rick to see them.

Milly Thieman got on the stand. She confirmed for the jury that she worked for Rick mostly in late afternoons and evenings, because his phones didn't stop ringing at the end of the work day. Besides answering phones, she did some paperwork. After she'd left Hector Lepore's house, Rick offered to let her stay at his place. She slept mostly on the sofa, though they had been intimate towards the end.

On July 14 Milly and Rick had gone out to dinner at Halibut Point, Rick's favorite restaurant, on Main Street in Gloucester. Rick ordered red wine with his meal. He had his cell phone with him, and at some point during the meal he called his brother Harry to discuss the computer server that Harry was creating for LaseHair. He was in a hurry to receive it. Harry needed Bruce's help to deliver it, but he thought they could get it over to Rick the following week. He also made several other calls, but these weren't answered and he didn't discuss them with Milly. With Milly driving Rick's Pathfinder, they went up the street to the Blackburn Tavern when they'd finished eating. Rick had more red wine and then a diet soda.

During the summer Hector Lepore stayed at another location, but he would often bring his son to the house he owned on Washington Street so that Milly could spend time with him there. She had been at Hector's with the boy earlier that day, and she had left the windows open. After the tavern, she and Rick drove to Hector's so that she could run in and close the windows in case it rained. When they arrived, she told the jury, Rick started to get out of the car too and she quickly said, "You can't come in." "Why not?" Rick countered. He reminded her that there was a desk in the house that she had said he could have, and he wanted to take a look at it. "Oh, what's the harm?" Milly admitted she'd said to herself. They climbed the stairs to the porch and then entered the living room. The gun was above the piano on a gun rack.

Milly testified that while she was in the other room closing the windows, she heard a noise. She thought Rick had tripped. The only light on was in the hall. There were toys all over the floor. "Are you okay?" she cried. He said he was.

They went out the front door. But before they could get back in the car Rick said he had to go to the bathroom. So they went back into the house again. Milly testified that she walked with him through the downstairs bedroom and into the adjoining bathroom and stood and watched him pee, to make sure he didn't make a mess because of how much he'd had to drink. When he came out she remembered the desk and they ran upstairs to see it. Rick wasn't interested in it. He turned and went down the stairs. She lingered behind for a moment, trying to locate a bottle of shampoo she wanted. She heard the front door slam. When they returned to Rick's, he realized he'd lost his pager. Fearing it might be at Hector's house, Milly said she'd go back and look for it.

The defense began their case in earnest by calling Rick's brothers to testify about the incredible abuse they had all suffered at the hands of their father. Harry, who was called to the stand first, held up the proceedings by arguing that he didn't want the cameras rolling during his testimony. He feared it would have an adverse effect on his business. He said he never told anyone about the abuse. After some consideration the judge agreed to forbid the camera crew from showing his face. The audio, however, would remain on.

Harry was fourteen years older than Rick, so he was out of the house by the time Rick's abuse began. But he acknowledged his own instances of abuse and some instances of Rick's that he had witnessed. He described his relationship with his father as "unique." Day in and day out his father called him stupid. He said his sons were all worthless, all losers who would amount to nothing. Once when Harry was twenty-one and Rick was seven, their father hit Harry over the head with a fireplace poker. He almost killed him. Their mother, who Harry described as "the greatest mother in the world," didn't escape her husband's wrath either. But her abuse amounted to a constant gnawing; it wasn't physical.

Harry told the jury that in his opinion Rick's abuse resulted in making Rick abusive. He cited an instance in 1978, when he was doing some electrical wiring in his Connecticut home and Rick, married by then, came over with Carmen to help. At some point Carmen offered to get lunch while the brothers continued working. Rick asked for Burger King, but Carmen picked up Kentucky Fried Chicken instead. Rick went crazy when he saw the chicken. He threw the bucket at Harry's freshly painted walls and the legs and thighs splattered everywhere. It took two days for Harry to clean and repaint the walls. It was the last time he asked his brother for help.

Again, I was forced to imagine a side of Rick that I had never seen. I weighed the new information. I wasn't on the jury so I wasn't judging Rick's future. But in a sense I was judging my future as his friend. How much could I tolerate? What kind of man was he?

Harry, who coughed a lot, testified that on the day of Carmen's death he received three phone calls from Rick, all about the server he was building. Rick kept thinking of new things he wanted included in the final product. The last call had to do with when the machine would be delivered. Harry couldn't give him an exact date until he confirmed Bruce's schedule, but he anticipated that it would be the following week, on Friday.

The point of Falcon's questioning was that even as late as nine o'clock on the night of the shooting, Rick was still arranging for events that would take place in the future—and hence the shooting could not have been premeditated.

During his cross-examination, Latto got Harry, who was coughing even harder by then, to agree that Rick had risen above family adversity and gone on to garner one degree after another. He catalogued Rick's many published scientific articles, his various businesses, his stock market prowess, his medical achievements…. Since the *Court TV* cameras had been barred from televising Harry, they focused on Rick, who sat with his hand over his mouth, his index finger at rest over his upper lip, his eyes squeezed closed.

Bruce was okay with the cameras, and in fact he looked handsome and calm sitting there in the witness box with his graying hair and matching mustache. He too chose an event from the year 1978 to describe for Falcon. Bruce owned a restaurant back then. Rick and Carmen had come in one New Year's Eve along with some other people. Rick had started arguing with everyone, to the point where Bruce had to tell him to leave. He dragged Carmen out with him, literally, in a way that was abusive. In another incident, in 1980, there had been an auto accident next to the Sharpe house, on an evening when all of the Sharpe family had gathered there. Bruce had gone out to see if everyone was okay. When he got back home, the police were there interviewing his family. For no observable reason, Rick became abusive with one of the officers and started calling him names. Luckily the family knew the officer and no charges were filed. "He would blow up," Bruce said calmly. "He was unstable. If someone did something he didn't like, he was on edge and ready to attack. Not always physically, but he didn't like anyone getting in his space."

While Harry and Bruce had refrained from cursing in their descriptions of their father's verbal assaults, Glenn, Rick's best friend, did not feel the same compulsion. On many occasions he had been there to hear Rick's father call Rick a "fucking bastard," and he would often say to both of them, in disgust, "Ought to put you kids in a bottle and ship you off to war." Glenn, a nice-looking guy with a beard and longish dark hair, said that there wasn't a single day that passed that Rick's father wasn't mean and abusive to him.

The defense called a few more people, including a woman who had only just begun working for Rick before the incident, doing some computer data input for LaseHair. She testified that during her initial interview he seemed to go in and out of focus and he actually fell asleep for a short time. The day before the shooting they'd had lunch together, a business lunch in which he talked to her about the future of the company and her potential part in it. Later she told her family that he had no expression the entire lunch, just a cold stare that frightened her. She said she never wanted to be alone with him again.

Cheryl Rice was also called to the stand. She stated that she had worked for Rick for more than two years, as a technician generating slides to test for cancer for Rick's dermatology patients. Rick was moody, she said, and he would go off easily over small things, but his temper tantrums would blow over just as quickly. They were friends. They talked on the phone a lot after Carmen left, and when he talked about Carmen he cried. Once when she went to check on him, Carmen happened to be at the house. When Cheryl inquired about Rick's whereabouts, Carmen stated that he was upstairs in bed in a fetal position. Cheryl went up and sure enough, he was curled up and weeping. He asked Cheryl to leave because he thought Carmen might come up again soon and they might continue the discussion they'd been having, which Rick hoped might lead to reconciliation.

Patsy, Rick's younger sister, cried through most of her testimony. Because Harry and Bruce were so much older than Rick and Patsy, the younger two had really grown up together. Patsy, an attractive blonde, said that their father would continuously call Rick a "fucking waste" and that Rick in turn would use that language with her. Her father was easier on her, maybe because she was a girl, and with Harry and Bruce out of the house, Rick must have felt singled out for the most extreme instances of mistreatment.

Patsy said that as kids they never played together, unless there were other children around, and then they interacted with the other kids but not each other. Once the principal at their school called her into the office to entrust her with a note for their parents detailing Rick's bad behavior. She agreed to deliver it, and as a result, Rick beat her up in front of the principal's office. He got worse in his teenage years. She remembered him urinating in a bottle of wine to play a trick on one of their brothers. She remembered him calling their mother a slut, because he thought she'd done a poor job of creasing his pants.

Rick's brothers and sister were turning their backs on him, whether because Falcon thought it would help or because it was simply the truth I could not tell. Could Rick have really been this bad? How was it that I had never seen any display of his rage, not even a hint of it?

A pretty blonde woman by the name of Felicia Rumman took the stand. Felicia, married and the mother of two young children, was an accountant. She had been a patient of Rick's in 1994, and after the birth of her first child, she came to him to ask for part-time work. She realized after only a few months that it wouldn't be easy working for him. He showed no respect for her personal life and would call at night or on weekends when he had a question. He would curse when he was angry. Once he got so mad he slammed his fist on a desk. She quit after that, but Carmen, who was still living with Rick at the time, convinced her to come back on board. They needed her. Carmen made her an offer: she would drive to Felicia's house and drop off files and pick them up again when Felicia was done with them. Felicia wouldn't have to see or talk to Rick at all.

This worked for a while. But then Carmen called Felicia from her motel room after she'd left Rick to say that she was finally out. Felicia's response was, "If you're leaving, I am too," and she quit a second time. Rick called her from his hospital bed, begging, unable to accept her abandonment. She told the jury he was a miserable person, a terrible person who would boast about risks he'd taken in the stock market, about his drinking and driving. He put himself above rules, she said.

The next person up to the stand was Rick himself. This caused a big stir among the talking heads who were convening over courtroom footage and before and after commercials. Viewers were invited to email the station and declare whether they thought this maneuver would help or hurt the defense. Most thought the latter, but as the talking heads confirmed, if a defendant wants to take the stand, he has that right. Rick was questioned not by Ben Falcon but by Ben's daughter and associate, the attractive and poised Joan.

Rick kept his eyes squeezed closed the whole time he was up there. Much of the time his hands were on his face, rubbing it, picking at his skin. In a barely audible monotone, he confirmed his father's abuse, always verbal and often physical as well. His father called him a worthless bastard and a dumb fuck. Even if Rick's friends were over, his father would call him such names. Patsy was verbally assaulted far less and virtually never beaten.

Rick recalled for the jurors that when he was about ten, Harry's marriage broke up and Harry moved into their grandfather's house, next door. Rick was over there one day playing with a ham radio when their father came in and started shouting at Harry. That was the day he beat his older son on the head with the fireplace poker, maybe five or six times. The blood flew everywhere. Once his father swung a baseball bat at Rick, but he missed, just grazing his arm. Rick began to fight back when he got older.

Then Rick revealed the details of the secret that *Court TV* viewers everywhere were yearning to hear. Once, again at age ten, he locked himself in the bathroom when his father was ranting and raving. There was a clothes hamper in there, and his sister's things were lying on it. While his father carried on on the other side of the door, Rick began to dress himself in the clothes of the cherished (relatively speaking) sibling. Sure enough, he began to feel safer and more relaxed. Thereafter, he dressed in Patsy's clothes regularly, maybe once a month, he said, but it escalated over time, and eventually he was dressing five or six times a week. By the time he was fifteen, he was working, so he had enough money to buy his own clothes, and a long-haired wig. He went out in public now and then just to see if he could blend.

Rick could never stand to be home at night when his father was there. If he couldn't find a friend who could have him for a sleepover, he would camp out in the yard. When Bruce made plans to move to California, he told his baby brother that he would take him with him, but in fact Bruce left without Rick. Rick called three or four times a day, begging Bruce and his wife to make arrangements for him to join them. When Rick's father got the phone bill, he flew into a rage. Thereafter Rick took some very valuable rare coins that his grandfather had given him and began calling his brother from a pay phone. He drank beer and smoked pot and stole his brother's car and got caught by the police. His father threw him out. His mother wanted him back in the house. "It was just a mess," Rick mumbled. The judge had to remind him to lean towards the microphone and speak up so the jurors could hear him. "Everything was a mess," he said more clearly.

In junior high Rick was "a little shrimp" and bullies fought with him in school once or twice a week. He never backed down, even when they were twice his size. Beating up Rick Sharpe became a joke. In high school he was beaten less frequently, because by then he had a few friends.

Rick told the jurors the story of meeting Carmen in high school, about the patch on the backside of her jeans that said "Built, Not Stuffed." It had come from a mattress label and she had sewn it on herself. Rick began to cry on the stand recalling it. Sniffling, his eyes still closed, he told the jurors that she had just moved to town, and, as it happened, she was in his English class. They sat together that first day.

There was a high school dance coming up, and Rick wanted Carmen to go with him but she already had a date with a boy named Joey. Her parents planned to drop her off at the school. But Rick had rebuilt a 1969 Cobra Jet Mustang with his own money; he could give her a ride. She agreed—and they never went to the dance. Or rather, they stopped in for a few minutes at the end of the night—by which time they were already going steady.

They saw each other every day thereafter. He picked her up for school each morning and brought her home in the afternoons. He visited her when she babysat. They talked on the phone every night of the week, and often they would fall asleep with their respective phone receivers in their hands.

Rick talked about Carmen's pregnancy, how they tried to keep it from her parents, and later, how they fought her parents to keep the baby rather than give her up for adoption. Stephanie had come along two months early. She was in the hospital for weeks. Carmen, meanwhile, was back home with her parents. She would tell them she was going for a walk and then meet Rick at the end of the street. It was the only way she could see him.

Once Stephanie was out of the hospital, Carmen's parents shipped mother and child off to stay with a relative in Pennsylvania. Rick freaked out when he learned she was gone. School was over and he was landscaping, saving as much money as he could to make a home for his little family, but now he couldn't go to work. He couldn't do anything. He had to find her. He called her parents constantly, begging them to tell him where she was. He even went to their house to plead with them in person. He asked to use the phone while he was there, and he happened to notice that their personal phone book was nearby. He grabbed the book and left. He had just figured out which number would lead him to Carmen when Carmen called him and confirmed her whereabouts. He immediately drove to Pennsylvania with some friends and retrieved his lover and their child. But Carmen was too afraid of friction with her family to set up a home with Rick immediately. Instead she and Stephanie stayed for a while at the home of one of Rick's friend's families.

Ultimately they married, before a justice of the peace and a handful of friends; no family members attended. They both wanted to go to college. They worked out arrangements for Stephanie. Carmen worked part time at a day care and was able to keep Stephanie with her when she was there. Carmen's parents watched her sometimes. Rick's parents did too. They made it work. At the University of Bridgeport Rick got degrees in chemistry, mechanical/electrical engineering and math. Carmen got an associates degree in nursing. They had school loans to repay and they were broke. Rick went to work as an engineer and did computer consulting for businesses on the side. Carmen took a job as surgical nurse in a hospital. Suddenly there was cash flow. Stephanie was five or six by then.

Those first years of the marriage were difficult, Rick admitted, his eyes still closed tight, his fingers at play on his face, his voice a lifeless monotone. Carmen had an affair with Nick Fox, the friend of Rick's in whose house she'd stayed when she'd first come back from Pennsylvania. He tried to beat Fox up, but in the end they just threw a few punches and called it quits. He did, however, have a big fight with Carmen, and he slapped her. Ultimately they turned all their anger and emotion into passion and made up.

Another time Rick hired a woman to work with him on a project for a company for which he was moonlighting. Necessarily, he said, they worked together at night, sometimes late into the night. Carmen showed up one night and accused him of having an affair. They screamed at each other for a while, and then she declared that she was leaving him for good and stomped out. He tried to go back to work, but her words kept echoing in his head and it dawned on him that she might mean it, that she might actually leave him this time. He tore out of the office and into his car and drove crazily, hoping to get to their apartment before she had time to gather up Stephanie and leave. In his hurry, he flew through a stop sign. A cop saw him and tried to flag him down, but Rick kept going. It was crucial that he convince Carmen to stay. But the cop had gotten his license plate number and he arrived at the apartment just after Rick, while Carmen and Rick were fighting. Rick went voluntarily to the station and they locked him up for a few hours. Carmen didn't leave.

They argued a lot, Rick said, mostly over trivialities. Most of their fights were verbal, but they would throw things too on occasion. A few fights were physical, but those were usually over perceived infidelities on one side or the other.

In 1980 Rick began medical school. Afraid of failing, he went overboard in the other direction, spending too much time studying and getting top grades. He graduated in 1985 and the family moved to Newton. Carmen had an affair with a doctor with whom she was working, he said, and he had an affair with a former classmate. But they ended their infidelities and made up once again and things got better for a while.

Rick completed his residency in 1990. He took a job as a consultant at a biotech company doing cancer research. That same year they bought their condo in Cambridge. They wanted a house in the country too, so they needed more money. Rick started his dermatology practice in Gloucester on the weekends.

Rick was sued for malpractice in September of 1990. He couldn't understand it; he hadn't done anything wrong, he said. Things seemed to be caving in around him again. He loved his research work, but it didn't bring in much money and Carmen wanted him to work full time in his dermatology practice. Meanwhile Stephanie was getting ready to leave for college. Rick became non-functional for a time, he told the jurors. He couldn't see his patients. He had a nervous breakdown. He sought psychiatric treatment with Dr. Pauline Feldman. She treated him for depression, schizoid personality disorder and anxiety. The meds that Dr. Feldman prescribed kicked in and he began to feel better. Rick and Carmen went house shopping and found the Gloucester house.

For a while they lived between houses, staying at the Gloucester house on the weekends, when Rick saw his dermatology patients, and in the condo in Cambridge during the week. Sometimes Carmen stayed in Cambridge alone. One night Rick was in Gloucester when he started to feel very sick, with vomiting and diarrhea. He didn't want to be alone, so he drove to Cambridge—and found Carmen with another man. They argued; the man left and Rick and Carmen continued arguing. It became physical. He picked up a fork and swung it at her and scratched her forehead. Carmen left him at the condo and drove to Gloucester. On the way she called Pauline Feldman from her cell. Pauline called to talk to Rick and found him nearly incoherent. She sent an ambulance for him. The next thing he knew he was in a hospital bed, unable to move because he'd been tied down. People were coming and going, asking him questions. He was transferred to another hospital, and then to a third, this last one a psychiatric facility. Carmen showed up eventually and told the doctors she wanted to take him home. According to Rick, she made him lasagna that night, one of his favorite meals, and afterward they surrendered to the kind of passionate lovemaking that always followed their worst fights.

He didn't see Pauline Feldman again after that. He was angry with her for committing him. He was a doctor; he could get meds if he wanted them. He began to treat himself.

Things got much better. Carmen became his nurse for his dermatology practice in Gloucester. Leo was born in 1992. In 1994, Rick raised a lot of money to start ClickMed, a more sophisticated version the women's health tracking database that he'd worked on previously. He operated it out of the Gloucester house. Meantime Carmen got pregnant with Judy. Rick was working hard, going to gym, taking care of his family and himself. In the mornings the kids would get into bed with them; in the evenings the family would go out to dinner.

By 1997 he had made his first million. He wanted to ensure that Leo and Judy would never have to work as hard as he and Carmen had to get their educations. He created irrevocable trusts for them, and he added to the trusts each year thereafter.

In 1998 he started LaseHair and Carmen became its titular president. He was also doing liposuction, collagen injections and other cosmetic treatments—along with his dermatology practice. In 1999 he transferred three million dollars from his name into Carmen's.

One evening in February of 2000 he decided not to go to the gym after work because he felt a cold coming on. Instead he went home and played with his kids in the sunroom. Carmen made him a cup of tea and suggested he go upstairs and rest. She said she'd bring up a snack and more tea. He slept for a few hours, but when he got up, no one was home. He panicked. He called Carmen's cell but there was no answer. "I freaked out," he told the jury.

He called Ann Marie Watson, his business lawyer, and she tried to calm him down. She suggested that Carmen may have been upset about something and would probably call him tomorrow and tell him what was on her mind. But he couldn't calm down. He started calling hotels, one after the other, any hotel within a twenty-mile radius, asking for her. He was scared, confused. Something could have happened to her and the kids.

He made phone calls until two in the morning. Then he fell asleep, and sure enough the next day Carmen called…to tell him it was over. He insisted that he had to have access to the kids. If she didn't allow that, he would call the police. They arranged to meet in Ann Marie's offices, in one of her conference rooms. Ann Marie stayed in her office down the hall. Nothing much was accomplished, but Carmen agreed to another meeting. She also informed him that she had a divorce lawyer. He begged her to consider trying to work things out.

The next day Carmen called to say that her divorce lawyer was willing to come to the house and meet with them. This was not Grange but a young woman she had hired before she found her way to Grange. Stephanie, who was living in the apartment over the garage at the Gloucester house, came over from next door. Rick remembered that she sneered when she was introduced to the attorney. Rick suggested they put the divorce on hold for three months and see if they could reconcile. Carmen said no. He asked for access to kids and maybe couples counseling. Carmen said she would be moving to the Wenham house with Leo and Judy. Under no circumstances was he to set foot in that house. She would allow limited visitation with the children. She still wouldn't say where she was staying for the time being, but Rick went out to her car and found her hotel receipt.

Things got worse. On March 5, 2000, Rick fell down the bridal staircase in his house carrying a heavy laser part and woke up hours later in great pain and with the laser on top of him. He crawled into the living room and buzzed Stephanie, who came and helped him to get to his feet. The next day he went into the hospital where he learned he had a broken tail bone, broken pelvis, back injury, internal bleeding, and a concussion. He was there for more than a week. Rick couldn't remember much about the hospital stay; he said it was all a fog. He was treated with narcotic pain relievers, meds for anxiety and depression, and muscle relaxers. This event precipitated his total collapse.

He laid off everyone at his dermatology practice, because he couldn't go to work. His patients went to his competitors. He was on crutches, camped out in the living room because he couldn't climb the winding stairs. What was left of his laser business was moved into his basement, which had a more straightforward staircase. He had been paying an RN named Alfreda

$100,000 a year to oversee the LaseHair operation and the associated websites, but seeing that his business was going down and hoping to protect her own interests, Alfreda started her own laser business while still accepting Rick's money for the running of his.

Rick's testimony went on for two days. Much of the time the *Court TV* camera focused on Carmen's father, sitting in the gallery with other family members. His expression was constant, his lips pulled back, his glassy eyes like those of a caged animal. One could not help but feel his pain.

Rick droned on and on, talking about how he refinanced the Gloucester house after Carmen left and added money to the trust for the smaller kids. He also sold the Cambridge condo to Stephanie for one dollar.

In April he and Carmen reconciled. He had been on the couch, resting when Carmen called. Milly Thieman was there with a couple of other people, working, and Mike was there grilling burgers for everyone. Carmen's tone was different than it usually was; she asked to come over and talk to him.

When she arrived, after the others had left, she sat next to him on the sofa. One thing led to another and they started hugging and kissing. It was an emotional time. They made love that night, and the next day she was there again, early in the morning, eager to take him to the Wenham house.

He lived with her at Wenham for the weekend and maybe the next three days, five days in all. They talked about Art, the painter. She said that Rick hadn't been paying attention to her, and Art had—and it just happened. She told him that she'd made changes to the three million that had been moved into her name. Based on advice from Grange, she'd sold equities and opened a new account with a new company. As a result of these transfers, the money had gone from three million to about half that. If you factored in capital gains, the three million, according to Rick, was now worth a couple of hundred thousand. Rick suggested she find someone else to help her with investments. One of his former patients knew someone really good at Merrill Lynch. They made some calls, and Carmen actually met with the Merrill Lynch guy and filled out an application for a new account, in her name. The day after filling out the transfer forms, she broke it off with Rick again.

Niles Petersburg, Rick said, had learned that Carmen had been embezzling money from the LaseHair account. He also confirmed that she had been writing checks to Art, the painter, from monies outside of the construction account. One check for $10,000 she had written out to herself and then endorsed over to Art. This particular check had come from the LaseHair account.

Petersburg was president of LaseHair at this point, and he filed a lawsuit against Carmen on behalf of LaseHair, sometime after the failed reconciliation. Carmen meanwhile filed a restraining order against Rick and also a motion to have him examined psychiatrically. In the twenty-nine years they had known each other, she had never filed a restraining order before and Rick was beside himself. He couldn't eat or sleep. He cried all the time. He talked about seeing Carmen and Art together on the sofa at the Wenham house, on the occasion when he'd been in the car with Milly and had gone up to the windows to peek. He added a detail that I hadn't known: He picked up a rock and smashed the headlights in on Art's car before returning to Milly. He was never charged in connection with this act of vandalism.

Rick testified that his relationship with Carmen was "confusing" in June of 2000. He was seeing the kids, and at least once Carmen came along when he took them to the movies. Once he showed up at a parade to which he had not been invited and hung out with his kids. He tried to put his arm around Carmen on that occasion but she pulled away.

Joan Falcon asked him about his plastic surgeries. He admitted that he'd had his lids and nose done, and liposuction on his neck and love handles. And of course laser hair removal. He didn't like hair, he said, and he added that it was an advantage not to have it when he cross-dressed. When he mentioned cross-dressing, one corner of his mouth turned up. His eyes were still closed and he still looked wretched, but in that split second I swear there was a hint of a devious smile. I couldn't decide if it was real or if his defense team had told him to snicker when he said those words, so that he would appear crazier. Or maybe it was just my imagination. He went on to say that there were times he'd taken Stephanie's clothes, because they fit better. And there were times when he stole birth control pills from Carmen's pack, because they made him feel more relaxed.

Joan made a list on an easel board at the front of the courtroom. On it were the various factors that had likely contributed to Rick's mental state on July 14, 2000—the restraining order, the loss of savings, Art the painter over there with kids in the house that Rick had hoped to retire in, the business falling apart, the medications, the alcohol, nightmares, being harassed by Grange, etc. Then she continued with her questioning.

Rick testified that he'd taken his meds just before leaving for dinner with Milly that night, antidepressants, muscle relaxers, pain relievers (including

Percocets), anti-anxiety pills.... He couldn't say for sure that he had pulled the trigger on the rifle when he got to the Wenham house just before midnight. He didn't really remember doing so. Nor did he remember loading the gun. Really, the only thing he remembered clearly was a persistent thought—that he must talk to Carmen, that he must get his family back. The next thing he knew, the blast from the gun woke him from his stupor.

Latto descended on Rick when Joan Falcon was through with him. He wanted to talk again about the times Rick had slapped Carmen, the names he had called her. He had called her fat. He couldn't stand fat, could he? Latto asked. He reminded Rick that he'd had his own fat removed from his body. Once he had given Carmen a black eye. On the way to the hospital he'd insisted that she say she fell down the stairs. He also reminded Rick that he'd had to study Behavioral Sciences in medical school, because it was required, and Rick had hated it. He thought it was a bunch of nonsense. The inference was: And here he's trying to plead insanity, when he doesn't himself believe in the rationalizations that are the framework of behavioral psychology.

Latto pointed out that Rick had been able to control himself when he'd seen Carmen and Art through the windows at the Wenham house, and he'd been on meds then. So why should he *not* have been able to control himself on the night of July 14?

Latto had a copy of a letter Rick had written in jail to the man in the cell beside him, Steven Smith, about a possible escape attempt. He knew he was being sent to the hospital for an MRI at a certain time on a certain day, and if the fellow inmate could arrange for him to be "snatched" while being dropped off, Rick would pay him handsomely, with a bonus to come once he was safely out of the country. Rick insisted it was a fantasy. Latto asked him about asking Hector Lepore if he had a gun for sale. Rick insisted he'd never had a conversation with Lepore about guns. Latto pointed out that he'd been rational enough to talk to his brother Harry about a business matter during the dinner with Milly. So how was it that he went into a dream state shortly thereafter?

Before Rick left the stand, he made some comment about how even if he was found not guilty (by reason of insanity) of first degree murder, he would still live out the rest of his life in a mental hospital. This was in response to a question Latto asked him about the Smith letter, and really his response had little to do with the question. It looked like he was trying to sneak that information in, his way of letting the jury know that a lesser sentence would still put him away for good, and thus they should consider the insanity verdict. But all it did was make him look manipulative. Again and again he turned out to be his own worst enemy.

Next the defense offered up none other than Vincent Kahn, the highly respected forensic psychiatrist who is the author of several popular books—some of them on mental disorders and others fictional thrillers—and who had, in recent years, become a sought-after daytime TV and radio show personality. After reciting his long list of degrees and affiliations for the jurors, Kahn, looking handsome and confident, confirmed that his specialty was patients at risk for violence or patients who had already committed violent acts. A practiced communicator, Kahn addressed himself to the judge, the defense and the jury alternately. For the first time since the trial began, Rick sat forward and opened his eyes, showing interest in everything Kahn had to say. Finally his hands came off his face. He looked young and vulnerable in his alert state. Though pale and thin and really quite awful looking, his expression was closer to the one I recognized from our encounters over the years.

Kahn testified that he had seen Rick eleven times for a total of approximately eleven hours. He had also reviewed many documents—police documents, medical records, etc.—related to the case and had interviewed many people, including other doctors, one of them an expert in Borderline Personality Disorders. He thought he had spent a good one hundred hours to date on the case. Ben Falcon asked him how much he had been paid and he admitted he'd received only a scant $6000 to date. I guessed the point of that exchange was to confirm that while he was being paid for his work, he hadn't been bought.

Vincent Kahn's diagnosis was that Dr. Richard J. Sharpe suffered from numerous mental diseases, including Intermittent Explosive Disorder, major depression, Alcohol Related Disorder, and at least three personality disorders: Borderline Personality Disorder, Narcissistic Personality Disorder and Obsessive Compulsive Disorder. He had referred to a well known psychiatric text book, the DSM4, to confirm the names for the illnesses he'd observed.

Kahn explained that Rick had never had a real sense of identity, that his father's relentless abuse had shattered it. He had been too busy coping with one trauma after another to ever feel comfortable acting as himself in the real world. He wasn't even comfortable with his gender, or with his face. He didn't understand why he was being tortured. When he met Carmen he was able to define himself somewhat through his relationship with her. In fact, he needed her desperately in order to avoid feeling totally obscure and alone in the world. His frantic attempts to evade abandonment were evident throughout his marriage. Carmen was his god and savior when his needs were met—and she was terrible in his mind when they weren't, so terrible that his anger exploded and he devalued her in public, calling her names and even striking her. He needed her nurturing to keep his fragile world from disintegrating. Since the age of seventeen he had managed to feel quasi normal only because of her.

Kahn went on to pinpoint instances throughout Rick's life when he was unable to conform his behavior to the rule of law. He was so violent with his sister as a kid that Patsy put ten locks on her door in the hope that he wouldn't break it down. Still he would find his way in and wrench the phone out of her hand and take it to the jack in his own room when he needed to talk to Carmen, which was all the time when he wasn't with her. His father beat him so frequently that it was not a big leap for him to become erratic and sadistic himself.

Kahn maintained that all of Rick's life was an attempt to appear normal, that his chronic overachievement was his way of trying to disguise the confusion and insecurity he felt inside. Kahn explained that drinking made Rick even more erratic than it would someone not taking as many medications—because antidepressants are metabolized by the liver, making blood alcohol levels much higher.

Kahn told the jury he did not believe that Rick was able to premeditate his conduct on the night of July 14, 2000. Rather, the nagging thought that he had to go home heralded a dissociative state and Rick lost his fragile grasp on reality in the face of it. He explained that people who are dissociative and unable to premeditate can still perform structured activities (such as asking Harry about the server delivery date).

There was a commercial while Falcon wrapped up his questioning and Latto got ready to take over. Before the *Court TV* cameras began rolling again, the talking heads took a moment to gush over Kahn. They were under his spell, actually "getting" that Rick had mental disorders. They liked the way Kahn presented himself. They liked his confidence and intelligence. I could only hope the jury was experiencing the same sudden fit of compassion.

Latto began his questioning by asking Kahn what impact Rick's intelligence and education had on his sense of responsibility. Kahn, still smiling good-naturedly, looking very much like a man who thought he had already won the battle, explained that there were some very intelligent people who simultaneously suffered from different kinds of mental illness. As an example he cited a nuclear physicist he had worked with, a man who had been able to hide his psychosis and violent eruptions well enough to make his way high up the ladder in his field. It was only after the guy lost his job for economic reasons and became homeless that his mental illness became blatantly apparent.

Latto wanted to know how stealing a rifle and later disposing of it worked into Kahn's "dissociative state" theory. Kahn said that the combination of drugs, alcohol, the perceptions brought on by his mental illness, his injuries from his fall, etc., all combined to create a "perfect storm" that collectively impaired Rick's capacity to control his behavior. And then he had the misfortune to stumble on the rifle. Kahn pointed out that Rick had made no attempt to keep from being arrested after the shooting. He used a credit card to make purchases; he parked his car right out in front of the motel. This was the same Dr. Sharpe who so excelled at plotting and planning that he had been able to raise hundreds of thousands of dollars to fund research projects and successful businesses all his adult life. Yet he had done no plotting and planning regarding Carmen's death.

Latto tried his best to trip Kahn up by saying that he was misinterpreting the definition of the standard used to determine whether a defendant knew the difference between right from wrong. Kahn said that his understanding addressed the spirit of the standard, and Latto said that wasn't good enough. The courtroom seemed to fall asleep while Latto and Kahn argued semantics, but now Kahn was no longer smiling, and when the next commercial came on, the talking heads were not raving about him as feverishly as they had before. Then the trial was on again and Latto was reminding Kahn that the psychiatrist for the prosecution, Dr. Jerome McNay, had interviewed Rick as well and had generated a report stating that he found the defendant not to be suffering from delusions or auditory hallucinations, that his speech was okay and he was oriented—in other words, he was perfectly sane. Latto argued that it was possible that Kahn had rendered his opinions based on Rick's answers to his questions, which Rick may have fabricated for the sake of his insanity defense. Kahn countered that he had evaluated records, family history, and other documents that had borne out Rick's responses to the T.

Latto complained about the book that Kahn had used to confirm his diagnoses, the DSM4. He said there were caveats in it about using its conclusions in forensic settings. Kahn countered that everyone in the field used the same book. The DSM4 was as good as it got. Latto went back to events before the date of the shooting, reminding Kahn that Rick had said he was in a fog after his fall, and yet he was able to arrange to leave the hospital, meet Zack Daw, get into Carmen's motel room on his crutches, and rummage around, the point being, How was his "fog" any different then than on July 14? On July 13, Rick had gone to dinner with Petersburg, Milly Thieman and Stephanie, and he and Petersburg had talked about offshore business profit shelters.

Since Carmen was killed with a .22 weapon and Hector Lepore had testified that the weapon stolen from his house was a .30 caliber, Latto wanted to know if Kahn had considered that there might have been two guns, which would confirm premeditation. Kahn said this prospect had not had an effect on his diagnoses, though he admitted that if it were to be proven that there were two guns, it was possible that it would have an effect. Latto suggested that Rick already had a .22 in his possession and took the .30 from Lepore's house to make it look like killing his wife was a last minute decision. Kahn said he wasn't buying that the stolen gun was the Weatherby.

Latto insisted that the escape attempt that Rick had fashioned with Smith, the inmate in the cell next to him, was a perfect example of his manipulative nature. Kahn said it was a boyish fantasy to think they could hatch an escape by passing notes back and forth, that Rick had never taken it seriously. Rick had an active and imaginative mind. It was as impossible for him not to use it as it would have been for him to shut down his dreams. Then Latto and Kahn were back to Rick's intelligence again, and Kahn explained once more that because Rick was a physician he was able to hide how mentally ill he was. If he had been homeless, people would have picked up on it right away.

Jerome McNay was called up next. His list of degrees and affiliations was as long as Kahn's, but he had nothing of the former's personality or stage presence. He had interviewed Rick only twice, he stated, at the request of the prosecutor. The interviews had been taped, and during a break he left Rick alone in the interview room and Rick, apparently not aware that the monitor was still on, could be observed rifling through McNay's notes. McNay told the jury that he had concluded that Rick was not in a psychotic state at time of murder and had been able to premeditate. This was evidenced by the fact that he had been functioning during the day in a way that allowed him to make decisions, even as to whether to take the desk offered by Milly Thieman at Hector Lepore's house, and the fact that he knew enough to park at the bottom of the driveway when he went to the Wenham house and to hide the gun when he peeked in the door.

While Latto fumbled with some papers as a prelude to his next set of questions, the *Court TV* cameras swept to the gallery, where Stephanie was now sitting. This was the first time I had seen her in the courtroom. It was impossible not to notice how much she looked like her father. But she was beautiful, sitting upright and seemingly composed, and Rick was slumped over, hiding his face in his hands.

It looked like a stalemate—two prominent psychiatrists who had interviewed the same patient and come up with totally different diagnoses—when Ben Falcon got up and, in my humble opinion, made McNay look like a man with his own agenda from the get-go—or maybe I should say, a man willing to accept the prosecution's agenda without question. Falcon made the case that the questions McNay had asked Rick during the interviews were vague, that he had ignored any questions about his family history and as a result had been told nothing about Rick's abusive father. McNay was made to admit that he had read Dr. Feldman's report from 1991 (in which she said that Rick was suffering from major depression and seemed at risk to himself and his wife), but that he had not thought it important enough to include that information in his own overview report. Likewise, he had read Carmen's affidavit about Rick throwing clocks, ripping up papers she had typed for him, stealing her birth control pills, punching her—but again he hadn't thought it was significant enough to include in his own report. He had read the police report in which Milly Thieman had been interviewed and had stated in his own report that Milly seemed to think Rick behaved fine on the night of the shooting. In fact, the police report revealed that Milly had said at one point he looked like a ghost. Nor did he include mention of the police interview with Britta McMahn, the neighbor, in which she revealed that Carmen had told her that Rick could potentially kill her if she didn't come back to him—or the fact that the day of the murder he was begging Britta to arrange a date for him with Carmen. Nor did McNay include mention of the police interview with Stephanie, in which she said that her father had been obsessing over Art the painter and that in her opinion that had led to the killing. Nor did he include that Rick had tried to reach Carmen on his cell phone over and over again on the evening of July 14, 2000. Yet he did say that Milly Thieman had told the police that Rick hadn't talked about Carmen at dinner, that he'd told Britta earlier in the day that he was taking the kids to the pet store.

There were other omissions as well, many, and in their place were the activities and events least relevant to the case. It was clear that McNay had tailored his report to exclude anything that might add to the evidence that Rick was insane at the time of the murder and had instead chosen to include what was left of each event once all traces of such evidence were removed. Falcon asked why he had been so selective. In essence, his response was that time and space did not allow him to include everything.

It looked like Falcon had worn McNay down, but then Latto got up and got McNay to say that a lot of what was missing from his report was stuff that had happened in the past, events that had nothing to do with Rick's mental state on July 14 or his ability to control himself and conform his conduct according to the standards of the law.

During his closing statements Ben Falcon reminded jurors that while they had seen plenty of emotion and passion in the courtroom, such as an incident when Latto had shouted and pointed at Rick with his finger only inches from his face, their verdict had to be made without emotion or passion. Nor did all evidence have the same weight. Rick was awake again, listening to Falcon attentively as he went on to say that some evidence had "a lot of sizzle but little pop," and while it played into the publicity the case was generating, it didn't really help to establish Rick's mental state. He reminded jurors that the Commonwealth would undoubtedly have them believe that Rick had a stash of guns, or at least two, but that Hector Lepore had proven himself a liar regarding some other matter having to do with the care of his son and had likely lied about the stolen gun being a Weatherby too. There was a picture of the Weatherby hanging on the rack over the piano—Latto had shown it to the jury numerous times—but the picture was from six years ago. Murder in the first degree, Falcon said, required the jury to prove that Rick's act was premeditated, when in fact he loved Carmen very much and as late as the day of the murder was still trying to get her back.

He also warned the jury not to let itself become distracted during their deliberations. He cited Steven Smith, the inmate, as a potential distraction. Smith, he said, saw that Rick was vulnerable and egged him on, all the time thinking Rick's letter—which was so full of hyperbole it might have come from a dime store novel—would allow him to make a deal with the Commonwealth for his own freedom. He even thought he could sell it and maybe get on "Inside Edition." It had nothing to do with Rick's mental state on July 14, 2000. There was also a Dr. Pack, a retired psychiatrist who testified that he had observed Rick at Bridgewater and noted that he was capable of watching TV and chatting on the phone and looking perfectly normal, but once confronted by Pack began to pick at his face and grimace and act much the way he had in court. Pack had called Rick a malingerer. His testimony, Falcon said, was another distraction, and frankly I could have told them that Rick was capable of being utterly miserable one moment and seemingly content the next. I had seen him jump from one side of the aisle to the other many times throughout all the years I had known him. It was almost as if his brain had two compartments, and one or the other was in charge at different times.

In his closing statements, Latto went after Vincent Kahn. This was not a surprise. Out of all the testimony, it was Kahn's that had the best chance to sway the jury. Latto tried to diminish him, saying that he needed the help of other doctors to reach his conclusions. He insisted that Kahn had based his evaluation on what Rick had told him, and as Rick was a liar, anything he said was irrelevant. Further, Latto declared that Kahn was the only psychiatrist who had found Richard Sharpe to be suffering from psychosis. Dr. Pack had not, and neither had Dr. McNay. "Put aside all the psychobabble," he told the jurors "and think of the facts," and he then went on to summarize them once again.

The jury deliberated for some eleven hours, over the course of two and a half days. At one point they returned to court to ask if, legally, the use of a gun automatically infers intent to kill. This led the talking heads to presume that the jury was vacillating not between first degree murder and insanity but between first degree and second degree. The jurors were sequestered in a hotel, and some of them complained that the service at the hotel's restaurant was terrible, that they'd had to wait forever for their dinners to be served. In the meantime, the big news on TV was that Osama bin Laden had ordered gas line explosions in the U.S.A. and people everywhere should take precautions.

On the day the verdict was handed down, Carmen's family assembled in the gallery and the *Court TV* cameras kept a zoom on them. They all began to cry for joy when it was announced that Dr. Richard J. Sharpe had been convicted of first degree murder. He was immediately cuffed and led away. It was a tragedy for everyone involved, Falcon later said to the talking heads.

Sentencing took place two days later, on November 29. Kitty Greene, Carmen's sister, and her husband Harold Greene, took the stand to thank Latto and the prosecution team, various police, and the judge and the jury.

The winner here was justice, Kitty proclaimed. Stephanie would not have her mother to help her pick out her wedding dress, and Leo would not have his mother to bring his first true love home to, and Judy wouldn't have her mom for her upcoming kindergarten graduation. No one could argue with that.

Next Judge Keating confirmed that she had received many letters from various people on Rick's behalf and she read their names for the jury. Among them were Skye and Patricia, as well as a few professors and attorneys.

Patricia's letter I knew about, because she had sent a copy to me. It was a long, heartfelt letter asking Judge Keating for leniency. She told the judge the story of how her mother, Skye, had gone back to school when she, Patricia, was a teen and how Skye had become Rick's classmate and good friend. Patricia began to babysit for Stephanie at that time and came to know the whole family. She always found Rick to be kind and generous, and when her mother called earlier in the year to tell her about the tragedy, she felt compelled to write to Rick to say that he could count on her to pray for him during his time of crisis. They had written regularly to each other since. She added that Rick would often make his own colorful greeting cards for her by taking a piece of his own hair and taping it to a swizzle stick to make it into a paintbrush. Then he bought M&M's from the prison canteen and rubbed them in water to make the paint.

Falcon spoke after the judge had acknowledged the letters, saying that Rick had in no way lived a life of crime. He was seriously abused as a child and as a result became an overachiever. Coupling the successes in his life with evidence of what had happened on July 14, 2000, including the meds and the alcohol, Falcon asked that the secondary charges, possession of an illegal weapon and breaking the restraining order, would not be used to add additional years to Rick's sentence but rather would be concurrent with it.

He was rewarded for his effort. The judge asked Rick to stand and stated that his sentence was life in prison without parole, which was no surprise to anyone as it is mandatory in Massachusetts when the verdict is first degree murder. Additional years would not be added for the other charges. Rick would go to the maximum security facility at Cedar Junction.

Court was recessed. When Rick realized he was not going to have the chance to make a final statement, he yelled out, "I have a right to speak." As the police were coming to remove him, he turned to the camera and said, "I'm sorry, I'm sorry." Then he burst into tears. "I loved Carmen," he sobbed.

He looked as if he was about to lean into one cop's chest, as if he thought the bigger man might support his collapsing body and let him cry on his shoulder.

Carmen's family and the prosecution team assembled on the court steps, under an overhang. It had started to rain, so the cables for the microphones from the TV stations had to be moved out of the rain and re-taped so people wouldn't trip on them. Latto stepped up first to thank the court and say that he was thrilled with the result the jury had delivered. Kitty Greene was next. She was asked by one reporter if it meant anything to her that Rick said he loved Carmen and was sorry. She responded that Rick meant nothing to any of them anymore. "How can you say you loved someone you murdered?" she asked. She was asked about the younger children, who had been in her custody since the shooting. (Carmen and Rick had always agreed that Kitty and Harold would be their guardians if anything ever happened to them.) She said they were fine, making friends, doing great, adjusting. She refused to discuss their reaction to the shooting itself. Stephanie did not attend the sentencing, but Kitty reported that she was okay, that she felt relieved by the verdict, and that she had begun to work with a domestic violence agency in New York, where she was now living. About her sister, Kitty said that Carmen was selfless, that she would give everybody everything and never think about herself. In a final remark, Kitty asked that judicial systems everywhere make breaking a restraining order more than a misdemeanor (and I definitely agreed with her). Then her brother Vance spoke, just a few words to thank the media for being considerate of the family throughout the duration of this highly publicized case.

The press conference was over. The talking heads did a brief interviews with Falcon and Latto. They wanted to know why Rick had not been allowed a final statement in the courtroom. Falcon answered that the judge hadn't asked him and he, Falcon, felt the court was too emotionally charged to listen to whatever Rick might say, so he didn't offer. My guess is Rick was just overlooked. Falcon said that in his opinion Rick was a good man who was mentally ill. He said that in addition to the letters that had been sent to the judge, he himself had received all kinds of letters from patients whose lives Rick had saved, or at least touched in some way. Falcon prophesied that Rick would be okay, that he would get medications in prison and that the other inmates would recognize his great intelligence and that one day his case would be retried.

On the same day the trial ended I received a homemade card in the mail. It was dated November 26, which meant that Rick had mailed it a few days before the verdict had come down. The picture on the card had apparently been drawn by one of his artistic inmate friends, maybe the same man who had drawn Sylvester. This time the picture was of Rick, a very good likeness of him looking aside, forlorn and preoccupied. The wording on the outside of the card—which had been rendered in a careful ornamental script—read, "I miss you and wish you was here." On the inside, in his own familiar chicken scratch, Rick apologized for his fellow inmate's grammar. I looked carefully at the drawing again. All I could think was that if he looked that wretched a few days ago, when he still had some hope, what would he be like now?

Chapter Seventeen – New Friends are Not Enough

WHEN I SPOKE TO RICK ON THE PHONE A FEW DAYS AFTER THE SENTENCING, THE first thing I noticed was that his voice sounded clearer than usual, as if he were right in the next room. He said it was because he was in the infirmary, where he had been sent for evaluation because he was back on suicide watch. I was upset but not surprised. I could hear in his greeting that his depression had reached a new low. "Please don't kill yourself," I pleaded. "There are people who care about you, your brothers, your sister, your friends...." Bruce had been hospitalized in the last day or so, to analyze a heart irregularity. But Harry had been calling me lately and saying he planned to get out to see Rick very soon. "Harry wants to come and see you, and so do I," I offered. Then, to lighten things up, I added, "As you know, my hair went gray when everything first happened. If you die, I'll be bald. You're just in shock right now, that's all."

Rick humphed. "Shock, that's a good word for it," he mumbled.

Christmas came and went, and by the first of the year, Rick seemed to be doing better, or at least he was back to his efforts to get everyone busy working on tasks that would both ensure our continued prosperity and generate monies for his appeal. By now Carmen's family had been awarded five million dollars in response to the wrongful death suit they had filed back in July of 2000, so Rick was down to the wire, literally without a penny to his name. Given that the defense had built their whole argument for his motivation in killing Carmen around the fact that she had all his money, you would think that he would be upset now to have gone from riches to rags. But to his credit he didn't say much about his financial loss at all. In fact, he wrote me a letter in January saying that Patricia was still having major financial problems and that he thought she was deeply depressed because of them. He wondered if I could manage to give her some sort of advance, from the income about to come in from all the websites he was still hoping we would create, until she got on her feet.

And I might have, but the truth was that we were still spending money trying to set up the websites according to Rick's instructions. With the trial behind him and the opportunity for an appeal not yet formulated (it would be tricky getting lawyers now that he was dead broke), he began again to send us instructions, focusing on meta tags that should be inserted into the "head" area of the web pages we were supposed to develop. Meta tag information, he explained, would not be seen by anyone viewing the pages in their browsers. Rather, the purpose was to communicate information to programs and web spiders that search engines use. The process he wanted us to use would eventually become known as "spamdexing" and would come to be thought of as underhanded and manipulative—and search engine web spiders would learn to identify it and would not give high rankings to spamdexed sites. But at that time it was still possible for a computer geek to repeat related phrases in such a way so as to exploit the relevancy ranking by search engines. But I was not a computer geek, and just reading his instructions gave me a headache.

Dear Gary & Linda,

Linda said that you put the Alpha Hydroxy products on the new website. The next step is to do traffic driver pages for the Alpha Hydroxy. We will do things a little different this time. Instead of duplicating the index, we will duplicate the Alpha Hydroxy page.

Use the following keywords (replace the keywords which are present with)

Alpha hydroxy, alfa hydroxy, alpha hydroxy acid, glycolic acid, beta hydroxyl acid, skin, face, eyes, wrinkle lines, lids rejuvenate, rejuvenation, laser, lazer, laser treatment, laser resurfacing, frown lines, forehead wrinkles, crows feet, retin-a, removal, facelift, plastic surgery, cosmetic surgery, nose job, posuction, moisturizer, exfoliate, topical, exfoliation, brown spots, blotchy skin, psoriases, psoriasis treatment, vitamin c, psoriases cure, treatment, cure, face cream, eye cream, dandruff, acne treatment, seborrhea, seborrhea devinatitus rash, rashes, skin aging, rough skin, dry skin, infection, fungus, whitehead, skin fungus treatment, blackhead, tinec vesicular, sun fungus, keratosis pilaris, razor bumps, in grown hairs, pseudo folliculitis, barbae, follicultis, ingrown, waxing, electrolysis, ingrown hair, peel, peal, obagi peel, skin zinc, TCA peel, power peel, micro dematrasion, dermabrasion, facial, eczema, shiny hair, hair rejuvenation, botox, collagen, fat transfer, exe lift, blepharplasty, eyelid, better than cellex-c.

Start by making a copy of the alpha hydroxy page. If a button does not exist on the page itself which says Home, put one at the bottom of the page. Link it to the top URL. Check it in Internet Explorer to be sure it works correctly. Also, be sure both of Linda's phone numbers are prominently displayed on the page. Also, put an email link that says EMAIL US and link it to Linda's email address..

In the description field put [keyword 1], [keyword 2], [keyword 3], [keyword 4], [keyword 5]

In a small font at the top of the page put [keyword 1], [keyword 2], [keyword 3], [keyword 4], [keyword 5]

Name the page [keyword 1], [keyword 2], [keyword 3], [keyword 4], [keyword 5]. Do not exceed 26 characters. Truncation is okay.

Submit the page with the savvy submit. Also, view it in Internet Explorer to be sure it looks okay.

Now highlight keywords 1 – 5 in the meta keyword list. "cut" the keywords and paste them at the end of the meta keyword list.

Now repeat steps 1 through 5.

Keep repeating the process until you have cycled through all the keywords.

To make life easier, keep an updated list of page names in the proper syntax to submit to Savvy Submit in a word file in RTF format on the desktop. Make backup copies of this important file.

Since Linda loves cats, I think it will be fun to sell a cat allergy shampoo.

When you have a chance, make a page for the cat allergy shampoo. Copy the stuff from Patricia's site.

Good luck.

Rick had it all figured out. He had done the math. If we could get three laser clinics—mine and two others, perhaps one of them Patricia's in Arizona—up and running and each made between $20,000 and $30,000 a month because of business generated from the websites, along with another $10,000 to $20,000 a month in collective product sales, we would be on track to make millions over time and his chances for an appeal would be greatly enhanced.

Sometimes I felt as if I were a princess in a fairy tale, being asked to perform impossible tasks that would, if properly completed, ensure my financial success *and* free the dark prince from his prison. I felt I couldn't fail him. But at the same time, I couldn't succeed either. I just didn't have the energy or the know-how. Neither Gary nor I realized that what he was asking us to do was totally unethical, though we did have some questions about the legitimacy of the project. We hedged. Rick's frustration was evident in his letters. Day after day they came, rephrasing the same impossible instructions.

To compensate for what I was only playing at doing regarding the websites, I did go along with some of the other things he requested. He wanted me to get a hold of the court tapes (from *Court TV*) and have four copies made right away. Then he wanted me to watch my copy—all twenty or thirty hours of it, not counting commercials—to see if anyone in the courtroom was making gestures or facial expressions that might have influenced the jury. (The other copies I would keep until their recipients—appeals lawyers—had been determined.) He even told me who to go to—a video production company in Shelton, Connecticut—to have the copes made. "Take no chances," he wrote. Tell Fred (the owner of the video company) to package them well and use FedEx to send them to you."

In addition to trying my best to keep up with the tasks that *were* doable, I sent him money for the prison canteen and I sent him scientific journals and also *Daily Word* magazines in the hope that he might find some solace in prayer. While his letters filled boxes and boxes in my closet, I wrote very little back to him. I knew that anything I sent might be read by the guards. Mostly I continued to send greeting cards expressing guarded declarations of friendship and reminding him that I prayed for him all the time—which I did. My hope was that all my prayers—added to those of others and whatever praying he was doing himself—would result in his death wish subsiding, or disappearing altogether. I also prayed that the guards would keep an eye out for him, just in case. But I decided—one day after Rick called to inform me that an inmate a few cells down had slit his wrists and died— that the guards probably didn't care one way or the other and any praying I did regarding their activities was a waste of whatever spiritual energy I had.

Rick's appearance on *Court TV* resulted in his making some new friends. One was a thirty-eight-year-old nurse from New Jersey named Nadine. Not long after she first contacted him, I received a letter from Rick saying that she might be calling me to discuss learning how to use the laser. He said I would like her, that she was kind and compassionate. He also mentioned that she was not in great health.

For a few days after that I didn't answer his calls. It was my way of conserving energy—of checking back in to see how my real life was going. It was also my response to his telling yet one more person that I would teach her to use the laser. Rick was allowed only a limited time each day to write letters—generally about fifteen minutes—and while he tried relentlessly to get me on the phone, his letters became less frequent after the first mention of Nadine. I assumed this meant he was using his letter-writing time to be in touch with her. Frankly, it was a relief to think that there might be someone else willing to take some responsibility for his wellbeing.

Nadine was one of the many friendships he would make as a result of *Court TV*. Gloria, a woman living in Indiana, had also watched the trial. I learned about her not from Rick but because she got my number from him and called me directly to introduce herself! She had decided that her mission in life would be finding him an appeals lawyer, and quickly. She said something about *us* having three months to make it happen. She indicated that she had a lot of health problems too, involving her liver. Rick had already been really helpful to her and she thought his ongoing guidance would have good results. He seemed to be a magnet for unhealthy women who also suffered from too much free time and an overabundance of compassion.

Gloria also got Harry's number from Rick and didn't hesitate to call him and get him involved in her plan for finding an appeals lawyer either. In turn, Harry called me to see if I knew what was going on. I was talking to Bruce on the phone regularly as well. Between Rick's calls, which I had started taking again by then, and all the others, it seemed that I was on the phone a good part of each day. And there was always something new to talk about. At that time, for instance, Harry had learned that "Dateline TV" was interviewing members of Carmen's family to see if there was enough intrigue to warrant a segment. He wondered if they would reach out to Rick's family as well, what he would do if they solicited him. There were lesser issues too. Prisoners don't pay for their phone calls; the recipients of the calls have to pay. Collect calls are very expensive, especially for people living out of state. Apparently Gloria, Rick's new advocate, was spending a lot of time talking to Rick and couldn't afford to pay her phone bill. So Rick took money that Harry had sent him for canteen and sent it to Gloria. Harry was furious, but he couldn't tell his brother that because Rick was still on suicide watch, and who knew what might push him over the edge? Rick was so miserable. He was constantly telling us that he couldn't live the way he was living forever, that if he didn't get an appeal, he would have to make other arrangements. In spite of the fact that he was wretched, the guards, who clearly hated him, kept finding reasons to put him into isolation, where he would go days without TV or radio and would be let out only an hour a day for exercise.

In February I visited Rick to discuss in person the issue of his looming suicide. I wore my favorite fragrance, so that I would have something to fall back on if things got out of hand. We talked—or rather I talked—about healing, how we all—not just him but me and his brothers and everyone else involved in his life—needed to heal from Carmen's death as well as from the results of the trial, that we had to expect that things would get better or at least change over time, because nothing stays the same. "Please let me know when you feel that depressed," I said. He agreed that as long as there was a chance for an appeal, he wouldn't do anything drastic. But when I looked into his eyes I got the feeling that he was indulging me, that he was fully capable of taking his life at any time. "Where there is hope, there is love," I continued, determined now that I would not give up until I had extracted a promise that felt authentic to me.

I tried to persuade him that the day might come when his younger children—if not Stephanie too—might want to reconnect with him, that he had that hope to live for. I reminded him that before Carmen's death, he had done lots of good deeds in his life; he had saved a lot of people. Now he was tutoring his new friends Nadine and Gloria regarding their health issues; even from prison he could be saving lives. I talked and talked, and eventually I saw a shift in his expression, as though he was being hit with a tidal wave of emotion. He whispered, "Linda, you're my best friend."

"You have lots of friends," I said.

"No," he countered, "you've been there from the start."

We didn't say much after that, but he didn't take his eyes off of me either—except once to glance at the clock.

A week or so after my visit, I got a call from one Dr. Cameron Hayes. Dr. Hayes informed me that he had notified his lawyer to say that the Botox and collagen text, as it was presented on my website, constituted a copyright infringement because it had been lifted from one of his brochures without his permission. He suggested I take the text down within five business days, or prepare to be sued. Of course the Botox and collagen stuff had been embedded in the text from Rick's original LaseHair site. Unless you "searched" for it, it didn't pop up, and I had forgotten it was even there. I promised Dr. Hayes that I would remove it as quickly as possible, and then I called all the other former LaseHair affiliates to make sure they removed it from their sites too.

Dr. Hayes' call totally stressed me out. It seemed like every time I got to thinking that Rick really appreciated me and would never do anything to hurt me, I was setting myself up for another slap across the face. When I mentioned the incident to Rick, he suggested that I offer ALI, Dr. Hayes' company, a $500 licensing fee for the right to keep the information up on the site. I guess I shouldn't have taken his manipulation personally but I did. It reminded me too much of the relationship I'd had as a kid with my father; every time he got in trouble I felt like he'd let us both down. Sometimes I thought that my relationship with my dad was simultaneously what allowed me to be so supportive of Rick Sharpe and also what most revolted me.

I didn't know how to remove the text from the site myself; I had to pay someone to do it. As I knew I wouldn't have time to redesign the page once the text was removed, I simply had the tech person delete the entire page and be done with it. All of the text on the site had come from Rick. I wondered how long it would be until I got another call informing me that I had unwittingly committed another offense I would never have committed on purpose.

In early March I got a call from a *Court TV* producer. I guess the trial had been a great success for the network and now they wanted to capitalize on it by doing some post-trial segments. Grant, the producer, said that they planned to interview Harry and also Glenn, Rick's best friend. I allowed Grant to fax me the questions he wanted to ask me—thirteen of them in all—but in the end I decided I didn't want to go on TV and answer them. I had lost enough clients as a result of knowing Rick Sharpe. I didn't want to lose more. Harry tried to talk me into changing my mind. He suggested I appear in silhouette so I wouldn't be recognized. When Grant called again, I asked him about doing an interview that way, but he didn't think it would work. He said it would lose some of the emotional impact. I told him to forget it.

When I visited Rick again that month, I noticed that there were more guards at each of the various stops and gates than usual. In the visitors room, there were six guards as opposed to the usual three. This happened sometimes when the guards were changing shifts, but time passed and none of the six left. It felt very awkward to have so many of them around. With nothing else to do, they hovered behind the inmates as they were attempting to have private conversations. Once we got settled, Rick explained that an inmate had been stabbed a few days before, hence the additional security. I noticed that he had a bruise on his elbow and some peeling skin on his face, as though from a scab that was still drying up. He said he'd tried to block someone and got hit. I still didn't understand but before I could ask any questions, a guard shouted for a headcount, and all of the inmates rushed to line up against the far wall on their side of the room. There were probably thirty of them, and Rick was at the end of the line, near the corner. He looked so small and scrawny compared to the others, most of whom were burly men with lots of tattoos.

Towards the end of March there were a few quiet days when I didn't get any calls from Rick and didn't hear from his brothers either. Too many quiet days in succession put me on alert; generally they meant Rick was back in the hole. I could have called Harry or Bruce to find out what was going on, but I chose to wait it out. Then I got a call from Harry saying that state troopers had been to Bruce's house the night before to question him about whether or not he had agreed to give money to someone on Rick's behalf. According to the troopers, Rick was trying to get another inmate to make a deal with someone on the outside to knock off Ronald Latto, the prosecutor from his trial. The charge was that Rick had told the inmate that his brother Bruce would pay for this service.

Bruce had his own problems, mostly with his heart. He needed state troopers snooping around like a hole in his head. Harry, Bruce and I discussed the matter at length. We knew Rick didn't like Latto, but he liked Grange, Carmen's divorce lawyer, even less. If he was really going to attempt to pay for a hit, it would have been on Grange. We decided that he was being set up, again. We could only hope these new events wouldn't hurt his chances of getting an appeal. In the meantime, he was in lockdown.

Generally Rick would be in isolation for a day or two and then be released back to his cell. This time they kept him in there for weeks. I checked in with Harry and Bruce every day, to see if anyone knew what was going on. They didn't know anything, but we were all tense and we sensed that something bad was going to happen. Then, on the last day of the month, Harry called to say that Rick was in the hospital. He didn't know why and he didn't know which hospital he'd been sent to.

I called the hospital nearest the prison. The woman at the front desk gave me the name of someone, maybe a social worker, to call. I called her and she said to call the family for information. I said I was family and she confirmed that Rick was there and in serious condition. But that was all I could get from her.

Later I spoke to Harry and Bruce, who had by then made some progress with their own calls, and learned, as I'd suspected, that Rick had tried to commit suicide, by tying a shoelace around his neck.

Rick, who was having seizures, was transferred from the hospital near the prison to New England Medical Center in Boston. Once again the TV news had footage, of him lying on a gurney as it was slid into an ambulance. Already talking heads were speculating. They seemed to agree that he had done it not because he really wanted to die but because he wanted to get out of isolation. They had called Carmen's father for a comment, and they got one. Mr. Corrado said, "He didn't die? That's a shame." The whole situation made me think about what it must feel like to be Rick, to have glimpses of pure brilliance, urges of pure compassion, and then spasms of desperation so black that no action, no matter how awful, seems implausible.

Chapter Eighteen – Transfer

Rﾠ{.}ICK'S SUICIDE ATTEMPT FURTHER EXTENDED THE TELEPHONING NETWORK I FELT myself to be at the center of. Nadine, the nurse from New Jersey, called to introduce herself—and to get information. Of course I knew who she was from Rick, and she had known about me too, but now that he was in the hospital, she felt the need to reach out to me directly.

Rick hadn't gone into details about his relationship with Nadine and I hadn't given it much thought. But now on the phone, in her moment of emotional grief, she told me all kinds of things I was probably better off not knowing. She had received over one hundred letters from Rick in the short time they had known each other, and she had probably written him that many too. She had fallen in love with him, she admitted between sobs. She was thinking of moving to Massachusetts to be closer to Rick. Rick was still having seizures; no one knew what would happen. Harry speculated that he might have gone without oxygen too long, that he might be a vegetable. Nadine cried hysterically when I told her that. She said if it turned out he was okay and the appeal went well and he eventually got out, she was going to marry him. They had discussed it extensively. They would move to Switzerland.

We were three hours on the phone, with her doing most of the talking. At first she blamed herself for what happened. It was hard for her to visit him from New Jersey; it had been weeks since she'd seen him, and she thought the interval might have been too much for him. Then she blamed the medical staff at the prison. She said that Dr. Psycho—apparently their pet name for the shrink who was treating Rick—had taken Rick off antidepressants when he learned that Rick was having trouble urinating. "So now he pees but he flips out!" Nadine exclaimed. Dr. Psycho could have found another antidepressant, one without that side effect, she insisted. She knew about this stuff. As an RN she had worked in psych wards with people with borderline disorders. It was why she understood Rick so well. "He always liked nurses," I mumbled in response.

We talked too about the accusation the prison was making that Rick had tried to set up a hit on Latto. Nadine said that Rick had told her about it in a letter. He'd been taking a nap when a fellow inmate woke him up and said, "Did you hear the news today?" Rick sat up and asked him what he was talking about. The inmate said, "You told someone you were going to kill Ronald Latto, your prosecutor." That was the first Rick heard about it. Rick said in his letter to her, "This is how it starts. A couple of inmates decide to get famous."

I thought it was important for her to know that she was not Rick's only pen pal. I mentioned Skye, Patricia and Gloria. She didn't seem to care. She said she had sent him a lock of her hair and that he slept with it under his pillow to have good dreams. I said that sometimes when I couldn't sleep I perfumed a note card and put it under my pillow for good dreams. "That's interesting," she replied.

While Nadine rattled on, recounting anecdotes about their relationship, I thought about Yolanda Rider, another nurse I met through Rick one day when I was at his office first learning to use the laser. She was one of the nurses that assisted when he was doing dermatology procedures. Yolanda was as older woman, matronly in her looks and in the way she dressed. But she was one of those kind, warm people that no one can resist. She came into the kitchen area when I was in there nuking a slice of pizza. We sat down together and started to chat. At some point she said, "You know, I would have lost my house if not for Dr. Sharpe." She went on to tell me that she had been unable to pay her bills for a while, and when Rick found out he gave her the money she needed and told her she could work it off over time. She confided that she had some kind of cancer, that she was in remission then and doing okay. Rick knew about the cancer and he knew that she would go under financially if she got sick again, and he didn't want to see that happen. A couple months later Rick called me very upset. I asked him what was wrong and he told me that Yolanda, his favorite nurse, was in the hospital. He hadn't realized I had gotten friendly with her. Soon after, she died, and Rick and Carmen attended the funeral.

Several days after his attempted suicide, Rick was released from the hospital and returned to his cell. Bruce, who had gone to see him at the hospital, reported that he had a nasty wound around his neck, but he was definitely not a vegetable. I spoke to Rick myself that week. He must have been heavily medicated. He didn't have much to say and he didn't have much of a response to anything I said, not even when I mentioned that I had met his future wife over the phone.

Days later Rick was moved from Walpole to the correctional facility in Bridgewater. Harry and I agreed that this would be an upgrade for him, that he would get more care and consideration. Dr. Jamelli, the psychiatrist who would be overseeing his wellbeing, wrote to Lucy, my lawyer but currently the only lawyer Rick could call on (since I had agreed to pay the bill), to say that he found Rick to be exhibiting signs of "suicidality, hopelessness, depressed mood, impaired concentration, poor memory, flattened affect, tearfulness, psychomotor retardation, anorexia and insomnia…and major depression." But as he was also demonstrating "splitting behavior" (attempting to create conflict among staff), he was refused one-on-one therapy, which is what he insisted he needed and wanted.

Things quieted down in the wake of the transfer. Bruce bought the laser he had been talking about, and I became his laser-leasing client. Nadine continued to call me, although she insisted she couldn't afford Rick's calls, let alone the ones she was making to me. Mostly she and Rick wrote to each other. She said it was not unusual for him to sell off his dinner in return for some paper and stamps so he could write to her, he loved her that much. She also wrote to me, a card to thank me for my friendship. Her writing was so pretty and uniform it could have been typed with some ornamental font.

I didn't need or want a new best friend. With all the phone calls, it was all I could do to find time to spend with Gary in the evenings, and he was my best friend. I found myself saying things to Nadine that I wouldn't have said to anyone else, little jabs insinuating that she was overstating Rick's adoration. She didn't seem to take them in, which made me want to do it more.

In April of 2002 Rick was taken off one of his anti-anxiety meds and was feeling a lot of anger. He was talking a lot, Nadine said, about his father's abuse when he was a kid, how he'd grown up never trusting anyone as a result. They had that in common, she said. She had losses in her life that she was angry about. He was also upset about his brother, Harry. Harry had discovered a large lump on his neck, and although Rick hadn't seen him in some time, Harry's description of it convinced Rick that it was cancer. He wanted Harry to get a biopsy right way, but Harry had no health insurance. In my almost daily conversations with Harry I could hear in his voice that he was genuinely feeling bad.

Since Rick was so busy talking to Nadine and Harry, he didn't call me quite as much as before, and as a result, I seemed to have more patience with him when he did call. Sometimes after we hung up tears would well up in my eyes. He was back to talking about how much he wanted Stephanie to visit, how important it was that he talk to her. He reminisced constantly about the happy times with the two younger children. One of his favorite stories was about how they, he and Carmen and the younger kids, would go to the Fourth of July parade every year with another family, the Bellemontes. They would go early, with baskets of food and drinks, and set up their lounge chairs in the best spot on the sidewalk and everyone would have a blast. Time heals everything, I told him. He laughed lightly. I told him I was going to try to come by and visit soon. He said he didn't look too good. One of the other inmates had punched him in the nose because Rick had stood too close to him. He said he'd been a few feet away, not close at all by normal standards. His nose bled for a long time afterward.

Harry and I spent more and more time talking on the phone. His health was failing him and he needed distraction. If nothing else, his brother's ups and downs were intriguing enough to lift him out of his own problems for a time. Nadine had told me that she and Rick had made a pact, that if he committed suicide first, she would too, and if she did first, he would. Romeo and Juliet. Harry and I discussed their relationship at length. Harry laughed. "She *is* kooky," he said. Harry had seen a doctor by then and learned that he needed thyroid surgery. Rick was also insisting that he have his lungs checked, but Harry was putting it off. One body part at a time.

By late Spring Rick seemed settled and his depression had subsided to the point where he could think about other things besides suicide. He was still getting a lot of support from Gloria, who was making all kinds of calls on his behalf and talking to various lawyers, none of whom were willing to consider an appeal for a man with no money. As a rule I didn't return many of the messages she left for me, but that didn't seem to deter her from leaving them. Some of her messages asked me to have Gary call her. Maybe she thought she'd have better luck recruiting him to work with her on the appeal stuff. He didn't call her back either.

I went for almost two weeks in June without taking any calls from Rick. I knew from Nadine and Harry that he was doing okay, so I took myself a little vacation. When I finally answered one of his calls one day in the middle of the month, he exclaimed, "Where have you been? I've been withdrawing from not hearing your voice!" Before I could answer he went into a monologue about websites and keyword meta tag generation, which ended with him requesting that I give whatever information I had managed to garner back when I was still trying to follow his meta tag instructions over to Gloria. This would include the domain names that I had paid for and had not put to use. It would also include the domain names I had put to use for my own website.

I put my foot down. "I'm not doing anything for her," I said. "I've paid lots of money to get where I am. I've done favors for a lot of people you know and I've gotten nowhere." He began to give me instructions, about how I could still make use of the domain names I had purchased. I interrupted him. "This is Chinese to me. I can't even stand being on the computer. This is nonsense. I'm not interested." As if he hadn't heard me, Rick went back to talking about how Gloria could set up what she needed from the old sites, that he needed twenty-five percent of the revenue from the sites for his appeal. I said, "I'm not getting involved. Stop this. Gary agrees that these calls from you are very stressful."

He was quiet for a while. Then he asked me if I wanted to talk sex with him. I could only think that they were trying out new meds on him, and one of them must have made him more manic than ever. I said, "That's not the kind of relationship we have. Talk to Nadine about sex. She's your girlfriend. Think of me as a sister." He said that if I talked sex, I would be considered a girlfriend too. I said no way. The next thing I knew he was in tears. "Linda, it's so bad in here," he cried. "I can't take it much longer." I said, "Put your energy into getting your appeal. Look forward to that."

Rick called five times the next day, approximately every three hours, and I didn't answer any of them. Nadine called asking if I knew why Rick had called her, as he wasn't supposed to call her until Sunday. Now she was in a panic thinking that something must be wrong. I called her back and said that as far as I knew everything was fine, he was probably just bored out of his mind. He called everybody all the time, every chance he got. I didn't see what the big deal was. She was really stressing me out. I managed to calm down, but then she left me a second message, saying basically the same thing. She added, "Listen, he doesn't want me bugging you, so don't say I called. He doesn't want me putting you in the middle of our relationship. But I don't know what else to do. Blame me, not him. I'm the one who called you. He's depressed enough. It's my fault. Bye."

Rick called me at my office the next day, and as I was between clients I picked up the phone. He was distraught. He said he'd had a dream that he and Leo and Judy were at the house in Gloucester. There was a man there, wearing a black mask and black clothes and trying to pull the kids away from him. They were out on the deck and the kids were screaming and hanging onto the railings for dear life. Rick grabbed their hands and used all his strength to get them away from the bad guy at the last second. Then he woke up, but it took him a long time to settle himself. He added, "I'm sorry about pushing you about Gloria using the websites."

Gary and I took a much needed holiday to visit his parents at the end of the year. Christmas in a prison cell would be hard for Rick, but I tried not to think about it. I was too far away to be able to help if he got super depressed again anyway. Instead I focused on present company, one of the joys of which was watching Gary bake bread with his dad. The entire family had been baking together since Gary and his sisters were kids. They even had little "from our family to yours" labels that they stuck on the packages that were gifts for family, friends, neighbors, the mailman, or for donors to the Cystic Fibrosis Foundation (their charity of preference), or for use as Communion bread for the church Gary's family attended. It wasn't what they said while they were baking; actually most of what I heard was, "Where's the new bag of flour?" and, "How much longer until the rising batch goes in the oven?" It was more the easy fellowship in the space between their exchanges, the warm aroma of the sourdough on the rise, the love…. This, I thought, is what real family feels like.

I found myself really connecting with Gary's mom, Dorothy. I told her all about Rick and the ambivalence I felt about being his friend. She seemed to understand. Her empathy made me say more than I might have otherwise. I told her how dumped on I was feeling, with calls coming in not only from Rick but from all the other people in his life. It wasn't that I disliked anyone. In fact, I had grown quite fond of Harry, and Bruce too. But I felt like a woman with too many kids; they all seemed to need something from me at the same time. It was exhausting.

Dorothy and I went shopping together. We went to a Mexican restaurant. I told the waiter I was a vegetarian and asked him to decide what I should order. I was too burnt out to look at the menu. He brought quesadillas made with goat cheese. Dorothy had lentils, flat bread and sprouts. It was the first time in months that I felt truly relaxed.

No sooner did Gary and I walk in the door than the phone rang. I picked it up without checking the caller ID. In a raspy voice Rick said, "I'm having withdrawals from not seeing or talking to you." I said, "You survived." "Barely," he countered. He asked about the trip. He wanted to know if airplane security had changed as a result of 9-11. In fact, they took me aside and patted me down on the way over. On the way home, they pulled Gary aside. He was carrying six loaves of fresh baked bread. They took one out and checked it over. "I can't survive without outside communication," Rick told me.

Chapter Nineteen – New Place, New Rules

LOLA, A DENTAL HYGIENIST IN BOSTON, HAD ALSO SEEN RICK ON *COURT TV.* She'd watched the trial in its entirety, and she was convinced he hadn't had a fair one and that his sentence had been harsh. She went to Bridgewater one Sunday morning to meet him and to offer her support. She said she might come by maybe in a couple of months and visit again. But he must have bugged her over by the phone, because two weeks later I heard she'd been there a second time.

It seemed to me he now had a sufficient number of friends and I could back off just a bit. I'd hired someone new at work and I asked Rick not to call anymore at the office because the new woman might not understand. When he complained that I was too hard to reach, I asked him about Nadine. He said that she was either writing about her sexual fantasies, which he didn't see the point of engaging in as he was incarcerated, or she was mad at him. I told him to be grateful for the little things. For one, he was in a much better place now, in Bridgewater. He could sit down with his visitors without a glass wall separating them. The treatment he received was significantly better than what he'd gotten at Walpole. There wasn't nearly as much violence. He agreed that Bridgewater was an improvement, but he reminded me that he had been sent there because of his attempted suicide. Once they determined that he was no longer at risk, they would send him back to Walpole. "Don't worry about the future," I said. "Just be happy for what you have now."

"Besides Glenn, you're my best friend," he said. "I get along better with women."

"You're not gay, so liking women better is normal," I said.

"Yeah, I'm not gay," he agreed.

I said, "I know that, Rick, I know you're not gay."

I had barely hung up with him when Harry, his brother, called. He said, "What's the worst that can happen?" He was referring to his thyroid operation. "I die, right?"

I said, "Harry, God's not ready for you yet."

Harry changed the subject. He wanted to tell me about a woman he had dated a few years ago, after his wife died. She was so in love with him that when he threatened to break up with her—because she was extraordinarily possessive and was always accusing him of being involved with women he worked with—she threatened to commit suicide. He took three months to break up with her. Every step of the way had to be carefully planned. He'd thought he'd done a great job of doing it gently and incrementally, but she wound up institutionalized anyway. He never found out what happened to her. He had no idea where she was or whether she was still alive. His surgery was coming up the following Tuesday. Bruce was going to pay for it. The doctors were saying that he'd probably had the tumor on his neck for years. I wondered if it was part of the reason he had insisted the *Court TV* cameras be directed away from him during the trial.

Over the weekend we had a three-way conversation, Rick, Harry and me. When I got on the phone, Rick made a sneezing noise so any guards listening in wouldn't hear the clicks of a third party coming on. Custom phone calls were not permitted. Rick talked about Harry's health and suggested he insist on some additional tests before and after the surgery. I kept quiet and took notes, in case Harry was letting it go in one ear and out the other. Rick again voiced his concern that Harry had cancer in his lungs. Harry said he was more troubled about pain he was having in his stomach. Rick insisted he have his lungs checked first and then worry about his stomach. Harry had been a heavy smoker for years.

Lola began to call me too, no surprise. But she had a sweet personality and I was happy to have the chance to get to know her. Years back I had worked as a dental assistant myself, so we had some common ground. Plus, relative to everyone else in Rick's life, she sounded fairly normal. She told me that the dentist she worked with had tried to fix her up with one of their clients, a lawyer. She was uninterested at first, but she was downright appalled later, when she learned that the lawyer was married, that his wife had lupus and didn't have sex with him anymore, that he went to prostitutes for services. Lola was freaked out to think her boss would try to fix her up with someone like that.

I figured it was only a matter of time until she started falling for Rick as Nadine had. I wondered what would happen when he had two women on the outside who wanted to marry him. If that didn't give him some hope then I didn't know what would. Also, there was another new friend, Naomi, who lived in Manchester. She too had seen him on TV. She had been to visit him a few times already by the time I heard about her. Rick mentioned that she had a serious weight problem. I guess he was set on helping her to overcome it. Lola reported that Rick had offered to work with Naomi to get her involved in one of his business ideas and Naomi had responded, "While I should not mind sharing your cell with you, I certainly don't want to end up in one of my own." We had a good laugh over that.

At the end of June I went to Bridgewater again to visit. I wanted to get there by at least 2:15 because shutdown was from 2:25 to 3:10 and there could be no movement in or out of the visitors room during that time. If I was late, it would mean waiting for the next visiting time, after 3:15.

It was a gorgeous day, sunny and hot, about ninety degrees. For some reason my car's air-conditioner didn't seem to be doing its job though. I felt overheated. I arrived in the parking lot at 2:18. I got my license, pen, sunglasses and lifesavers out and rushed in. I said to the guard, "I'm on time. Can I go to the ladies' room and lock up my stuff?" He said I could, but that I was the last one who would be allowed in before shutdown. I looked behind me. There were some seniors, a few of them in wheelchairs, who were being turned away.

Rick was already in the visitors room when I entered. He stood when he saw me. It was hot in there too and his hair was pulled back into a stubby ponytail. He was dressed in a blue uniform with a white T-shirt beneath it. His clothes looked like he'd had them on a few days running. He gave me a big hug and a kiss on the cheek. He said, "I missed you so much. I'm so glad you came."

I had to wiggle out of his embrace. His neediness was always so apparent. He said, "You look beautiful today." I was still overwhelmed from my air-conditioner not working. I had spent the morning at home exercising on the treadmill. I ate lunch in the car and then drove too quickly so I could do the fifty miles to Bridgewater in forty-five minutes. And I had forgotten to douse myself with my favorite scent. Now I felt dizzy and flushed, like I might pass out. My heart was racing. I said, "I don't feel that good. Can I rest? I don't want to talk." For ten minutes we sat and said nothing. He held my wrist, evaluating my pulse. When the guard wasn't looking I rested my head lightly on his shoulder. He whispered, "Breathe deeply. You're going to be okay."

His soothing words brought me back to an incident that had occurred four years earlier. I'd had some spider veins in the back of my leg and they were really bothering me. Rick said to come into the office and he would give me an injection. The process is called sclerotherapy and it is very common and relatively painless. The doctor injects a liquid agent through a tiny needle directly into the veins, causing them to contract and collapse.

The procedure should have taken about a half an hour, but I had a reaction. I should have known better because I'm allergic even to flu shots. Suddenly I couldn't breathe. I felt a horrifying tightness in my throat and chest. I couldn't talk because my tongue was swelling up in my mouth. I was in anaphylactic shock. In a matter of seconds I found myself staring at Death's door. Meanwhile, Rick had run off and returned with an epinephrine. He administered the shot into my arm, but nothing happened. He began moving me, jiggling me. I was like a dead weight. If anything, I felt worse. The blood had drained from my body, and I was turning blue. As if he were my mirror image, Rick looked bloodless too. I could see that he was horrified, which made me even more certain I was dying. He ran back to his cabinet a second time and prepared another epinephrine injection, this one a full vial. It worked almost immediately. I began to feel a little better. Or at least I was breathing again.

Rick stood staring down at me, holding my wrist and checking my pulse, for some time. When I was able to talk again, he left me long enough to call Carmen from the office phone and tell her what had transpired. In minutes she was at the office, with Leo and Judy in tow. Carmen said, "Let's stay together. We'll go have some lunch."

We went together to an Italian restaurant on Main Street in Gloucester. I sat down at a table with Carmen and the kids. I still felt really weak, but I was alive, so I was happy with my progress. Rick didn't sit at our table. Or rather, he sat there at first but then he got up and moved to one to the left of us, in the furthest corner. He sat sideways, as if he didn't intend to eat. When the waitress came, he ordered a small salad, which was also what I ordered. Carmen chatted amiably throughout lunch—asking me every five minutes for an update on how I was feeling—while the kids picked at their food and simultaneously colored with the crayons the waitress had brought and teased each other. Every time I turned around, Rick was either staring into space or staring at me in a spaced-out way, his salad untouched. I think he was in shock. He didn't handle losing patients well, and he had almost lost me. After lunch we went to their Gloucester house and they made me sit there and relax while they went about their business. Much later they let me drive home. The next day he called me to say that he had written a prescription for me for four EpiPens, one for the office, one for home, and two in case I switched bags—and that I needed to pick it up and have it filled right away. "Don't leave them in the car," he warned, "because the inside car temperature fluctuates with the weather and could reduce the shelf life."

My thoughts returned to the present. There were twenty or so other people in the small visiting room and it remained so bloody hot. There was one small fan on the guard's desk in the corner, but it was only circulating the hot air. Rick said Lola had come to visit that morning, at 9:15, but two prisoners had been fighting and visiting hours were pushed back as a result. She didn't get in until 10:15. Glenn and his girlfriend were supposed to come but never showed up.

We talked for a while about Harry, who had come out of anesthesia following a seven-hour surgery. The hospital staff had told him that his was the biggest tumor they had ever seen. It had been fast growing; in another couple of weeks it would have hit an artery. They thought they got it all. Harry had told Rick that his neck was now five times bigger than normal. Rick was afraid he might have a hematoma. He was also upset because they were waiting three weeks to even look at his lungs.

When there was nothing more to say about Harry's health issues, Rick talked about selling his practice. Except for the medical equipment that Patricia had allegedly removed, I didn't see what there was to sell. He said there remained in his garage at the Gloucester house boxes and boxes of files, from the five thousand plus dermatology patients he had seen over the years. There might be other stuff too, files or equipment that Patricia had overlooked or hadn't known what to do with. He said he needed someone to go over and clean out the house before it was sold.

I pictured the house in my head, not as it had been the last time I'd been there but from back in the days when Carmen had thrown big parties, when the kids were always out playing on the lawn and dogs from the neighborhood were stopping by to play with the Sharpe dogs and flowers were blooming everywhere. I think I loved the house as much as he did. It had everything I had always wanted in a house, the large rooms, the oversized kitchen, the solarium, the woods, the location near the beach. It was a dream house. It was as close to *my* dream house as I had ever seen. I wondered how long it would sit on the market before it sold. I wondered if the reason it hadn't sold already was because he had lived there.

With all the weighty stuff behind us, we talked about androgyny, about people who walk the fence between male and female. Surprisingly I knew more about it than he did. Or, he was pretending to know less so that I wouldn't feel inferior to him intellectually. He did that sometimes. He had done that, in fact, when we had first met in my office. Either way, I said I would print something from the Internet and bring it for him next time.

He said, "Did you know that when I was sure Carmen didn't want me back again, that day after we went to the lawyer, I went to the bank where she had an account?"

"What are you talking about?"

Rick sort of smirked. "I dressed up. I went to the bank. I thought maybe I could pull it off and get at least a little bit of money. But someone recognized me and I ran out."

"You dressed up as what? A woman?"

"Yeah, to look like Carmen."

I stared at him. I had never heard this story. I didn't know if he was telling me the truth or not. In the end, what did it matter? To change the topic, I asked him if he enjoyed porno movies. "Next subject," he interrupted, and he reminded me that he hadn't had sex in two years. When he smiled, I realized that it was the first full smile of our entire visit. I said, "If you get through this appeal and the suit about the Latto threat, you will have shown yourself to be a very strong man. But you have to get through each hurdle one at a time. Stay strong and say your prayers."

"One more minute," the guard yelled.

Rick smiled again. He said, "You're a great therapist. You should work here."

I went again to see him a week or so later, but this time I brought Lucy, my lawyer. When he saw that I had a stranger at my side, he hesitated, almost looking like he might turn back and vacate the visitors room. But then he came forward and after a few minutes he was fine, talking up a storm about URLs and websites and ways to make mega bucks on the Internet. After we left, Lucy and I went to Dunkin Donuts to get some coffee and I asked her what she thought of Rick now that she had met him in person. She said, "You can really feel his sensitivity when you meet him face to face. You can feel the vibes. He's gentle—and charismatic." She shook her head. "He is *so* bright; if he really wanted to kill his wife he could have planned it so he would never get caught. He had to have been insane when it happened."

Chapter Twenty – Jealousy

NADINE CALLED ONE EVENING TO SAY THAT SHE HAD WRITTEN A LETTER TO THE editor at one of the local papers about how the prisons only discipline people but don't take the opportunity to help heal them. I could have told her that. To be polite, I asked her if Rick had seen her letter, and she screamed, "Don't you send a copy to him!"

I said, "I don't have a copy. What are you talking about?"

But I did mention her letter to Rick on the phone the next day, and that evening Nadine called again and left a message while I was in the shower. In it she screamed, "If you want a copy of my letter to the editor, don't go through Richard. Come to me. Stop fucking with me! You'll regret it!" Click.

This is not the kind of thing you want to hear after a long hot relaxing shower at the end of a work day. I called her back and she immediately repeated herself. "Don't fuck with me," she yelled. "I'll kill you."

I said, "This is a threat. Do I need to report you to the police?"

She said, "You're fucking with me."

I said, "I never even met you. What are you talking about? What did I do to you?" I was thinking, Borderline Personality Disorder. I had heard it discussed so much during the trial that I thought I knew the symptoms.

Then she suddenly forgot that she'd decided to make me the target of her anger and switched gears to tell me some of her gripes with the prison system. For one, a lot of her letters were not reaching Rick. I could have told her why. If she was writing to him about her sexual fantasies, the guards were probably saving her letters to enjoy over coffee at the end of a shift. She said, "I'm so confused."

I said, "So is he."

She said, "I want to move up there and visit him and keep him alive."

Besides a teenage daughter who lived with her father, Nadine had birds and dogs and cats. I said, "If you move, how are you going to pay the security for all of those pets to move with you?"

Even though I maneuvered to get off the phone in a relatively short amount of time, there was a part of me that felt bad for her. She didn't talk much to me about her health issues, but Rick mentioned them regularly. There were a lot of them, and they were serious.

The next day Nadine called again and said in one of his letters Rick had said he would never do anything detrimental to our friendship, meaning his friendship with me. "I'm so confused," she cried, and then she burst into tears. I knew then that it was in fact jealousy that had caused her to be so angry the previous day. I said, "Nadine, I have a wonderful man in my life. I don't know what you're talking about."

She said, "Rick wants us to get along."

I said, "Fine." But I was thinking the task was near impossible.

A few days latter I happened to notice Nadine's name in my appointment book. I asked Rachael and she said yes, that Nadine had called and said that I had been recommended by Richard Sharpe. She wanted a laser treatment on her face. I sat down at my desk and called her right away. I said, "Did you make this appointment for the 18th?"

She said, "I'm visiting Rick that day too. I'll be nearby. I wanted to surprise you!"

She'd succeeded. I was surprised, and a little nervous about letting someone like her into my place of business. But I couldn't think how to cancel the appointment without being rude. I said, "You're on a lot of medications. That could make you photosensitive. You need to check with your physician."

She said, "Oh, I didn't think of that."

We left it that I would hold the appointment open until she had a chance to confer with her doctor.

Our conversation stressed me out. I can't work on someone if I'm nervous. I got home from the office and Rick called, four or five times, and I didn't answer. I tried to take a nap but I wasn't tired. Finally I got in the car and drove out to Gloucester and sat near the sea at a picnic table under an umbrella and watched the boats coming and going. In the foreground a few locals were snorkeling and trying to catch lobsters. They caught one and measured it and put it back. The weather was still hot, but it was nice by the water.

The next day Rick called and when I answered he wanted to know where I was that I didn't take any of his calls. He seemed more frantic than usual. I wondered if his brain was gradually altering because of his last suicide attempt. I asked him outright and he said, "My brain is fine." He said the only difference was that he couldn't remember numbers as well as before. I told him I'd been to Gloucester, to the ocean. He asked me what it was like.

The next time I went to visit I was there in plenty of time before shutdown, but for some reason they didn't bring him in. I sat in the visitors room for an hour or so with no one to talk to. One of the inmates had a lady friend there with a baby and I talked to them a little. The inmate wanted to know who I was waiting for, and when I told him, he said, "Yeah, he's very high profile." He said that the guards were watching Rick closely and listening to his every word on the phone. They picked on him a lot, the inmate confessed. I asked him what he was in for. He said he'd had killed someone too. His friend asked me my name. I said, "Susan," my instinct to distance myself kicking in, I guess.

Rick finally appeared. He was holding a flower, a small wilting daisy that he'd picked from the prison yard. He gave it to me. He said the reason he had been so late was because he'd an anxiety attack and had to go back to ask for an anti-anxiety med and somehow he missed getting to the visitors room before lockdown. And then there had been a bunch of fights, three at least, so lockdown had been extended. I had claustrophobia by then. I got up to pace a little but the guard yelled at me to sit down. It was hot in there again, and crowded. There had to be at least thirty people. The kids who were in there were falling asleep from the heat.

Rick had seen his new friend Lola again and he was hoping Lola and I might go together to clean out the house before it was sold. There were some pictures he wanted, photos of Carmen and the kids, and some personal items that he hoped I would store for him. Also, there were some medical charts that Joan Falcon seemed to think he might be able to keep.

Our visit was short and frustrating. Before I left I told Rick to be careful with Nadine, that she scared me. He said, "Did she threaten you too?" I didn't answer and he went on to say that he felt sorry for her, because of her health and some other messy issues in her life, but that he thought it might be good to back away a little, because she could be so mean sometimes. He told me that he'd gotten one of the artistic inmates to draw a rose on the envelope for one of her letters. When she said something about how beautiful the drawing was, he made the mistake of mentioning that the inmate had drawn one on an envelope that had been sent to me as well. When she flew into a rage, he explained that under her rose he'd written, "I love Nadine the nurse." Under mine it simply said, "For Linda." I hadn't received the letter he was referring to yet.

On the way out, there were seven of us together going through the gates. When we got to gate four, the guard there asked me for my name. I had to say "Linda" in front of the same woman to whom I'd said "Susan" earlier.

Chapter Twenty-One – Death and Taxes

RICK CALLED FRANTIC ONE NIGHT A WEEK OR SO LATER, JUST BEFORE I WENT TO bed. He said, "There has to be a way out of here."

I said, "You try to get out, they'll find you."

He said, "I can't go on like this. Don't you hear that noise? That's an inmate trying to kick his door down. They do it all the time, all night long. Last night a guy succeeded."

I could hear the noise in the background. *Thump thump thump thump.* Rick said that he'd had to trade his bottle of shampoo for two stamps because he'd run through all his canteen money.

I said nothing, just gave him a minute to hear himself, and sure enough he began to calm down. He told me that he'd helped Lola to make a few small investments in the stock market and she was happy with the way they were going. Then we talked about his house again, what a great investment it would be for someone. When it first went on the market it was listed at $600,000, which was not a bad price for five-thousand square feet of living space on a wooded lot four miles from the ocean. Now it was down to $569,000. First it had been listed with Century 21, then Remax, and now it was back to Century 21 again. It had been on the market for over two years. Besides the Richard Sharpe stigma, there was some problem with the septic.

I went to sleep that night thinking about the house, and the next day I called Lucy, my lawyer, and asked her what *she* thought about me buying it as an investment. She had never been there of course, but she knew the area. I asked her if she thought the stigma would hurt its resale value in the future. She said people forgot that sort of thing over time.

When I went into work that day I found that Nadine had left a message canceling her laser appointment, not because of anything her doctor had said but because she wasn't coming to Massachusetts anymore—because she was no longer having a relationship with Rick! Rick called several times that day, at work and at home, but I didn't answer any of them. I didn't want to hear his side of the story. Nor did I want to hear more from Nadine, but she called too, and one of her messages was so long that I couldn't help getting an earful anyway. She said, "Linda, I'm sending you copies of all his letters and maybe then you'll understand. The originals will go to Kitty Greene, Carmen's sister, so she can give them to Stephanie, so Stephanie can see what's going on. I'm going to destroy him. He sent me a letter saying he wanted to get to Bridgewater to get contact visits. I hope Stephanie writes a

book from these letters and makes a lot of money. I'm out to destroy him."
I was thinking, This woman is crazy and she's going to destroy me too,
because I'm sure I'm the topic of at least some of their conversations. "He's
not borderline," Nadine the nurse continued. "He's narcissistic and he uses
people. He's a womanizer. He finds your weak spot and hones in and gets
you addicted. Maybe Stephanie can get rich from this. And another thing,
Linda, you are the cause for our break up."

Click. Gone. Call ended. Jack Nicholson in *The Shining* came to mind.

I was so shaken that I actually called her back, but I got her answering
machine. I called Gary at work but he wasn't there. I didn't leave a message.
I called Harry, who was just getting off his oxygen allocation for the day. I
said, "I have to talk to you about Nadine. I don't want to upset you when
you're trying to heal, but I have to talk to someone."

We talked about Nadine for a while and Harry succeeded in calming
me down. Then we talked about Rick and Carmen. Harry said Rick never
intended to hurt her. He said that before she ever left him, she had tried to
open a separate checking account under LaseHair in her name. The bank
asked her for the corporation papers but she didn't have them. So instead,
allegedly, she stole some fifty or sixty thousand in cash from the company.
It made me think about the time she'd called my office screaming because
we had sent our laser money by check instead of cash. Harry said Rick could
have put her in jail for embezzling when he found out about the missing
money, but he loved her and he couldn't admit to himself that she was strat-
egizing. He said, "He was so fucked up that night when he went with Milly
Thieman to Hector Lepore's. And what did he find there but the devil, setting up to do his thing."

I responded, "I never heard you curse before."

He said there was no other way to put it. Rick did everything all wrong—
like the way he presented himself at the trial. He didn't know how to deal
with people. He only knew business and medicine. But he had also seen him
cure people and help the needy, and that was why he stood behind him.
He reminded me that Rick had done lots of pro bono work for so many
Gloucester fishermen who had no health insurance and probably would
have died without proper intervention. "I love my brother," he said, "but he's
not playing with a full deck."

"He's so bright, he's crazy," I said.

"Well put," Harry replied.

෮෬

I had sent Nadine a phone card a few weeks back, for her birthday. It was my way of trying to get her to see that I was not the enemy. So when I started getting calls from "unknown," I assumed it was her using the card and I didn't answer. She sent me an email:

Linda, I would appreciate it if you could give Richard a message to send me $700 for all the collect calls. All I want to do is end this all but I will not allow him to use me like he did to others. As you know, I have information that could seriously harm lots of reputations.

Keep ignoring my demands and you will leave me no other choice.

Nadine the nurse.

I waited until the weekend, when I had a chance to get to Bridgewater, to tell Rick about what was going on in person. His eyes teared up. I said, "She's out to destroy you. And probably me too. Do you have anything to say?"

"I'm sorry I'm sorry I'm sorry I'm so sorry," he whispered.

I said, "I can't tell you what to do, but if I were you I would stop all correspondence with her."

"I will," he promised.

Somehow I got to talking about my stepdad after that. Al had been very sick, with pneumonia following heart complications, for about a month before he died, back in 1999. Just before he was hospitalized, he came to my house with a trunk-load of stuff, art prints from Sears, copper pots and pans, all sorts of things, some of it probably stolen. He said, "I'm not going to live much longer and I want you to have this stuff." I said, "Come on, you're not going to die." But he looked old and weak and tired for someone age seventy-seven. He told me he had stuff for Harriet, my sister, his real daughter, too. Except for her annual Father's Day visits, at which time she would bring him a baby rose bush in a ceramic pot, they hadn't spent time together for years. Harriet, who was a master barber, had cut his hair regularly until he married Phoebe, who was also a hairdresser. Without the regular haircuts as an excuse to visit, they drifted apart. Sometimes you need an excuse to see somebody. I was closer with him than she was, but that was because I worked so hard all my life at our relationship in return for his care and for his never abandoning me.

Harriet was not a crier. Even when she was a kid, when she got emotional she would run away. Once Al got to his death bed, all hooked up with IVs and oxygen tubes in his nose, Harriet went to visit, and instead of crying she took pictures of him and then ran away. Later she gave me the pictures.

After he was gone and the funeral services were over, I met Phoebe at a restaurant for breakfast. She said, "Did you know that the only thing he left me was $2,000 in the checkbook to pay off his bills? And that's not even enough to cover them."

This was an awkward moment because he'd left me an IRA worth $10,000. Phoebe had been his IRA beneficiary initially, but at some point he'd taken her name off and put me down instead. He'd left some money for Harriet too. Phoebe broke the silence, saying, "He gave you *my* money. I've had it with this family."

I thought about this for a while. I was working and she was retired. In the end I cashed in the IRA and gave her the $10,000. But when tax time came, I had to pay taxes and a penalty (about a third of the money) for cashing the IRA prematurely.

I was at the office with a client at the time of Al's passing, and suddenly this peaceful feeling came over me and I knew that his spirit was leaving him. That feeling was like nothing else I had ever experienced. It was like the whole world went quiet for about thirty seconds. My client said, "Are you okay?" I said I was and sat back to rest. But a minute later the phone rang, and then Rachael tapped on the door and stuck her head in to say there was an important call about my stepdad. I told Rick, "If you were to leave the world, I think I would feel your spirit pass too."

When I got home the phone was ringing. I picked it up and Nadine screamed, "Don't fucking ignore me." I hung up. I called the local police, but they only told me to call the police in New Jersey. I put both my lines on hold so that if she called again she would get a busy signal. Later I called Harry and he said she was threatening him too. She wanted $1000 from him. It was almost comical. Almost. Harry had called a lawyer friend, to see if there was anything we could do. He was waiting for a call back.

Chapter Twenty-Two — Dream House

THE NEXT TIME I WENT TO SEE RICK, GARY CAME WITH ME. THERE WERE ONLY A dozen or so people in the room, several of them interracial couples—white women with black men. They looked over at us but didn't smile. One couple had their legs crossed over each other's. The guards didn't say anything at first. If Rick had done something like that, he would have been in big trouble immediately. The rule was both feet on the floor at all times, inmates and visitors alike.

Rick was quiet. He said he'd received a letter from Nadine saying she was never writing to him again, but she asked him at the end to call her. He said, "I won't respond to her because she hurt you. I won't tolerate that." He thanked us for visiting, and the three of us hugged.

It was a good thing we'd gone when we did, because very soon after Rick was prohibited from *having* visitors...because of Lola. Lola wore a brace of some sort because ten years earlier she'd had her ribs removed on one side. (She was vague on the reason for the rib eradication.) She had been to visit Rick and he had put his arm around her and it had somehow unsnapped a section of her brace. Because of the nature of the thing, it took a minute to re-hook it, and Rick tried to help and got called out by the guard, who insisted that Rick had been touching her breasts. The guard wrote up a report, and now Rick was forbidden to have visitors for the next two months. Lola said that he'd asked the man sitting across from them to stick up for him, because the guy had been watching the whole time. But the guy was too afraid of getting written up himself. Lola was so upset she called the superintendent the minute she got home. First she was calm but then she yelled at him. "Oh, that's a good way to speak to the superintendent," I told her.

It wouldn't end for Rick. He was miserable when he couldn't have visitors. A few days later he went to call Lola on the phone, but a bully inmate beat him to it. "Fuck you, faggot," he said to Rick. This same inmate had offered Rick protection if Rick would give him canteen money, but Rick hadn't had any money when he'd asked, and now Rick was afraid the guy had it in for him. He told me that a lot of the prisoners would find crushed cigarette butts on the ground and remove what little tobacco was left in them and, when enough tobacco had been collected, use toilet paper to make a whole new cigarette—a rollie, they were called. Two stamp books could be traded for a rollie. A real cigarette would bring in four stamp books. You had to have something to offer at all times, whether to satisfy your own needs or to avert conflict. Nadine had sent another note, this one insisting he give her back photos she had sent him. But the photos were among the ones that had been stolen from his cell back when he was at Walpole. "What should I do, Linda?" he asked. I had no answers.

Meanwhile, Lola was doing everything she could to get Rick's visiting privileges reinstated. She called Lucy, my lawyer, to ask her to subpoena the visitors video from the day she had been there. I was impressed. I hadn't thought of that. When Lucy was denied the footage, Lola set up a meeting with the superintendent. That night she called me in tears. It was so clear that everyone at the prison, from the inmates to the superintendent, hated Rick. She felt sure they would send him back to Walpole now, and we all knew he wouldn't survive there.

It was August by then, and I was still thinking about the sea. Just for the heck of it, I called the realtor, Chase, who was handling the sale of the Gloucester house, and introduced myself as someone who had been in the house and liked it. We got to talking and he said the house should have sold the first week it went on the market, but as soon as people found out who had lived there, they weren't interested anymore. However, he had recently taken an offer from a couple; it looked like it might sell after all. Impulsively, and I guess because I had that sick sensation of having moved too late, I said I wanted to meet with him to make a backup offer, in case the one he had fell through. He said that would be fine, but I shouldn't get my hopes up. Theirs was a good offer.

When we hung up I had this strange feeling, as if the world had all gone mute for a half a minute, almost like the feeling I'd had when Al died. I felt so certain that I was destined to have the house that I went to my bank that same afternoon to see what the chances were that I could refinance my house in Newton so that I could restructure my loan and put a down payment on the Gloucester house. It was complicated but doable, I was informed, as long as my house had the value I thought it did. Gary was a little surprised when I told him what I was up to later. He liked the Gloucester house too and he thought the purchase would make sense from an investment perspective. But he was concerned about the Sharpes having lived there. Even though the shooting hadn't happened there, there had been yelling and tears and bad vibes. But he said he'd support me, just as he supported my friendship with Rick, though I'm sure he would have preferred that Rick and his entourage didn't take up so much of my time and energy.

It felt good to know that I could actually afford the house if we got that far. I could afford my dream house, mostly because of Richard Sharpe.

Rick, Harry and I had another three-way call, though we had to be more careful than ever now that we suspected the guards had it in for Rick. Harry had discovered that he still had some cancer cells near his thyroid and had gone to the hospital for some version of interferon that was highly radioactive. He'd insisted on this treatment only after numerous entreaties from Rick, who felt sure it was the best option for him. Rick had driven us all crazy with this. When he hadn't been able to reach Harry, he had called me, insisting that I make sure Harry get the help he was recommending. Now Harry was able to report that he had gotten the treatment and was back home, but he couldn't see anybody. When the radioactivity of the pill ceased working, he would have to throw out his bed sheets. He was eating from paper plates. Radioactivity gets everywhere. But in three to four weeks he hoped to learn that his thyroid cancer was totally gone. Rick reminded him of his lungs, which he still hadn't had checked. "Don't screw around with this," he warned him. "You smoked for thirty years and you were exposed to secondhand smoke even longer. I want you around when I get out. I miss you and I love you." He added, "And Linda is my savior. Without her I would be dead. She sends me *Discover* magazine and *Investor's Business Daily*." I was embarrassed but I couldn't say anything because I wasn't supposed to be on the call.

Lola's hard work on Rick's behalf achieved no results. In fact, things got even worse for him. They decided to cut back on his phone time and forbade him to use the library, which was the equivalent of cutting out TV privileges for another kind of inmate. When Rick saw Felix Robare, the Bridgewater superintendent, walking down the hall, he called out to him, "What you're doing is a violation. It's morally and ethically wrong." Robare said, "You're entitled to your opinion." Rick cried, "That report was all about busting my balls." Felix Robare glanced at him but kept on moving.

Around this same time I learned that my friend Oscar, my latest father figure and confidante, had non-Hodgkin's lymphoma. He'd only found out about it two weeks earlier, and in that short time he'd begun to feel really bad. He was only sixty-eight. He said he couldn't even walk now, it was so bad. His throat and ankles were swollen. They'd used a needle to withdraw some of the fluids. He was scheduled for chemo the following week. His heart, lungs and cholesterol were all great, he said. His blood pressure too. Except for the lymphoma, he was as healthy as a horse.

The next time Rick called I picked it up right away and told him all about Oscar. He immediately began to rattle off all kinds of things that Oscar should be asking his doctor, including about some experimental drugs that might work if the traditional stuff failed. He also recommended other doctors Oscar should consult. I had a sheet of paper handy near the phone and wrote down everything. My heart was broken just knowing Oscar was sick. I didn't know what I would do if anything happened to him.

I called Oscar back to give him the information, and once he promised to look into everything, I told him I was making a backup offer on Rick's house. I knew he'd want to know. He was the one who had inspired me to buy my condo, as well as the house in which I now lived in Newton. Oscar thought it was a great move for me—if it actually came to pass. The inspection for the Gloucester house was coming up. If there were enough problems, it might scare the buyers away.

Sure enough, Chase called within the week to say that the problem with the septic, along with some other issues, had put the potential buyers on edge. They had been told by the home inspectors that the house needed about $200,000 in repairs. Their contract deadline had just about expired and Chase could only give them a short time to make a final decision.

Now I was convinced that the Gloucester house was meant to be mine. I wasted no time in calling an appraiser to come over and give me a value for my house. Then I called Chase back to find out if the other people had come to a decision. They had; they were backing out! I was thrilled. But then I had a second thought: I wondered aloud what Stephanie, and her fiancée, Harrison (who was overseeing the house transactions), would have to say when they learned I wanted to buy the house. Chase assured me that he'd already taken the liberty of telling them I was the one making the backup offer, and they were fine with it, as long as I could get pre-approved for a loan right away.

Driving out with Gary to meet Chase, I felt nervous to the point of thinking I might faint. It was a good thing Gary was behind the wheel. Except for Oscar, we hadn't told anyone yet. I didn't want to tell Rick until it was definite—just in case anything went wrong.

Chase was out in front of the house when we arrived. He said that now the other people were saying that they did still want the house, but their time had expired on the contract and they weren't showing signs that they were really serious. Still, their offer had been better than mine, and I still needed a letter from the bank saying I could do the loan. I looked around.

The front yard was a mess, not anything like it had been back when Carmen had been there. The house looked sad and run down. The turquoise Ford handicap-style van that Rick had used for laser deliveries was still parked in the driveway.

The inside of the house was a mess too. The garage was full of empty bottles for Alpha Hydroxy (I guess Patricia hadn't been able to cart everything away after all) and boxes and boxes of files from Rick's dermatology clients. I also found a shipping box from the McKernan Packaging Clearing House, addressed to ClickMed Corporation. Dust and cobwebs were everywhere. Rick hadn't had much furniture near the end, but whatever he did have was still there, including some shelves and desks in the area he'd used for the business. I gave Chase an earnest money check to go with my offer.

I called Lola as soon as I got home. She saw it was me on her caller ID. and answered, "Hello, Sweetheart!" Her greeting almost made me cry. My father always called me sweetheart, and his letters from prison always began with "Hello, Sweetheart." Lola said, "So I hear you went to the north shore?"

I said, "How did you know that?"

She'd spoken to Rick and he'd told her I was going to an art show out there. He'd wondered why I wouldn't stop at the house and get the medical charts. I said to Lola, "You need a lawyer for that. No way would I have touched them." But then I broke down and confided that I had actually been at the house. I began to laugh and cry with emotion. "I bought the fucking house," I squealed.

"What?!"

I repeated myself. I never swear, but this occasion demanded it. She started crying right along with me. She was so happy. She asked if she could tell Rick, and I said no, not yet. She said, "I can keep a secret." She was quiet for a moment. Then she mumbled, "Now Rick and I can get married there when he gets out." I thought to myself, Oh, here we go again.

Later Rick called. He was in a pretty good mood because a lawyer by the name of Burt Tucker had come in to talk to him about possibly handling his appeal. He wanted to tell me about their conversation but I didn't think it would be a good idea to discuss it on the phone. I said, "Let's talk about something safe."

"Safe sex?" he asked.

We both giggled. I said, "I'm not good at phone sex, especially when it's being recorded."

He said, "Besides, it wouldn't look good for me with the guards here watching."

We laughed again. Then we talked for a while about his kids and how much they liked animals. They'd had two iguanas in their aquarium, and the two dogs, Spotty and Pearl. Pearl was overweight, because Carmen would feed her dinner scraps. She had been Stephanie's dog. I guess none of the guards were watching the time because no one yelled at him to get off the phone. The only yelling going on was some inmate down the hall, a guy named Joe who Rick said was always yelling, but the guy liked him so he didn't mind.

It was so nice to talk to him when he was in a good mood. It was almost like the old days. I told Rick about how the day before I'd taken my car cover to the laundromat to wash it. But it got fried in the dryer and some areas were badly crinkled when it came out. Now it didn't fit all the way. I pulled it so hard to try and make it fit that it busted open. Then he told me about how when he was twelve he and Glenn would pick up golf balls and wash them and try to sell them for extra money. Then they got the idea to save time by bringing them to the laundromat first. They washed okay but they melted in the dryer, making a terrible mess. When the boys saw what happened, they took off, before the clerk there figured out they'd ruined the machine. They went back to washing them by hand after that.

Chapter Twenty-Three — The Nadine Letters

V ALERIE, MY ASSOCIATE, HAD A FUNERAL TO GO TO ONE THURSDAY AFTERNOON. I had to take her clients as well as my own and so I was already feeling overwhelmed when I got a call from Sara at the news desk at Channel 7, our local TV station. My first thought was, Oh God, What is Nadine up to now? My heart was racing and I could feel my face turning red. Sara said they were doing a story on Rick Sharpe that night on the 11:00 p.m. news show and it would feature an interview with a nurse by the name of Nadine Garret. I said, "Oh, yes, I'm familiar with her," but I was thinking, If this woman is calling me, I better get myself a lawyer. Sara asked me to hold on because she wanted to get Phyllis, one of the producers, on the line for a three-way conference. Phyllis got on a few seconds later and said that she had seen all of the letters from Rick to Nadine and she was wondering if this Nadine was a criminal or a psycho or what. Then she dropped the bomb. "Your name is mentioned in the letters," she announced. All life ceased to exist for me during that split second before she continued. "But Nadine asked us not to use it."

I took a breath. Sara went on. I wasn't sure whether Phyllis was still on the line or not. As it was, I heard Sara's voice as if she were under water—or I was. She said, "Nadine says that you fund Richard Sharpe's canteen and that you purchased his clothes for the trial." This was pretty much true but I decided not to respond to it. "Nadine says that Richard Sharpe has photos of her. She wants them back now that she has ended the relationship." Again, there was no reason for me to say anything—beyond what I was saying in my head, which was, This is exactly the kind of drama this woman Nadine thrives on. Sara said, "Apparently Nadine has a sister in jail." Yeah, so what? I thought, but again I didn't comment.

When Sara asked me if I had anything to add to the story, I lost it. I just didn't see how they would talk about me in an interview without mentioning my name. "I will get leukemia if you air this tonight," I cried. "I will lose clients if people know I'm close to Richard Sharpe. Don't do this to me. I'm furious. You hold on. I'm calling one of Rick's brothers and we'll conference *you* in."

I called Harry and filled him in as quickly as possible. Then I clicked Sara back on the line. "Harry," she began post introduction, "can we interview you tonight?"

"No, I'm sick," he said.

"Well, can you comment on what Linda does for Rick?"

"Yeah, she helps us to get things for him. My brother and I are in Connecticut and she's right there. She makes our lives easier for us."

I was still flaming. "I'm calling my lawyer," I interrupted.

Before Sara could respond, Harry interjected, "If you air anything tonight that involves my family, we will sue. Nadine is not playing with a full deck. She's crazy; she's looking for attention."

Sara said, "Call your lawyer, Linda, and call me back and let me know what's going on. We can do this without using your name."

I hung up and wiped the tears out of my eyes. My lunch hour was coming to an end and a client would be appearing in the waiting room within minutes. I called Lucy and told her the story as quickly as possible. She promised to handle it.

With that settled, I got up from my desk and prepared to go back to work, but the phone rang again: Rick. I picked it up and snapped, "Why are you calling here?"

He said, "I had to hear your voice. I'm so lonely.… What's wrong?" he continued when I didn't answer immediately. I burst into tears. I heard him mumble, "Oh oh, it's Nadine, isn't it?"

I said, "I can't talk now." And I hung up on him.

Lucy called later in the day, from the studios at Channel 7. She'd reiterated that any mention of my name would be an invasion of my privacy and potential slander. Thanks to Lucy, the interview on Channel 7 was actually rescheduled for two weeks from then, so that the news team could do an investigation. What a good idea! Take a breath and get the truth before you ruin people's lives.

I was almost calm when I sat down to watch the segment two weeks later. Nadine told the interviewer that Rick was living in a fantasy world, that he believed that one day he would get out and he would have the opportunity to practice medicine in Switzerland. She failed to mention that she had contributed in large part to his life-after-prison fantasies. If he didn't get out and got sent back to the maximum security facility, he'd told her in one of his letters, he would find a way to have a sex change operation, so that he could be placed in the women's section.

Rick's fantasy life was rich indeed, but not surprising. After all, he'd used fantasy as a kid to make himself feel safer when his father was screaming at him. It occurred to me that maybe he fantasized so much growing up that he had long since lost the ability to know when he crossed the line from reality to fantasy and back again.

The show producers interspersed the interview footage with pages from Rick's letters. Key sentences had been highlighted with yellow marker to direct the viewer to the words that coincided with what Nadine was saying. Then the camera would cut back to Nadine again, with her long thick wavy dark hair draped over one shoulder and her puffy white arms exposed and accentuated against her dark-colored sleeveless shell. She was an attractive woman, but her bad attitude was evident in the way her mouth set after she answered each question, in the way she let her jaw protrude and her lower lip sort of hang. She said that Rick wrote often that he dreamed of Carmen and the kids. She thought he was mentally ill in the beginning but now she thought he was a hardened criminal. She broke up with him, she said, because he was a womanizer. I guessed that she was talking about me there, her conviction based on the fact that I, like her, had received an inmate's drawing of a rose on one of my letters. She also mentioned that she owed the phone company $1000 for the collect calls she'd accepted from Rick—her real gripe, in my opinion. Maybe she thought someone watching would send her a check to cover the bill. In a blip following the interview, another newscaster announced that Stephanie Sharpe, who would soon be getting married, was seeking custody of her younger siblings, as a result of a problem with her aunt concerning financial issues.

All in all I was pretty pleased with the segment. Harry had seen it too and he called me the day after to say that he had all of Nadine's letters to Rick in his possession and would send them to me. I really didn't want them, but with him being so sick he thought my place would make a better storage facility. A few days later an interview with Nadine ran in the Boston *Herald*, and after all the hoopla with the TV piece, it seemed like small potatoes. Shane Field, a local journalist who loved to talk about Rick (he wrote about him regularly during the trial and had become one of the talking heads' favorite interviewees), wrote that Nadine had said Rick was a womanizer who owed her $1000 for her phone bill. What else was new? My only fear was that all this nonsense would result in Rick being sent back to Walpole.

As I didn't hear from Lola for a while I made the assumption that she had dumped Rick because of all the publicity regarding Nadine and therefore had no reason to call me either. But that was not the case. She left me a message at the end of the month asking for my take on the *Herald* piece. There was nothing in it that hadn't already been said in the TV interview, so my take was basically that Nadine's brief moment in the sun was over and done and good riddance. But I decided not to respond right away and tell her that. Rick hadn't called either for a few days, and I was enjoying the peace and quiet. But then Lola left a second message, explaining the reason for all this tranquility: Rick had been sent back to Walpole.

Chapter Twenty-Four – The Green Pill

OSCAR HAD ALREADY SEEN SOME OF THE DOCTORS THAT RICK HAD RECOM-mended, and as a result, he'd had blood transfusions and other proce-dures. Even though he had plenty of problems of his own, he insisted on advising me regarding the purchase of the Gloucester house and the selling of my house in Newton. The market was at an all-time high and Oscar sug-gested I make some improvements to the Newton house to ensure that I got the best possible price for it when I put it on the market. Having been in the business for much of his life, he knew all the right people. He called a guy named Duane to come and do the floors in the Newton house. Oscar pretty much told him the limit on what he could charge me and Duane agreed. Then he set about getting prices for me to add an addition to the house that would include a two-car garage with a master-suite bedroom above it, hop-ing there would be more profit after the sale.

Plenty of work needed to be done in the Gloucester house as well and Oscar handpicked the best contractor/designer he knew, a man by the name of Andy, to do the job for me. Gary, Andy and Oscar and I all went out to the Gloucester house one Sunday afternoon and spent a couple of hours making lists of things that would have to be done once I took ownership. First a general cleaning would have to be executed, because there were bugs and spiders everywhere. The garage doors needed to be replaced; the carpeting had to be ripped out, and I wanted to replace it with tile; the kitchen needed to be totally remodeled; closet doors throughout had to be replaced; and everything had to be painted. Andy figured it would cost about $100,000, and another $150,000 for the work on the Newton house. The numbers were staggering, but on paper it all seemed to work out, and anyway I was too excited about the chance to live in a place like Gloucester to back out. I trusted Oscar; it would work.

In the meantime I learned from Lola that Rick was on a "mental health watch," as opposed to a suicide watch, at Walpole. He was in a cell with a TV and he was able to receive mail. He was not, however, permitted to see other inmates, though he could talk to them from his cell. Lola, who had been making lots of phone calls to Walpole superintendents, said, "If he's good for two or three years, they'll move him someplace less strict."

I said, "Guess what, Lola, he won't make it that long."

He was not allowed any visitors, but as inmates are supposed to have twenty-four-hour access to their lawyers, Lucy agreed to visit him on behalf of the rest of us and see how he was doing. But when she called ahead she was told that she wouldn't be allowed in either. She drove down anyway, with some documents that she felt sure would gain her access. They still wouldn't let her in. She was very upset. She planned to call the Massachusetts Corrections Legal Services and report Walpole. She also planned to call Burt Tucker, the lawyer who was considering handling Rick's appeal. Lola and I discussed the situation at length. The only thing we could come up with was that the prison didn't want Rick communicating with anyone on the outside—probably because they were hiding something. What could they be hiding? Well, for one, the terrible care he'd received from his psychiatric team at Bridgewater, including them not giving him the right medications. He'd written to both of us about this matter, and we'd believed that it would somehow be resolved.

Though Rick could receive letters, he was prohibited from writing them and also from using the phone. He got around the former by getting another inmate to write for him, though of course the length and frequency of his letters was greatly restricted by the inclinations of the inmate assisting him. His letters to me begged for help. He begged me to pay Lucy, who was the only one with the power to help him in any way at this point. I was already paying Lucy, but to date she had still not been able to penetrate the illegal wall that Walpole was building around him.

Lola got a letter too, from a different inmate. It read: "I love you; I have no access to phone, pen, paper or mail. I haven't showered or brushed my teeth in three weeks. I need you to call Lucy and get Linda to pay the legal fees. I'll pay her back when/if I get out. Ask Lucy to do anything in her power to get me back to Bridgewater."

Lola wrote back to Salvatore, the inmate who had penned Rick's letter, thanking him for what he had done. She didn't mention Rick's name in the letter as she feared it would only get him into more trouble. Heartbroken over the way Rick was being treated, she called everyone she could think of, from Lucy, to the prison superintendent, to Burt Tucker and even Ben Falcon. No one could help, and whoever answered the phone in Falcon's office explained that they hadn't even received full payment for the trial yet. Lola was about at her wits end on how to get assistance when she got a call from the prison pastor, who had gotten her number from Rick. He prefaced his conversation by saying that she must never tell anyone that he had called her; it was totally taboo and he would be excommunicated if anyone found out. He then went on to report that he'd visited Rick, that he'd found him curled up in a fetal position in twenty-four-hour lockup. Lola said, "Make him sit up. If he sits up, maybe they'll take him off mental health watch and it will be better."

The pastor explained that there were fifteen cells like his, all for the severely depressed. He said that until Rick "snapped out of it" they were likely to keep him there. Lola asked how the heck they thought people would snap out of their depression when they were being treated like animals. The pastor said that once he got out he would be in a cell block where everyone was stealing and fighting all of the time. At least he was safe in his isolated cell.

Lola was so hysterical when she called to tell me all this that I thought she was going to say that Rick was dead. I said, "Breathe, relax. I'm here to listen." In addition to everything she'd learned from the pastor, she had also received a letter from Louis Wilson, the prison superintendent, saying that she was banned for one year from seeing Rick, even after he got out of the hole, because a contraband green pill had been found in a letter she'd recently sent. She couldn't believe her ears. She'd called him immediately and explained she didn't know anything about any green pill. He said she could write and request a hearing within fifteen days if she wanted to. I said, "Do you have any green pills at your place?"

She cried, "The only green pills here are my calcium pills."

"Could one have slipped into the envelope by accident?" I asked.

"No, of course not. This is fabricated! This is a setup! Why would I do anything to make life even worse for Rick? I would never do that."

She was yelling at me. It was clear she was too upset to talk. I said, "Go calm down. Tomorrow call and see if they checked the pill for fingerprints. Then call Lucy and tell her what happened." As I said this, I remembered that Lucy and I had spoken earlier. I had given her a retainer a while ago to cover work for Rick, and now it was used up. She was billing me sparingly. Still…. "Lola," I added quickly, before she could hang up, "scratch that. Call me first and I'll call Lucy."

Lola hadn't made any progress on anything when I called to check on her the next day, but at least she was calm. She was calm and she wanted to talk. She had spoken to someone named Nel at the Massachusetts Correctional Legal Services about the green pill accusation. This Nel was married to an ex-prisoner and she had heard stories like Lola's hundreds, maybe thousands, of times before. She didn't have much hope that the situation would be resolved in Lola's favor. "If they want you out, they'll keep you out," Nel said. Nel suggested they had targeted her (as opposed to me or Naomi or any of the others) because they wanted to make him suffer.

This only made Lola more defiant. "Fine, I'll wait it out," she said. "I'll wait one year. They can't keep us apart forever."

Nel told her that Walpole was a city onto itself, and Louis Wilson was its king. You couldn't enter his domain without his permission. Lola had asked Nel if she thought they'd let her take a lie detector test. Nel said, "They don't have to do anything. If they don't respond to your request for a hearing in two weeks, then you might as well forget it." Nel had called Burt Tucker at Lola's request, but Tucker said he was a criminal lawyer and couldn't help. This was not a surprise. Lola had called him a day earlier and he all but told her that Rick's chances for an appeal were slim to non-existent. He no longer seemed to have any interest in the case.

When we had exhausted the topic we moved on to a discussion about the drawing of the rose, the one that had sent Nadine over the edge. In fact, Lola had gotten a rose on one of her letters too, early on, before she had become so tight with Rick. She said that Rick had told her the artist was an inmate named Sean, a real lunatic who had blinded his psychiatrist by punching his eyes out with a pencil. Now the shrink had two glass eyes—and Sean was serving three to five for insanity and would ultimately be released to a halfway house.

Our deep concern for Rick's wellbeing made us reluctant to get off the phone—and our conversation became more intimate. Lola told me she hadn't had sex in ten years—in part because she was embarrassed about her body. Part of her lung was gone, along with the several ribs. The pressure garment she wore helped her to breathe better. She only took it off to shower. She didn't know if having sex would throw out her back.

Finally, she told me the story. Years back she had fallen in love with a jeweler who hoped to make some extra money with a different kind of crystal: cocaine. He borrowed $2000 from Lola to get his second business going, and he told her he could either pay her back in cash or in coke. She chose the latter and ultimately began to freebase and became addicted. She wanted so badly to end the addiction that she decided to commit suicide.

Her mother had died from breast cancer, so Lola collected all her morphine pills and ingested them. Though her stomach rejected them—she vomited—she went into a coma. Her brother found her five days later and brought her to the hospital, where they put her on life support because she had pneumonia and couldn't breathe on her own. Eventually she lifted out of the coma, but she still couldn't breathe. Back then, in 1983, the solution was to remove all the ribs on one side to get to the infected lung.

It worked. She lived. But she didn't go a day without pain. And the embarrassment about her condition and the compression corset she had to wear had left her reclusive. As for the jeweler boyfriend, his suicide attempt (he used cyanide) was successful. His body (Lola had attended the funeral) was a ghoulish gray, a result of the fact that cyanide blocks the oxygen supply to the cells, or, as Lola put it, burns the body from the inside out. Lola said to me, "I can only work twenty-four hours a week because of my back. I can get by with the money, but I'm not rich. I've got about $30,000, and Rick said that's enough, that he's going to make me a millionaire."

I said, "Have you checked your account?"

"Well, Rick said—" she began.

I said, "I don't care what he said. He's in an isolated cell right now and he's not watching your stocks. Please watch your principal. You need to control it."

We were silent for a moment. Then Lola said, in a small voice that I could hardly hear, "Sometimes I wish I never got involved. Maybe I should have had some vision."

"If I didn't already know him for eleven years," I agreed, "if I hadn't seen the goodness in him...."

Chapter Twenty-Five – Knocking at Death's Door

I GOT THE CLEARANCE I NEEDED FROM THE MORTGAGE COMPANY TO REFINANCE THE Newton house so that I could use some of the equity for the down payment on the Gloucester house, but until the septic problems were resolved, I would not be able to get the final mortgage. In the meantime, I met Andy, Barry (the owner of a kitchen and tile store), and Lindsey, Barry's designer, in Gloucester so that Lindsey could look at the kitchen. Andy had priced out the Newton house extension work for $160,000. I was disappointed to see the figure higher than what we had talked about the last time we'd met, but Andy insisted the job he would be doing was really a $250,000 value, so he had already come down significantly, as a favor to Oscar.

Oscar was back in the hospital by then, in a transitional care unit, which is a step down from ICU. In addition to his lymphoma, he had pneumonia too. I didn't want to bother him with complaints about Andy and his pricing. But two weeks later Oscar called me and said he was home again and he felt great. "I'm going to beat this cancer," he proclaimed. He had lost thirty pounds, and he had quit smoking. He said he had talked to Andy for an hour before calling me and he would be changing his Newton estimate back to $150,000. He said, "I told Andy he'd better make you smile. When all is said and done, you'll be going from what began as a $200,000 house in Newton to a million dollar house in Gloucester." He couldn't see me over the phone, but I *was* smiling. It was the best news I'd had in weeks.

The Gloucester closing was scheduled for December 30, 2002, but the sellers still had not come up with a satisfactory plan for the septic. The bank needed an inspection certificate from a septic system company which could then be approved by the Board of Health. Stephanie and her family were perfectly willing to pay for whatever the new septic would cost, but that fact wasn't helping to get the certificate taken care of. In the meantime, I met again with Lindsey the designer and gave her the okay on the plans she had drawn up for the new kitchen. We also looked at catalogues for appliances. She would be ordering the appliances locally and getting the cabinets from Canada. They would take two months to be delivered.

With all the house stuff going on, you would think I wouldn't be pondering Rick's dilemma at all, but it was there when I went to bed at night, and sometimes it popped up in my dreams. One morning I awoke with the certainty that Lola was handling the situation with the superintendent all wrong. She'd been coming down hard, begging him to see things from her point of view. I called her up before I even got out of bed. I told her that she had to change her attitude, make Louis Wilson believe that she had only friendship—as opposed to love—to offer Rick, that she respected the system and understood *their* point of view. I said, "Lola, they don't want him to have an ounce of pleasure. You sent him pictures of your condo, for God's sake, and told him this is where he's going to live when he gets out! Hello? He's serving a life sentence for murder. He's not going anywhere!" She started to cry. I said, "Cut it out. You have to be strong if you're going to be in this with him."

Lucy called another superintendent there, someone named Kimmel. She insisted that the law provided for her to get in to see Rick. She threatened that if she wasn't allowed, she would go to the Supreme Court and get an injunction. "This is cruel and inhuman, how you are treating him," she said. She called other people too, but she still couldn't get herself let in.

In the meantime, Lola received another letter from Salvatore, but this time he wasn't writing on behalf of Rick. He was writing to share personal information about himself. His letter read: "I'm 5' 10", 207 lbs., brown hair, brown eyes, armed robbery, five years here, did one so far. You put a smile on my face. I study, exercise and read. What are your hobbies? I don't need a girlfriend, just a sister. I can offer you my heart and mind. I hope I didn't bore you. Send pictures."

Lola was a sucker for the crestfallen. I said, "You'd better rip that up before you get suckered in."

She laughed. She said, "Can you hear that, Sweetheart? That's the sound of me ripping it up, right now."

Finally we got some good news. After leaving several messages, Ben Falcon called Lola back and said he would send a private investigator to check out what was going on and whether Lola had been framed. Because he had been Rick's trial attorney, he would be able to get his man in. Not a day later Lola got a call saying that Rick had been upgraded to a daily shower and was being allowed time to brush his teeth. She also got a letter from Louis Wilson saying that her hearing was scheduled for the following month.

One night during one of our long phone calls, Lola admitted to me that she felt better all this time that she had been unable to communicate with Rick. She still insisted that she loved him and would do anything for him, but in the meantime, and even with all the work that she was doing contacting people to try to get him out of the hole, she was sleeping better and feeling less agitated by virtue of not having spoken to him directly in so long. She said, "I have to put things in perspective, not make him my whole world. My phone bills are ridiculous. My deepest hope is that he gets out." Again I reminded her that he was in for life, that it didn't help anyone for her to believe in an alternative future for him—or herself.

෨ලෂ

In the beginning of October Gary woke me up with the words, "Rick's back in the hospital again." I rolled over and grabbed the remote and flipped through the channels. I couldn't find a story, just some crawl at the bottom of the screen. Apparently he'd been found unresponsive in his isolation cell. His condition was deemed stable and his location remained undisclosed as he was considered capable of plotting an escape.

I immediately called Harry, who said he'd make some calls and get back to me, and then I called Lola. She was of course very upset. She said he'd promised her back in April that he would never try to kill himself again. She said, again, "Sometimes I wish I'd never written that first letter to him. I never had a clue it would turn out like this. All the pain, the crying, the worrying…." Nevertheless, Lola spent her every free moment making phone calls and was finally able to ascertain (from the pastor) that Rick had been found partially unconscious and having convulsions. The pastor himself had not been permitted to see him in the last few days, but he'd been told that Rick had been deprived of sheets and even underwear. The pastor thought he'd been taken to Shaddock Hospital in Jamaica Plain, Massachusetts.

There was a story that night on the news. The newscaster suggested that Rick may have overdosed. "Being a doctor he would know how much he'd need for an overdose," he commented. Footage of an interview with Stephanie from earlier in the day was spliced into the segment. She said, "I encourage the media to focus any attention they might otherwise give to the actions of Richard Sharpe on the silent plague of domestic violence that impacts countless women and children across the country." I had read that she was now an advocate for victims of domestic violence through the R.O.S.E. Fund. I had even caught some footage of her, a week or so earlier, on one of the news channels, giving a speech at a fund-raising dinner at the Plaza Hotel in New York. The newscaster also mentioned her custody suit, which was still in progress.

Rick's hospitalization had the effect of drawing attention to his plight, and as a result, the prison relented and his phone and letter writing privileges were restored. Two days after his return from the hospital he made his first phone call to Lola. He was calling from the psych ward where he was still recuperating after having had his stomach pumped. Lola told me later, "I told him you were buying his old house. His voice went up three decibels. 'Really?' he said."

I said, "Lola, you told him? I told you not to tell him yet."

She replied, "I had to give him a fucking ray of hope. His whole past has been unloaded. He has nothing. At least he knows you have the house."

The next day I got a call from Lucy to say that Rick had been transferred back to Bridgewater. I immediately called Lola. She was ecstatic. "He'll be able to go to the library again," she said through sobs. "He'll be able to read."

In spite of his long period of isolation, I guess Rick had been apprised of the local news, because the first thing he did after contacting Lola was write to Kitty and Harold to say that they should insist on the custody of his younger children. He also asked Kitty to try to find it in her heart to let Leo and Judy know how sorry he was for what he had done and how much he loved them. He signed the letter, "with sadness, grief, remorse, and yet a remaining flicker of hope that I may somehow help to heal the people I have hurt."

His meds must have been readjusted too, because when I finally spoke to him he didn't seem all that downtrodden considering everything he'd been through. He didn't even mention his ordeal, and I didn't bring it up either. Instead we spoke about the Gloucester house. He said he would send me a map showing the location of various neighbors that he and Carmen had been friendly with. He thought they would want to meet Gary and me. He suggested I have the house blessed. And he recommended a local landscaper who, he thought, would do a good job of keeping up the grounds for a reasonable price if I was not inclined to do it myself.

His letters in the weeks that followed reverted back to being directives: he wanted me to contact his brothers, whom he hadn't had a chance to talk to yet, and have them make high quality copies of any of Rick's family photos in their possession and send them to me for safekeeping; he wanted me to get busy again with the cat allergy product; he wanted me to allow a woman by the name of Regina (who was married to one of his fellow inmates and had four kids to support) to work part time for me so she could learn the business, but only after she had signed a confidentiality agreement—as Rick believed that was better than non-competes.

For the most part, I read each letter and then pretended I hadn't, though I did give in to his request for renewals of subscriptions to *Discover* magazine and *The New England Journal of Medicine* and other science and financial publications. I did read the letters he sent about the Gloucester house. He wanted me to get it in writing that there were no IRS tax liens on it. He wanted the exhaust for the dryer checked over; he thought it might need a hose clamp. He wanted an infrared bulb (with a switch) installed in the box where the steam shower pipes were located, so that the pipes wouldn't freeze.

That same month there was a story in the "Living Arts'" section of the Boston *Globe* about Stephanie. It was called "A Daughter's Trial" and basically it talked about all that she had been through as a child, the abuses she suffered at the hands of her father, how she became her mother's protector because Carmen wouldn't or couldn't stand up for herself, and how afraid she was for her mother—for all of them really—after her mother left. The article also talked about the suffering she had experienced since her mother's death. She and her fiancé had lost their Battery City apartment—which had been a stone's throw away from the World Trade Center—on 9-11; her fiancé had been in the stampede after the towers had collapsed. It must have felt like the worst possible nightmare to have been so directly affected by the worst national tragedy of our times at the same time that she was going through the worst personal tragedy of her life. The article reminded anyone who might have forgotten that during the trial, Stephanie's father had revealed himself to be a cross-dresser who took his wife's birth control pills to make his breasts grow, wore his daughter's underwear, underwent liposuction and plastic surgery, and had most of the hair removed from his body. Stephanie got married the same day the article appeared. I thought to myself, I wish her the best; she deserves a chance to move on and have a happy life.

A week later I went to visit Rick at Bridgewater. While I sat in the visitors room waiting for him to be brought out, one of the guards walked over and said, "I gotta tell you that I work long hours."

I looked at him. "Yeah, I work long hours too."

He asked if I was a doctor—I was still wearing my work smock—and I said I was not. Then he shook his head and said, "You know, they're really blowing this whole thing out of proportion, always going on about it in the press."

I studied his expression. I could tell he didn't like Rick. I said, "Richard Sharpe is an amazing man, a brilliant man. I've known him for years."

Rick walked in just then, and the guard moved away. He'd been brought in late, so there would only be a half hour to talk before the visitors—myself and about ten other people—were asked to leave. But talk we did.

Rick said, "I'm so happy to see you," but he sounded and looked like he was about to cry. He sat down close to me and for a while we just looked at each other. Then I told him about Stephanie getting married and the lengthy article that had appeared in the paper to mark the occasion. I said, "Do you think you're crazy, Rick?"

He said, "I don't know. I know I was when the gun went off."

Rick became even more somber after that and told me in detail about the time he had spent in the hole at Walpole. He confirmed that he'd been locked in his cell twenty-four hours a day, except for the days that he was allowed a shower—and experienced complete sensory deprivation. He was naked except for a poncho, and there were no sheets on his beds. The guards would come in looking for contraband. They would cuff his hands in back and put his feet in cuffs too. He showed me the scars he still had on his hands from the tight cuffs. He showed me a dark line on his right ankle. The guards would tell him to get in the corner, up against the wall. Then they would check the room. But they never found the pills that he was saving up to swallow all at once—because he'd wrapped them in plastic wrap and stuffed them up his ass. He'd used margarine as lubricant.

He experienced severe memory flashbacks during his time in the hole, so vivid that he couldn't tell whether they were real or not. Now that he was back at Bridgewater he was doing a little better. The new psychiatrist that had been assigned to him was nice. His meds had not leveled out yet but he thought the psychiatrist would work with him to make the necessary adjustments. Yet even with the medication, he felt afraid almost all of the time. He felt that he couldn't trust himself not to lose control and try to kill himself again. "Why did I do this to my children? To Carmen?" he asked me. No amount of medication could keep him from dreaming about them each night, from waking up drenched in his own tears. Some nights he woke up in a panic, unable to breathe. "I can't handle it," he said. I asked him if anyone had been to visit. He said only Glenn, but he'd only been able to stay for fifteen minutes.

I asked him in the most gentle way possible if it was true that he had banged Stephanie's head and dragged her down the steps, as had been reported in the *Globe* article. I had to know. He said it wasn't true, that he never would touch or hurt his children. When he saw by the look on my face that my doubt persisted, he added, "Carmen wrote up that whole long affidavit when she was working with Grange on the divorce papers. She threw everything she could think of into it. But there was nothing in there about any abuse of the kids. She would have included that if it were true. I never laid a hand on my kids. I love them."

He changed the subject again and told me that he had a foot infection and had to be put on antibiotics. I asked him how that had happened and he said he'd had a crack in his heel and bacteria had gotten in, probably when he was in the shower. I asked him where his sandals were, and he said that like his other possessions, they hadn't followed him from Walpole. Neither had his glasses. He was wearing cheap canvas sneakers with very little sole. I said, "What about your good sneakers?" He shrugged. He said, "Someone stole them."

Before his transfer back to Walpole, Rick had been working on an idea to build a site called Cat Love Medical Corp. He'd asked me to contact a woman named Bonnie, who had once been his secretary, to see if she would visit him to talk about helping him out with it. I had contacted her, and now I reported to him that Bonnie said she couldn't visit him because she was afraid of the media. She'd said, "He's in my prayers daily, but I can't be in direct contact with him."

It made me think about all the other people who supported him emotionally but couldn't bring themselves to visit. Joan, my dentist, was another. I had just seen her a few days ago. She'd been Rick's dentist too, for years. While I was settling into the chair she asked me if I'd talked to him recently, and when I said I had, she said, "It was the drugs, wasn't it?" Then she went on to say that while she had always liked him and enjoyed talking to him— even felt a connection to him—she couldn't go to visit because she didn't want to be involved. She said she'd seen his emotional deterioration during his last visits with her. The last time he'd come to see her, she'd put a temporary filling in tooth number thirty-one, the second to last molar on the bottom right side on his mouth. Now she was afraid that he would never be able to get the permanent filling. She asked me to check to see how it was doing.

As she worked on me that day, she elaborated on her theories. She felt certain his breakdown had come about as a result of overdosing on vitamin E. I looked at her. I did remember that he talked about taking massive doses of vitamin E back in 1998, before everything began to fall apart. He'd even tried to talk me into taking vitamin E in high dosages. He'd read some studies about how mice receiving massive doses of vitamin E not only lived forty percent longer than mice not receiving it, but also enjoyed enhanced neurological performance throughout their increased life spans. Joan, the dentist, said that it was after his vitamin E obsession that he started coming undone. She felt so sure this was responsible for his decline that she sometimes thought she should have offered to take the stand as a witness for the defense. She'd known him for years. He was fine, she said, before the vitamin E. It was interesting to imagine her up on the stand arguing that the real weapon was not a rifle but a vitamin.

The vitamin E theory sounded crazy to me, but just to be sure I mentioned it to one of my clients, a psychiatrist. "Why would anyone want to take gross amounts of vitamin E?" I asked as I was plucking out some of her unwanted hair. Madison, the psychiatrist, said that Rick probably wanted to address his movement disorder, to make himself feel more stable.

Movement disorder? I had never heard of it, but sure enough, when I went home that night and looked on the Internet, I found a lot of information. The consensus is that people with schizophrenia or other related mental disorders sometimes experience repetitive involuntary movements of the arms or legs or mouth after taking anti-psychotic medications. Massive doses of vitamin E can reduce these telltale movements.

Joan changed the subject. "What does he do all day?" she asked. I told her he read and wrote letters. She said, "I was so hurt over all of this." Joan's husband was a mortician; they lived on the second floor above his place of work. Her husband was the one who got the call to cremate Carmen Sharpe. Small world. She said, "Send him my best; tell him he's in my thoughts." I said, "You can write him if you want." I had to say it with my mouth wide open because she had her tools and mirrors in there, looking around. She didn't respond.

Rick gave up talking about the Cat Love Medical Corp site and switched to an inmate who had befriended him. The guy was due for parole and Rick wanted to know if he could count on me to remove a tattoo the guy no longer wanted when he got out. I said, "No, I'm not trained to do that. I don't want the liability. I don't have the proper laser anyway."

He said, "It's easy," and he proceeded to give me instructions.

I interrupted him. "No, if you get out, you can do it. You're the doctor."

He let it go, but our clash caused me to flash back to the trial, when Carmen's father was on the stand. When asked how he felt about Rick in the early days, he stated that he'd never liked him, because he would talk Carmen into doing things she didn't want to do, like skipping school. I told Rick what I was thinking. He said, "I never liked him either." Then he bounced back to what we had been talking about earlier, saying, "Linda, I never hit my kids. Carmen and I fought physically during the first seven or so years of our marriage, but not much after that, but I never hit my kids. I wouldn't do that." I wanted to believe him, but I couldn't think why Stephanie would say such things if they weren't true.

Then somehow he got on to the Beatles, talking about how much he loved their music. He said he and Carmen had moved from one apartment to another and somehow his Beatle albums got piled near a window and the heat warped them. He'd been so upset. The night before Lennon (his favorite Beatle) was killed, he told Carmen he had a bad feeling that something was going to happen to him. He was shocked the next day when he heard that Lennon had been shot. Carmen called everyone she knew and told them Rick had had a psychic experience.

The guard shift changed in the room. The one that had tried to talk to me left and in his place came another, a tall dark handsome man, maybe Spanish or Middle-Eastern. I noticed he was wearing a wedding band. I also noticed that he was watching our every move. He began to walk down the aisle in our direction and said to the couple nearest us that their visit was over. They looked at the clock. There were still about eight minutes to go. The guard kept on walking, towards us. His expression was mean. I shuddered to think what his thoughts were. When he got close he said, "Time to leave."

I jumped to my feet. "Thank you very much," I said. You had to be more polite to the ones like him. They were just waiting for the chance to make peoples' lives miserable. They liked the control. I gave Rick a quick hug and a peck on the cheek, which was permissible at Bridgewater. Then I whispered that I felt bad about the day I'd come to get my epilator, after he'd fallen down the stairs. "You were sitting in the corner in that empty room in that empty house all alone, hurting physically and emotionally. I wasn't nice. Maybe I could have helped somehow." It was something I'd wanted to say for a long time, but somehow it had never come out before.

He was tearing up again. He said, "For a while I had everything. Beautiful wife, beautiful kids, beautiful house. Carmen loved the sun. She was full of vitality and energy. I've done a terrible thing."

"Yes, you have," I agreed.

Later I called Lola. Since she was forbidden to visit him herself, she liked to hear the details of my visits. She said, "I say four prayers a day, one on his behalf for forgiveness for what he did, one for friends and relatives, one for children everywhere, and one that I'll live long enough to be with Rick someday before we are both dead and buried."

I had nothing to say to that. I changed the subject. I told her I'd skipped my first period and I thought menopause might be around the corner. She laughed. She said, "I'm a year and two months older than you; I've got a head start."

Chapter Twenty-Six – Blessed are the Peacemakers

THANKSGIVING WAS ON THE HORIZON, AND RICK HAD ONE SURE THING TO BE thankful for: Ben Falcon, working pro bono now, accompanied him to a hearing to determine whether he should remain at Bridgewater or be returned to Walpole. The judge ruled that he could stay in Bridgewater for at least the next six months. After that, they'd see. Rick was so happy that he broke down in the courtroom and began to sob in front of the judge. On the way out, he waved to the TV cameras and yelled, "Happy birthday, Judy; I love you, and hello to Leo!"

When I spoke to him on the phone a little later he was still in a good mood. He told me about an inmate at Walpole who had found a piece of metal, four to five inches long, out in the yard. It took the guy three months of working on it—with bricks or stones or whatever he could get his hands on—for eight to nine hours a day to carve it into a knife. This guy had taken a liking to Rick, and in return for some medical information that Rick had given him regarding one of his relatives, he showed Rick the knife's secret hiding place—just in case he ever needed it for self defense. Rick said it was so tucked away in the crack of a wall that he couldn't have found it again if his life depended on it.

I invited Lola over for Thanksgiving. She arrived with a bottle of wine, dressed in a pricey fur coat that was—I will admit even though I'm not a fan of killing animals—absolutely smashing on her. Though we'd been friends for a while now, this was the first time I'd met her. Her face was as beautiful as her personality, all sweetness and light. She was tall, slender and graceful in her movements. My mother hadn't arrived yet, so Lola sat down with my father and he began to tell her prison stories. He started off with one about a man who had killed his wife with a hammer and only did ten years before he got probation and got out. I guess this was his way of trying to make her feel at home. He said, "Tell your friend Rick not to be a tough guy. Wise guys get stabbed by bullies. Don't instigate the bullies." Lola and I shared a smile over the image of Rick strong-arming prison thugs four times his size. Then he told her about an inmate who wouldn't shower and how the other inmates wanted to kill him because he smelled so bad. One of the nicer guys, a guy named Paul, made him a deal. The stinky inmate liked coffee, so Paul offered to bring him his morning coffee every day in return for the guy showering a couple times a week. Blessed are the peacemakers.

Lola loved my Newton house—both the interior and the yard. Four inches of snow had fallen and it looked gorgeous outside. As Rick was up to his old tricks again and had been pushing Lola to work with me to refill and sell laser canisters, I showed her one and explained how it worked. She said, "If this is illegal, I can't do it."

I said, "I don't know if it's illegal or not. You need to find out whether you need a license for the refrigerant."

Lola said, "He says you need to get some kind of valve to fill them."

"Forget the valve," I said. "Find out whether it's legal before you give it a second thought." Then I added, "I wish all schools had field trips to prisons the way they do to museums. If kids saw what goes on, there would be a lot less crime. And I wish people got paid to turn in their guns, like they used to, like they used to get paid to give blood until some people started giving bad blood."

I was on a rant. Lola changed the subject, saying, "Rick says he doesn't know why you're redoing the kitchen before you sell the house. I have to agree with him. It's really nice already."

"I'm tired of knowing that you and Rick are discussing me," I said calmly. "Talk about something else."

She said, "It's no big deal, it's just the house."

"But the house is my business!" I reminded her that they listened to his phone calls, steamed open his letters and likely photocopied them.

I had off the day after Thanksgiving and I didn't answer the phone all day. Towards the end of the day, Lola left a message: "He's been calling and calling you and you're not taking his calls. *Please* take a call from him. I can't do this all by myself. He's driving me crazy."

So the next time Rick called, an hour or so later, I answered it. Before he could get a word in edgewise I said, "Look, I'm in a bad mood. If I'm in a bad mood, I'm not going to take your calls."

He said, "Please don't abandon me."

I said, "I'm not abandoning you. I'm just not taking calls when I don't want to."

He said, "When you move to Gloucester, can I visit the house?"

I snapped then. "And don't discuss my business on the phone, with Lola or anyone else."

He changed the subject quickly. He said he needed glasses badly and asked if I could get a pair and wear them in and give them to him during the visit when no one was looking. I rolled my eyes to the ceiling. I said, "I'm not doing it that that way. You want me to help you, you do it the right way. Get a permission slip and a prescription and I'll get it filled. And don't discuss my business with Lola again! It's over…not our friendship, but you talking about my stuff." I took a breath. "I wouldn't even be your friend if I didn't know about all the people you saved."

He said, "You are my friend and I love you. I'll call you Sunday night. Goodbye."

Lola was the next to get mad at him. She received two letters from him but the envelopes were not in his handwriting. Her first thought was that someone was sending her anthrax. She was afraid to open them. She even considered calling the police. But finally she forced herself to look and both turned out to be in his writing, instructions about lasers and canisters. The letters, we figured out by process of elimination, had come from Naomi, the woman with the weight problem who had been his friend all this time. Sometimes he sent mail to her to redistribute, so that he could include several letters to several people and save on postage and envelopes. The idea that he had sent Lola letters—albeit about business—through a third party upset her even more than the idea of the prison guards steaming them open. He ended one of the letters by suggesting that Lola get $2500 together so that she could start her canister-refilling business. He thought it would be such a great opportunity for her. "I can't take it anymore, Linda," she confided. "I don't have extra money. He sits there and directs everyone."

I said, "His sister Patsy's husband only allows him to call twice a month, because he stresses her out so much."

When I spoke to him that night I told him off for both of us, because I doubted Lola would say anything to hurt him. "I'm not interested in doing any business with you unless you have permission from Bridgewater. Don't you give my address to anyone, including Naomi. Don't call Lola for a few days. Don't ask me to sneak in glasses."

"But—" he began.

"But nothing!" I pulled the cord. A minute later I heard the extension phone ringing. I didn't answer it.

I couldn't sleep that night. I kept thinking he might get suicidal again. I got up in the middle of the night and walked into the kitchen so as not to awaken Gary and called the main desk at Bridgewater and asked that someone go check on Rick. While I waited on the line I noted that the room still held the aroma of the blueberry muffins Gary had baked earlier, so that we could have them in the morning for breakfast. I almost forgot why I was sitting at the phone in the dead of the night when the person got back on the line and said Rick was sleeping like a baby. I doubted that, but at least he was alive.

⋈⋈

I was right about Lola. She couldn't bring herself to tell him how angry he had made her, but thanks to my lecture, he backed off about the canisters. In fact, Lola was so happy with him again by the time Christmas season rolled around that she decided to send one of her very dear friends, a woman named Sally, to visit him on her behalf as her gift. Lola said Sally was attractive and vivacious and entertaining. Lola knew that the holidays were the hardest for Rick, that his depression always got worse then because he couldn't be with his kids. She thought Sally might be an antidote.

On the day of the visit, Lola dropped Sally off and went to a coffee shop to wait. But there were several people smoking in there and Lola couldn't breathe. She pleaded with the waitress to do something, but there was nothing she could do. So Lola drove back and sat in the parking lot at the prison. She thought she wouldn't be noticed that far back from the facility, but sure enough there was a security cop out there in the freezing cold writing down license plate numbers. Her first thought was that she had to pull away; after all, she'd been banned from the property. But then she saw Sally approaching. She opened the window and waved for Sally to hurry, and once the door was shut behind her, they took off.

The incident reminded me of a time when I'd arrived at the prison a few minutes early and took the opportunity to eat a yogurt in my car. A security guard knocked on my window and told me to leave. I did, pulling away for long enough to finish my yogurt and then pulling back in again. You have to do things their way. Lola, on the other hand, was very upset that she hadn't been able to relax for five minutes while she waited for her friend. I said, "It's a jail, Lola. Who's to say you weren't waiting for an inmate to escape?" Her naiveté and vulnerability concerned me.

Still, Sally's visit had been a nice thought and it might have been helpful to Rick if not for the fact that the prison authorities chose that time to have him moved from Max 1 to Max 2, where the more violent prisoners were kept. Now he had to change psychiatrists, and he liked the one he'd had. Also, he could no longer visit the prison library, which was the only activity he really enjoyed. But even worse, in Max 2 inmates had to stay out of their cells, which meant that if he felt a crying fit coming on, he'd have to do it in public. Lola had gotten a snapshot (from Ben Falcon) of Rick with the little kids climbing on his back. When Rick received it he had to lock himself in a stall in the bathroom to keep the inmates from observing (and possibly reacting to) his meltdown.

I was anticipating that my own holiday season at least would be relaxing when two things happened. First, Rick found an attorney (through Gloria's research): Robert Shapiro of O.J. Simpson fame was willing to handle his appeal for $50,000—but Rick couldn't come up with the money. Lola said she would be willing to put up $25,000 if I would put up the other $25,000. I said, "No way! I have too many bills!" She said, "You mean you won't do this for him?" Later I told Lucy about our conversation. She said, "Lola doesn't realize how much you've done already." Still, the incident was upsetting.

And just after that, I got the shock of my life, a phone call from Nadine the nurse! She reminded me that she'd given Rick several pictures, one of them of her daughter, Jillian. Now she had it in her head that Rick was sure to be locked up with pedophiles into whose hands Jillian's picture might fall. I didn't have the energy to tell her that his possessions hadn't transferred with him to Bridgewater. Nor did I tell her that he'd been tortured for seven weeks at Walpole, or that a guy had tried to rape him in the shower (Lola had told me about this), or that he was full of bruises and scars, or that he had no glasses and someone had stolen his shoes. In fact, I don't recall that I said much of anything.

But on she went, as if I had given an indication that I was truly listening, saying that she hadn't gotten one single cent from the TV or newspaper interviews. In fact, after the interviews were over, a few detectives got to her and pumped her for information. One wanted to know if she knew how much money Rick had. Another wanted to know if she really planned to work in Atlantic City as a hooker—which was something she had written to Rick in one of her letters and to which he had responded in one of his. Since she hadn't mentioned this "joke" in her interviews, it confirmed that someone had made copies of the letters and given them out. She said she was shocked when she learned that Rick had tried to commit suicide again. "Are you recording this conversation?" I asked on a whim. She said she wasn't.

I visited Rick again. In spite of the difficulties he was going through, he walked in happy and gave me a long tight hug. The other couples in the visitors room were smooching up a storm. The guard on duty didn't seem to mind. I was stunned when a neighbor of mine, a lawyer, came in to see a young man who must have been her son. What are the odds of running into someone you know in a prison visiting room? I was afraid to say hello. But I made a mental note to give her a call later in the week. When I looked back at Rick, his eyes were brimming with tears and I could see that he was going to spill his guts any minute. He mumbled something about his younger children, Leo and Judy, about not being able to take the pain of not seeing them during the holidays. Ordinarily I would have said something hopeful, that maybe when they got older they'd contact him, but instead I said, "Are you even sure those kids are yours? I mean, didn't Carmen get pregnant with Leo during that time when you two were—"

"Those are my kids no matter what," he interrupted.

He didn't exactly snap at me, but he said it forcefully. I had only been expressing a personal opinion, not anything based on any facts. We stared into each other's eyes for a moment. "Let's just sit here and relax for a while," I suggested, and that was what we did.

Later we talked about Lola. He missed her so much. Then I told him about a TV movie I'd seen about the Green Berets. I said, "Here are all these people fighting for us, twenty and thirty years old, and we take them for granted, but what they do is incredible…sleeping out in the cold, out in the open or in holes, always in incredible danger…."

He said, "I would trade places with them if I could."

I laughed. I said, "You can't even play pool. You're not fit."

He said, "I used to be fit."

"Well, start working on being fit again. There's no reason you can't be fit now. Just pray."

I called my neighbor who I'd seen in the prison visiting her son. She said her husband went to see him too, driving three-hundred-and-fifty miles each way every weekend to visit for one hour. Their son was manic and bipolar. She was so glad he was there because at least she knew he was safe. (Later he would get himself straight and go to school to become a barber.)

She said her son said that Rick was always eating oranges. Other inmates would give him theirs. Her son attended some of the same therapy groups that Rick went to. He said that Rick was always crying, crying and talking about missing his kids.

Chapter Twenty-Seven – A Reason to Be

Back in the 1930s, during the Great Depression, a lot of people went to dance halls to compete in contests and dance marathons. It was a way to find relief from hard times, and maybe even to win a little money. My maternal grandmother, whose name was Jenny, had a crush on her regular dance partner, whose name was Pat. But Pat was married and had a few kids and one more on the way. So, when Jenny learned that she was pregnant too, having spent some post-dance-floor time with Pat on a few occasions, she kept it under wraps. Jenny was a hairdresser and capable of supporting herself. Pat was a womanizer who was capable of sleeping with three different women on a Saturday night. Much as Jenny liked Pat—he was a charming man and a fabulous dancer—she knew she was better off raising my mother on her own.

Not long before she died, Jenny decided it was time to tell my mother who her father was. She showed Mom the barbershop where her father, my grandfather, had once worked in Dorchester. How interesting it was to me, because my paternal grandfather had also been a barber. And Harriet and I were both master barbers, and of course I was an electrologist too. I guess getting rid of hair was in our blood.

My father's father had been a great storyteller. As a master barber working for the Breakers Hotel in Palm Beach, Florida, he'd given haircuts to many celebrities over the years and had lots of amusing anecdotes about them. He'd also been a political activist most his life, a Democrat who actually ran for Congress during the Kennedy years. I can still remember how proud I was at the age of twelve to see our last name—though it was spelled differently back then—all over Dad's lawn. Ironically, my grandfather kept a photograph of President Ford and his wife Betty, Republicans, in his dining room. It had been sent to him to commemorate his fifty years of marriage to my grandmother.

After Jenny's death, my mother decided she had to meet her father in person. She went back to the same barbershop and made some inquiries and walked away with a phone number for Al, Pat's brother, and eventually found her way to Pat, who lived in the Bay area of California.

She called him. He agreed that he could very well be her father. He remembered Jenny. They had won several dance contests together, he said, receiving $25 each time. It was a lot of money back then.

Eventually Pat came to Massachusetts. Harriet and I went with Mom to meet him at Mildred's, a restaurant famous for its chowder on Cape Cod. We planned to ask whether he would submit to a DNA test to see if he was really Mom's dad, but Pat said, "I don't need no blood test. She's my daughter!" Then he pulled some snap shots out of his jacket pocket and showed us his other grown children, and we could see the resemblance. In one fell swoop my mother went from being an illegitimate only child to a part of a big family. Harriet and I were a part of it too. My mother was thrilled. We were thrilled for her. We all got up and took turns hugging there at Mildred's while our chowder got cold.

Thereafter, my mother went to San Francisco to visit Pat (whose wife had died by then) and to meet her half siblings. Pat died of Hepatitis C not long after the initial round of reunions, but my mother stayed in touch with her siblings (Pat had six children as far as we knew), especially with the daughter who was only four months her senior.

It has always been remarkable to me how people can unexpectedly appear in one's life and utterly shift its direction—like the way the force of one asteroid can change the course of another if it gets close enough.

Of course people disappearing from one's life can cause a shift too. In the year 2003, I lost two people who had altered my life, Oscar, my confidante, mentor and surrogate father figure, and Rick's brother Harry, both from cancer. Naturally Harry's death was Rick's loss more than mine, but I had grown to care about him so much—in spite of the fact that I had never met him in person—and he had shared secrets and stories with me as if I had been his sister.

Rick was devastated over his brother's death. He had tried so hard to save him from his prison cell, and Harry had been unable to cooperate as fully as Rick would have liked. Rick had given me the task of making a list of all the meds Harry had been on, because he thought there might have been side effects from the combinations. But Harry never felt well enough to put it all together, and I couldn't do it for him. After the thyroid operation, Harry's lung cancer was confirmed. The interferon worked for a while to clear his lungs, but then we learned he had cancer on his kidney too. He was on oxygen by then; whenever I talked to him, he huffed and puffed and coughed; he was so tired all the time. Then he developed huge cysts on his face. Rick had wanted him to go directly to the Cancer Institute and request high doses of non-standard, experimental medications. He'd wanted him to get copies of the biopsy reports and have them sent to him at Bridgewater. There were a million things Rick wanted—but Harry was too sick to follow his orders.

If he hadn't been in prison, Rick was sure, he could have saved him. It was one more reason for him to beat up on himself, and it kept him somber for a long time. But then Riley Carter appeared in his life, bringing with her her own gravitational pull, and suddenly, for the first time in a long time, Rick could see a modicum of light at the end of the tunnel.

Her timing couldn't have been better. Rick was telling people that he had maybe three months left in him. He had nothing to live for. He'd been writing to Stephanie again, but as he knew she would never accept a letter from him (some of the letters he had written to her in the past wound up on the *Court TV* website), and as trying to mail a letter to Stephanie would only result in him being put in isolation, he wrote the letters and then ripped them into tiny pieces and flushed them down the toilet. It was almost as if he thought some vestige of his effort would reach her anyway. On top of that, his admirer Naomi went and told him that the book *Twisted* had come out. Maybe she read him excerpts over the phone; maybe she sent him a copy; I don't know. I only know that he begged me to call Lucy so that she could begin proceedings to sue the author, John Glatt, on Rick's behalf. He said the book was full of lies. He was in a panic about it. The book emphasized the cross-dressing and partying. Rick said, "I know I did a bad thing, but not all of this. Carmen never had any broken bones; I never prostituted Stephanie. That son of a bitch was writing fiction. Even Carmen's family wouldn't say this kind of stuff about me."

Riley Carter was what my father would call a "tough cookie," though you wouldn't have known it by looking at her tall, rail-thin exterior. She was a lawyer, but she didn't have a full-time practice anymore. Rather, she sought out select cases and took them on only one at a time. She had all the money in the world, so she didn't need to concern herself with making a living. Her mission was saving those she deemed worthy, from death row or from life imprisonment.

Like so many of the other women Rick currently knew, she had watched the *Court TV* segments and had come to believe that Rick could profit not by being behind bars but through rehabilitation. She called him, and yes, he said, he did want to be rehabilitated. He wanted that badly. So Riley decided to become his savior. She couldn't actually become his lawyer because she was not licensed to practice in the Commonwealth of Massachusetts. But she could get other lawyers involved and run things behind the scenes—like a puppet master.

Riley lived in the southwest. She and her husband owned numerous car dealerships. They donated hundreds of thousands of dollars to charities over the years and, being great dog lovers, they gave free cars to organizations that picked up strays and brought them to shelters. As soon as Riley came into the picture, she began sending Rick canteen money, $500 a month, which was a lot more than I had been able to give him. Nor did she have any problem accepting and paying for his phone calls. In all this time he had been pushing everyone to help him find an appeals lawyer, to help him find a way to pay for an appeal should a lawyer materialize. And now here was Riley, appearing in his life out of nowhere like a genie emerging from a bottle, saying, "Don't you worry; I'm going to get you an appeal," and sounding every bit capable of doing it too.

Like the other women who had appeared in Rick's life since his incarceration, Riley had some health issues. And her father, who had been a renowned scientist and a chemistry professor, suffered from pulmonary fibrosis. Riley had already lost her mother; she didn't want to lose her father too. She wanted Rick to cure him. She would see to it that, unlike Harry, her father would be a willing patient. Rick had heard of her father's scientific contributions even before he knew of Riley. The man had published over five hundred articles, many on anti-oxidants, and Rick was in awe of him. He wanted to know everything about him, his entire medical history. Once again he had a *raison d'etre*.

And so it began. Rick began talking to Nick, Riley's father, regularly on the phone. He told me almost immediately that Nick was a father figure to him, that he'd never met a nicer man. He told Nick about his own father and how his old man had abused him. Not only did Rick plan to find a cure for Nick, but he was also going to pray for him. As for Riley, she began taking private jets from her home in the southwest to Massachusetts to interview Rick. She took limos from the airport to the prison. During one visit, she bought Rick a copy of *Grey's Anatomy*, which made him deliriously happy. In between her visits with Rick, she had her driver take her past the Wenham house, the restaurant where Rick had gone that night with Milly Thieman, the tavern, Hector Lepore's house.…. She was looking for loopholes—with Sherlockian determination.

It was inevitable that Riley and I would become friends. She began to call me early on, and once when she was flying in on her private jet, I offered to pick her up and drive her to her hotel so that we could meet in person.

I was late that afternoon getting to the airport in Norwood, but she didn't seem to mind. She impressed me by emerging from the plane with a fat binder of transcripts, entitled *Commonwealth of Massachusetts vs. Richard J. Sharpe*. I took some photos of her and her plane, and she invited me on board to meet the pilot and have a look around. The plane was beautiful, a ten-seater with cushy beige leather seats, some facing each other. Riley told the pilot he could borrow the plane to visit family for the next week and a half while she was staying in Massachusetts.

One night at dinner Riley revealed that she didn't think Rick had purposely shot Carmen, that the shooting could very well have been an accident. A bullet might have been embedded in the gun before Rick ever took it from Hector Lepore's house. The ballistics investigators had already shown that the bullet fragment that was found at the scene of the crime was not the same kind of bullet as the ones that had been on the shelf in Lepore's place, which were assumed to be the ones Rick grabbed. A wrong size bullet could have been jammed in the gun before Rick ever stole it. Rick wouldn't have even known it was there in the chamber. He probably never even cocked the gun. He would have thought it was empty, if he was thinking at all at the time. It could have been all for show, something to scare Art, the painter, had he been there. At the very least, the confusion surrounding the ballistics evidence was sufficient cause for a new trial, Riley believed.

I agreed. I had always wondered what more we could have learned if only the weapon had been found. I remember thinking back then that I should go and look for it. Of course I knew that teams of police had already searched the area and come up empty, but somehow I thought that if I looked, intuition would guide me. But I never did get around to it.

Riley prompted me to talk about the other women in Rick's life. Her thinking was that if he appeared to be a man with lots of female friends, it would only hurt his appeal. Better that he should seem all alone in the world. I told her about Naomi, who, since she didn't drive, had to take the train to visit Rick and wasn't able to do so very often. Naomi lived in a one-bedroom condo with her ex-husband. He'd left when their one son was eleven, but then, some years later, he'd come back again. Naomi, who had flaming red hair and a serious weight problem, didn't have much of a life. But she had a huge heart, and she understood Rick and genuinely cared about his wellbeing. She was also something of a personal assistant to him, typing and distributing paperwork on his behalf, researching, making copies of tapes and transcripts, whatever he asked her to do. I didn't see how his friendship with her could hurt his chances for an appeal.

I had nothing to say when Riley brought up Gloria. Frankly, Gloria had been driving me crazy since earlier in the year. She had gotten a hold of Lucy's phone number and email address, probably from Rick, and had been contacting Lucy and complaining that she was in debt to AT&T for Rick's collect calls and couldn't take them anymore. But more than that, Rick had suggested that if she were to start producing cat shampoo, she could make a lot of money and pay her phone bills and contribute to his appeals fund too. She'd had the audacity to tell Lucy that she, Lucy, should persuade me to put up $6000 in startup costs for said cat shampoo company. Her argument was that I had learned everything I knew from Rick, and therefore I should be paying him back! "She is obligated," Gloria had written in an email that Lucy eventually shared with me. Lucy wrote back to ask her why she didn't contact me directly and Gloria responded that for some reason I didn't take her calls or answer her emails. Duh! Finally Lucy had to tell her that she was going to have to charge her $125 an hour to read her emails and act as a liaison between us. I wasn't about to give Gloria any money; I had paid Lucy $7100 recently, mostly for work she had done for Rick.

Still, for all that Gloria had been driving me up the wall, I knew she genuinely cared about Rick and had been a good friend to him. I couldn't count the phone messages she'd left me over the last year begging me to forgive Rick for some offense or another, because she couldn't stand to see him upset. And she had in fact made many earnest attempts to find him an appeals lawyer, including contacting Robert Shapiro, whose bill Lola had wanted me to help pay. And Rick cared about her too. He'd even sent Gloria a formal letter confirming that he would donate a part of his liver to her if she needed it, and she would, eventually, as hers was failing.

Nadine the nurse's name came up. She had recently written to Rick out of the blue to tell him she'd received a letter from Court TV saying that they were going to run the trial yet again and asking if she would like to do an interview with some of their talking heads in conjunction with it. Nadine wanted Rick to advise her on whether or not she should accept their offer. Now that she was no longer angry with him, she thought she might be able to make up for the damage she'd done with her previous interviews. "I will not hurt you ever again," she promised in her letter.

Riley and I talked about Skye in Pennsylvania, Patricia in Arizona and Kate in Oregon, who sent him postcards with photos of the Beatles and

Dylan and Janis Joplin and Mick Jagger and promised to take him to a Jackson Brown concert if he ever got out of prison. I had a lot of Kate's rock and roll postcards, because Rick sent them to me for safekeeping. Her notes were sweet and upbeat and platonic. It would be a shame if Riley decided to discourage Rick's friendship with her, or with Skye or Patricia either for that matter.

When Riley brought up Lola, I froze. If there was one person who might *seem* to invalidate the still-mourning-husband image Riley hoped to project, Lola was it. I gathered my wits after a minute and explained that Lola wasn't allowed to see him anyway, because someone had set her up, and I told Riley all about the green pill incident. My hope was that she would conclude that Lola could not possibly be an impediment to her efforts.

In fact, Lola was the person Rick spoke to most often about his most intimate memories of Carmen. Only recently Lola told me Rick had a meltdown while on the cafeteria food line. He had to tell the other inmates that he was having some kind of allergic reaction to something on the menu. But the truth was that he was remembering Valentine's Day, back when Stephanie was about two. Rick and Carmen had wanted to go out but neither her nor his parents would agree to babysit. That was when they first hired the homeless girl who would eventually become part of their household. To celebrate Valentine's Day, they went to a restaurant that they really couldn't afford and had prime rib. Now he was standing on a food line, in a prison, itchy because the previous night the COs had screamed at him to get out of the shower before he'd had time to rinse the shampoo out of his hair. He'd cried on the line and he'd cried again on the phone when he told Lola the story. He'd said Carmen was everything—beautiful, smart, nurturing, maternal, wonderful, loving—a better human being than he could ever have been.

Riley and I sat quietly for a while. I couldn't tell what she was thinking. I recalled a conversation Lola and I had just before Riley came into the picture. I had been upset with Rick and hadn't taken his calls for a few days. Lola had called to tell me that his new psychiatrist in Max 2 had taken him off his anti-psychotic pills and started him on some new medications and they weren't doing the job. He didn't even know what they were because now the nurses chopped up all his meds and mixed them together. The new meds were causing him to have auditory hallucinations. Voices were telling him that he needed to be with Carmen—authoritative male voices, saying, "Carmen loves you and wants you back." When he felt rational, he knew they were hallucinations. But when he was having them, he wasn't sure what was going on. Lola begged me to start taking his calls again. She said, "It's you and me, Linda. We're all he's got. He needs us. I can hear in your voice that you're too busy, but...."

I was too busy, that was certainly a part of it. Besides work and my life with Gary, I had guys tiling the floors in the Newton house, other guys bleaching the walls in the basement and painting. The closing on the Gloucester house had been set back yet again because of ongoing septic tank issues, and here I'd jumped the gun and already had the kitchen cabinets designed and built, to the tune of almost $25,000. Harrison and Stephanie had okayed the new cabinets being stored in Gloucester, but they were not going to be responsible should they be stolen or damaged. Every day was a new headache with one house or the other...more often both. We humans can only handle so much. "Without us he'll die," Lola had continued. "Together we can extend his life, give him a reason to hold on."

All of this discussion of the women in Rick's life left one question in my mind. If Riley decided the women were hurting the cause, would her axe fall on my head too? And if so, if she convinced Rick that our friendship must come to an end, would it be a good thing or a bad thing for me? I was still angry at Rick because there was no doubt in my mind that he had been the one to tell Gloria that she should persuade Lucy to persuade me to give her money to make cat shampoo. But I was so used to seeing this side of him that I knew even through my resentment that it wouldn't leave a permanent scar. For better or worse, I had developed an "oh, that's just Rick being Rick" mentality. I knew to expect his manipulations as surely as I knew that he would follow them with tears and pleas for forgiveness.

Sometimes I thought it wasn't even about me and Rick and the friendship we had developed. Sometimes I thought he just needed someone to listen, and it didn't matter who it was. Once recently when he called I asked Gary to talk to him so that I wouldn't have to. They had quite a long conversation.

Rick told Gary about how he had a pilot's license back in the late 70s and how he used to rent planes whenever he could afford it. Once, when he'd had his brother Bruce up in the air, he shut off the engine on the glider he'd rented in order to do an aerobatic maneuver called a corkscrew dive, often described as a "death spiral," before landing on a frozen lake. Bruce freaked out and said he would never fly with him again; in fact, he never liked flying at all after that. Rick had liked night flying. He said that when you lose your orientation because of darkness, your instincts kick in—and he liked that alertness you discover when you give yourself over fully to intuition. (When Gary told me this later I thought of how John F. Kennedy Jr. lost control of his plane back in 1999 as a result of spatial disorientation, during a descent over water at night.) Rick told Gary how once he'd flown in a snow squall and couldn't see the ground. He'd had to call the flight service station. They got him on radar and talked him through the landing. He said that flying over Long Island Sound it was easy to find yourself upside down at night because you didn't know if you were looking at stars or boats. Long ago, after he'd quit flying but before everything went haywire in his life, he had taken up making model airplanes as a hobby. He'd had over two hundred of them dangling on fishing line from the ceiling in one of the downstairs rooms in the Gloucester house. Someone had taken them all down before the house went on the market.

With the exception of Nadine, none of the women Riley and I discussed were ousted from Rick's life immediately. Although I was the one who was able to go into the prison and visit him, Lola continued to be his touchstone, communicating with him daily by phone or letter or both. In our conversations she would relate the smallest details of his day-to-day affairs to me. She liked to tell me his prison stories, such as when he had a run-in with Cuba, who was his best friend. Cuba had a glass eye, because he had once stabbed himself in the eye in an effort to kill himself. It wasn't a good glass eye either, and it didn't look real. One day when Rick went to pick up his laundry, he saw that his pillowcase had not been returned to him. Cuba immediately offered to give Rick his. But later one of the guards noticed the bulge in Rick's pocket, and when Rick revealed its source, the guard wanted to know why Rick had Cuba's pillowcase. Rick would have been better off to lie. Cuba and Rick both got in trouble. That same night, not only was Rick without a pillowcase, but he was cold and asked for a second blanket. The guard on duty said no. Rick had to wrap the sheet and the one thin blanket he had around and around until he was wrapped up like a mummy. He kept his socks on. When Cuba finally got over being angry at Rick, he got permission to make a plastic cover for Rick's window to keep out the draft.

Lola confessed that she'd told Rick she would marry him if that served to overturn the ban on her visits. But she warned him that such a marriage would only be for the purpose of getting in to see him. "You can't keep me captive," she told him on the phone. "If I meet another guy and you're not out, you'll have to divorce me." But to me she said, "I don't really plan on meeting anyone. I'm forty-nine years old. I'd be loyal to him forever."

In the beginning Riley's actions would lead one to think she wanted Rick to have all the female friends in the world. I learned, from Rick, that Riley had offered to give Kate money to take a plane to visit him from Oregon. But Kate had been afraid to fly since 9-11 and so had refused Riley's offer. Then I received a call from Naomi saying that she was hoping to visit Rick on the same day that I'd said I was going. She wanted to know if I could pick her up at the train station in Newton and drive her over in my car. I had never met her before. When I spoke to Rick, he said that if I didn't want to drive her, it was fine because Riley had promised to give her cab fare, and train fare too. But he hoped I would. I said, "You told me she has cats. Tell her I'll drive her but she has to wear clean clothes and not touch the cats once she's dressed….and wash her hands right before she leaves the house. Otherwise I'll be sneezing." He replied, "Linda, be nice."

Naomi was, as Rick had said, very nice, and forthcoming too. On the way back to the train station we talked about Nadine the nurse. Naomi said she was so upset when the article came out in the *Herald* that she had to leave work for the day. I said, "You're in love with him, aren't you?" She smiled shyly and whispered, "Yes."

Around this time Lola lost her job. Perhaps her boss was still upset with her because she didn't want to go out with the man whose wife was too sick with lupus to sleep with him. Or perhaps it was because some other people in the office suspected that she was friends with Rick Sharpe and didn't think that was an appropriate friendship for a dental hygienist. In order to make sure her boss didn't try to fix her up with any other patients, Lola had begun to tell her office colleagues, she admitted to me, that she was dating a dermatologist. She would sometimes bring Rick's letters to work and read them during break—so they knew this was a letter-writing dermatologist. And everyone knew she was interested in Rick's trial, because she listened to re-runs on the overhead TV while she was cleaning teeth. On the day she was let go, she'd had one of Rick's letters in her handbag, in the lunch room where anyone could have rifled through her bag while she was working with a patient.

Lola was extremely upset about this turn of events. She hadn't missed a single day of work in seven years. She'd even had someone plow her parking space once during a snowstorm so that she could get in to work in case any of her appointments made it in. All her reviews with her boss had always been excellent. Her patients, many of them repeats, loved her. She immediately contacted a temp agency. She needed to work.

In her hysteria over the loss of her job and the likely cause of it, Lola had a complete sea change and decided that loving Rick was getting her nowhere. It was too painful to continue. He called her crying all the time. She couldn't sleep at night thinking about their conversations. She called me one day while I was at work and told me she was going to change her number so he wouldn't call her anymore. She was so upset that I suggested she drop everything and get to my office right away. She said she couldn't; she couldn't bring herself to leave the house. I told her she needed to call a psychologist or psychiatrist, find someone to help her through this. "I'm not worth the trouble. I'm not worth anything," she sobbed. I said, "Yes you are. You're beautiful inside and out. You're in a state of shock right now from losing your job. It's not a good time to make more changes. Cutting off Rick overnight won't be good for you." Or for him, I was thinking.

When she finally calmed down I asked her if she had mentioned Rick to anyone at work. She admitted that she'd told a few patients who had become friends about their relationship. I knew it! I told her she couldn't do that anymore—if she ever wanted to have a normal life. People didn't understand. As far as they were concerned, Rick was that one moment when he screwed up, just that one moment in time and nothing more—and therefore not worthy of support or compassion. It infuriated me when I thought of it. Who gets to decide who's worthy of compassion? Isn't everyone worthy of our concern?

Lola said that she had seen Tammi, the woman who had married Erik Menendez, on a TV interview show. Tammi said that she had no friends anymore. But she knew that she had given Erik some hope in his life. Didn't he deserve that? Doesn't everyone? How the tables had turned. Here it was *me* telling Lola to take Rick's calls. I warned her not to blame him for what happened, her losing her job. "If you blame him, he'll fall apart." I suggested she tell him that she needed to cut back a little so that she could focus on finding another job. If she was going to break it off, she could do it gradually.

In the end, she did do it gradually, but it still didn't feel gradual to Rick.

Chapter Twenty-Eight – Friendship

NOT LONG AFTER THEIR RELATIONSHIP ENDED, LOLA CAME TO MY HOUSE IN Newton again. Even though she'd lost weight, she looked beautiful, her gorgeous skin radiant. She'd come to deliver those of Rick's belongings that she'd accumulated over the span of their relationship. She'd asked him who to give them to—Glenn? Bruce?—and he'd said me. There were some family albums, some loose snap shots, the psych tapes from his interviews with Jerome McNay, some legal documents, etc. She looked around while I poked through the box. The house was a lot different than the last time she'd been over. She said, "What a beautiful home." Then she turned to face me and added, "I hope this ending with Rick doesn't mean our friendship will end too."

I had prepared lunch—egg salad sandwiches. She had maybe four bites. I found a can of pears in the cabinet and got her to eat those. Afterwards I cut her hair for her. She said, "Don't tell Rick I told you this, but he was giving me too many errands; he was pushing me." Most recently, he'd been corresponding with his former doctors, trying to get information that would be useful in a new trial. Thinking that an envelope with Rick's lab results from one particular doctor would be too big for her mailbox, and knowing she wouldn't be home when her mail came, she'd had it sent to the office. But her boss got the mail that day and opened it before he realized it wasn't for him. He said, "Why are you involved with this guy?" It was only days later that he asked her to leave.

This was a story I hadn't heard before. Little by little I was coming to realize that she'd let her personal business slip out left and right at her former place of employment. I didn't say anything; I focused on her hair and let her do the talking. She said, "I can never get that low again. I miss him already, but I can't let myself get that low."

The phone rang just then. I stepped away to look at the caller ID. "Do you want to talk to him?" I asked. She looked shocked; she didn't answer me. I picked up the receiver and said hi. He immediately said, "I need you to visit; I need to talk to you in person. When can you come?" I mouthed to Lola, "Do you want to talk to him?" She nodded reluctantly and I passed her the phone. She said, "It's me, Lola. Linda's trimming my hair. Listen, you're in my daily prayers. I need to get a job and move on. God bless you." She hung up. We looked at each other for a long moment. Then I started cutting her hair again.

Lola finished up one temp job and began a second one. This second one was for another dentist and she thought it might turn into a permanent position. She began to sound a little better over time. Now that she wasn't talking to Rick before going to bed, she was sleeping better, she said, often a full eight hours. Still, she missed the energy his voice brought into her house, him saying he loved her. I said, "It was negative energy. You'll fill the void." She said, "If he gets out I'll be friends with him. If he doesn't get out, he's going to die. I don't blame him. I couldn't live like that either."

❧☙

Hobbies, I had always believed, were for people with extra time on their hands, and as far back as I could remember, extra time was not something I'd had to deal with. But somewhere along the line I had begun collecting interesting newspaper articles about prisoners and putting them in a box, and when the box was full and I had to get another, I realized that I had made the study of prisoners my hobby. No one I mentioned this to was surprised. People who suffer anguish as kids sometimes become shrinks to figure it all out. I was a hairy kid, so I became an electrologist, a person able to control her volume of hair. Likewise, I was the daughter of a thief, so I became a student of criminality.

Some of the articles I clipped were about how prisons mistreated particular inmates, and some were about inmates mistreating one another. Some journalists pondered—as did those involved in Rick's case—what constitutes insanity and how we should deal with the criminally insane. Some were about men who became criminals after being abused as kids; some were about people who committed terrible crimes and then killed themselves. I didn't draw any conclusions about anything from these articles. The one subject that I didn't find many stories about, at least in the newspapers, was the women who befriended prisoners. There were a lot of us. I thought someone should write about us.

After months of not hearing from her, Gloria called and left a message and a few days later I returned her call, mostly out of curiosity. She said that Bridgewater had sent her paperwork regarding the liver section she was supposed to receive from Rick. I found it hard to believe that Riley would allow an organ donation to transpire on her watch. I asked Gloria if Rick had mentioned Riley to her. Her response was, "Who's Riley?"

Gloria left another message a few weeks later, basically saying that now that Rick had a new lawyer working with him, and all these other women who would do what needed to be done, she was through. "I wish him luck. Tell him not to call me anymore. I won't be taking his calls," she said.

The women in Rick's life, it seemed, were dropping like flies. I had no way to know how much of it was due to Riley's intervention. Surely she was telling Rick that he was better off without Lola, at least.

Naomi called during this time to tell me that the prison had set up some new rules regarding phone use. As of the beginning of the following week, all inmates would have only thirty minutes on the phone for the entire day. The COs would have to stand there and record everyone's phone time. Naomi believed this new rule had come about as a result of Rick and a few others who were addicted to the phone.

Rick had loved the phone even before he was incarcerated. Some people are shy about using the phone, but he was never one of them. He would think of something he needed to ask someone and pick up the phone and call and ask. If he thought of something else a minute later, he would call again. It never occurred to him that he might be making a nuisance of himself. He loved communication, especially when it had to do with his projects.

There was another guy in the prison, Paul, who loved the phone too. This inmate had tried to kill his grandparents. Now that he was in prison, he called them nonstop, according to Naomi, but they had caller ID and they never answered. Naomi said that Rick thought the prison should get him a fake phone, so he could call all day long. Rick didn't think he'd know the difference. Naomi had just had a biopsy for a cyst on her breast. Rick was monitoring all of her interactions with her doctors to make sure no stone was left unturned as she went through the analysis process. Unaware that I knew Riley as well as I did, Naomi updated me in that department too, saying that Riley was working sixteen hours a day for Rick, that she was reading the transcripts of the trial and had already found a slew of mistakes that Ben Falcon had made. When we got around to talking about Lola, Naomi's comment was that if she hadn't always been thinking about Rick, she wouldn't have lost her job.

It occurred to me that it was not out of the realm of possibility that Riley got the prison to change the phone limits, expressly for the purpose of keeping Rick from talking to women. Nor was I the only one who surmised that she would go to whatever lengths were necessary in order to have things her way. Lola thought Riley had some ulterior motives for helping Rick, and she didn't understand why she was offering to give Naomi money to visit and Kate money, most recently, to pay for calls. It seemed fishy to her. Before Riley came into the picture, Bruce, Gloria and others had found various lawyers who had agreed to work with Rick in some capacity. Now the only lawyers on board were the ones that Riley had signed on. Lucy was less wishy-washy about her suspicions. She thought Riley worked for the FBI.

For one thing, Lucy wasn't impressed by her business card, which combined the auto business, a real estate business, and her legal designations. Lucy revealed that her dad had been a con man, and it made her suspicious of people like Riley. We got sharing stories after that. She knew about my dad, of course, but I told her about my stepdad, how he would put on a work uniform and go into a public building and take the paintings off the walls. I told her about my grandfather, my mom's dad, a bookie barber who had gone through half his life with two bullet hole scars, one in front and one in back. He liked to show them to people; he liked seeing them go all bug-eyed. Lucy suggested that my relationship with Rick probably had something to do with working out my feelings about my father and my stepfather and my grandfather. "Hmmm," I said, as if I had never considered that before. But in the end I stuck up for Riley. I believed she was working heart and soul for Rick.

Not long after my conversation with Naomi I took my first call from Rick since the day I cut Lola's hair, several weeks earlier. The first thing I said was, "Go easy on me," because I was mentally and physically exhausted and I wasn't in the mood for taking orders or dramatics or anything else. I could handle only a very quiet and casual conversation, and only for a few minutes at that. Rick yielded, talking first about Naomi's cyst and then about cancer generally. He predicted that in the next twenty years, half the population would develop cancer, due to all the pollutants on the planet. He went on to identify the specific pollutants that he thought would wreak the most havoc. I said, "You're on a roll, Rick."

"I'm dying to educate you," he responded.

That made me laugh. He won me over as usual with his scientific mind. Before we got off, I said, "I may visit soon if the rain ever lets up." I didn't tell him that I had dreamed about him the night before, that I had woken up wondering this: if an authority were to ask me in my opinion whether he should be let out or not, how would I answer? Maybe I'd say, Yes, let him out, with a twenty-four-hour bracelet, with distance monitoring…or with a full-time guard on his premises, and people coming and going to dole out his meds and psychotherapy sessions. Then he could do some teaching and research; he could compensate, at least a little, for his wrongdoings by making the world a better place for the sick. But then I thought, What happened with Carmen was a result of him being pushed to his limit. Who was to say that he wouldn't reach it again? For all that he was my friend, maybe my answer would have to be no.

Chapter Twenty-Nine – Trust

THE RAIN LET UP AND I VISITED RICK AND WE TALKED ABOUT TRUST. I ASKED HIM if he trusted me and he said he did. Then I asked him if he trusted Riley, and he said yes again. He said Riley thought even in a worst case scenario she could get him paroled in twenty years. I said, "Twenty years! You'll be sixty-five! Will you still be able to get it up by then?" Rick laughed.

We talked about people we had trusted in our lives who had turned out to be untrustworthy and how much that hurt. He mentioned Ellie, who had been his liposuction assistant back before the tragedy. He had come to suspect that she was selling bottles of Alpha Hydroxy out of the office and pocketing the money when he wasn't around. It was really bothering him, not so much that she was stealing money as the fact that she would do something like that to him; he had always considered her a close friend and confided in her about personal matters. Finally one day he had a friend of his stop in at the office and buy a bottle of AHA for cash, $60.00. Later he asked Ellie when they had made their last AHA sale. She answered, "Gee, that was weeks ago." He confronted her then, saying, "No, it was today." Ellie turned bright red. Rick didn't say anything more about it. He figured once she had been caught she would stop. She'd been with him for more than seven years, and he wanted to keep her.

But then there was another incident. A few weeks later, he had a client up on the table, anesthetized and ready for liposuction. But when he went to get the sterile tubing that attaches to the metal cannula that sucks out the fat, there was none! He'd laid the tubing out the night before. He wasn't losing his mind; Carmen had been at his side as he went through his pre-procedure checklist. Ellie had been flying out to someplace in the Midwest one week each month to work at the side of a doctor there. It hit him all at once that she was stealing things from his office to help the other doctor set up. He freaked out. He had to call Carmen to rush over and stay with his patient while he ran to the hospital and begged a nurse he knew to give him some tubing. He got back just before the patient's anesthesia wore off.

He changed the subject suddenly. He said, "You may be called as a witness for the second trial, because you've known me so long. Don't get nervous. It's probably years away." I said, "God must really be looking after you to send someone like Riley into your life. She's like an angel." He nodded, and then he began to cry.

೮೦೮ಚ

Days after my visit, Rick wound up back in the hole again. Riley, who would soon be flying in again from the southwest, called me with this news. "I don't know how he'll survive," she exclaimed. She said he was so nervous since going into the hole that he'd begun to pick and scratch at his skin—so the guards cuffed him. She didn't know yet what he did to deserve this current punishment. Her best guess was that he'd abused his phone privileges. She had arranged for him to be interviewed by one Dr. Greenberg, for yet another psychiatric evaluation, but now it couldn't happen. He couldn't see anyone except her while he was in the hole. Dogs were barking in the background of our conversation. It was hard to hear her over them. I asked her about this Dr. Greenberg. She said he was gorgeous and, like Vincent Kahn, something of a celebrity. He was on TV all the time, a favorite of Larry King.

Riley arrived at the prison a few days later and was on her way to the private room where lawyers could meet with their clients when an inmate in one of the cells began throwing shit at one of the guards. She walked on. A moment later another guard, one she had always thought of as a nice guy, said to her, "Do you want to know about the size of Sharpe's penis? I can tell you." She was not having a good day. She called me from her hotel when she got back to complain that Rick's letter writing was hurting him. She said, "How can we get him to stop writing to these bimbos?" I said, "Cut off his canteen so he can't buy stamps." She chuckled. She'd just given him $700 for canteen. By prison standards, he was a millionaire.

Riley and I met for dinner again not long after. She looked even thinner than she had the last time I'd seen her. Nevertheless, she was a great looking woman. On this night she wore very little makeup. She was dressed in a lacy white blouse and tight black jeans and a brown leather belt. She wore an emerald and diamond ring with a matching bracelet and a black rope choker at her neck. As soon as we ordered she started up again about Rick's friendships, his letter writing. "Things come up in the letters—marriage, having relationships…. It doesn't even matter if it's them saying it or him. He still welcomes it. It's all fantasy for him, a dream of having something like a normal life, with a partner, like anyone else. But it makes it sound like…. He's got to show more grief about Carmen." I nodded. I had seen so much of his grief over time, and I knew it was genuine, but I knew what she meant too. Riley informed me that Nadine the nurse had written to him again, to say she was moving to another country. Riley told Rick not to respond but he did anyway, because he wanted to let her know that Harry had died and that she should be careful in a foreign country with the car bombs and all. Then of course Nadine had to write back to say that she was sorry about Harry, and then he wrote back....

Our plates came. Hers featured a rare steak and broccoli, mine a salad. I tried to get her to talk about personal matters; I wanted to know more about her life in the southwest, but she stayed focused on Rick. She said she wanted to keep the publicity to zero over the next year; the shit had to die down. When appeals were filed, we could begin to generate positive publicity. She planned to fight at the federal level to keep the cameras out of the courtroom this time, but she conceded that she would probably lose on that point. She said, "I'm going to need you, Glenn and Bruce." Relax, I thought, but I didn't say it. She was as single-minded as her client.

Rick got out of isolation and my phone started ringing off the hook again. He mentioned in one call that Riley wasn't feeling well and had actually passed out while visiting with him. "How could that happen?" I cried. Rick had given her a lecture. He wanted her in the hospital for an IV. He said it would only take thirty minutes and then they could get back to work again. She said that all her medical records were back home, that he didn't need to make such a fuss.

I asked him about her condition again the next time I spoke to him, which was the next day, but now he clammed up, saying it was confidential and he couldn't discuss it with me. This was the first time he'd ever said anything like that to me. It made me angry. I said, "Is it anorexia?" He said, "I can't discuss it." I said, "I bet her electrolytes are messed up." He made no comment. I exclaimed, "Well, at least tell me if it's contagious in case she calls to have dinner again." He said it wasn't contagious, to just forget it.

Gloria called too. Now she had joined Lucy and Lola in thinking that Riley had to be some kind of a imposter. She'd made calls to some universities in the southwest trying to get more background information on her. She wanted to see if I could help. I told her I didn't know anything, which was practically the truth.

Dr. Greenberg, the handsome, celebrity forensic psychiatrist who Riley had asked to interview Rick, finally got in and conducted his interview. His fifteen-page report followed soon after and Riley sent me a copy. He began by addressing the fact that the Bridgewater doctors had concluded that Rick was a manipulative, narcissistic malingerer who acted as if he was entitled to whatever he wanted. Hence they responded to him with confrontation, scorn, and antagonism instead of caregiving. There were records that confirmed that they refused to acknowledge that his sleeplessness, tearfulness, grief and depression indicated that he needed more treatment, not less. Because he appeared to be animated when he was on the phone, they, like Dr. Pack, the old guy who had put in his two cents at the trial, assumed that he was faking symptoms to get attention, and for this reason they felt justified in withholding the medications he badly needed. ˙

Greenberg had sat with Rick for hours. In addition to administering several assessment tests, he interviewed other inmates, and in a summary of their remarks wrote that Rick spent most of his days curled up in the corner of either one of two rooms on the unit; that he broke into tears spontaneously for no apparent reason; that he never played cards or took part in other group recreational activities; and that he always talked about his wife, kids and brothers at group meetings. Greenberg also spent some fifty hours reading all available written records. He found Rick to be not only utterly depressed but also suffering from post-traumatic stress disorder. The self-mutilation that he'd been engaging in of late was because he didn't know how else to relieve the tension and pain that he lived with constantly. His greatest fear, Greenberg concluded, was being alone—hence his animation on the phone.

Greenberg concluded that if the doctors and nurses at Bridgewater changed their attitude toward him, he wouldn't be such a difficult patient and might not try to commit suicide again. In fact, if Rick had access to a computer and medical books, he might actually become productive. He'd already read the *Grey's Anatomy* that Riley had given him some five times. "There is no more pertinent redemption for the killing of another," Greenberg wrote, "than to save lives. Dr. Sharpe's knowledge and skill can save many, and he is motivated. It is a debt of servitude he would be glad to pay." If changes weren't made, on the other hand, Greenberg warned, he would remain at high risk of suicide, depression, anorexia and self-mutilation.

Riley was furious with Bridgewater after she got the report. She planned to sue everyone there for all sorts of reasons. She said she had to have two guards in with her whenever she met with Rick. And here there was an inmate who had cut his wife up into small pieces (because she'd burned his dinner), and he didn't have to have any guards when he met with his legal team. She said, "Rick's not abusive; he's *being* abused." She was telling me this over the phone, and she banged the surface of something—a table probably—so hard I jumped. She said the last time she had been to see him, she'd been strip searched. When Michael Goodman, the Massachusetts-licensed lawyer that she'd hired to work on the case, had gone to see him, the guard had made him unzip his pants and push them down to his knees. She wasn't going to take it anymore. Robare, the administrator, was going to have to call off his dogs.

She had her husband write a letter to Robare saying that here everyone at Bridgewater was running around with shanks and drugs, yet on the one day that Riley had showed the guards three innocuous letters that she, a lawyer, wanted to leave with, she was not permitted to do so. Moreover, on a few occasions when she went to the locker to get a medication she needed, her visits were terminated and she was made to wait an hour to get back in again. Her husband, Gregory, threatened to come to Bridgewater with his own attorney if she wasn't treated better.

While Gregory was busy letting Robare know that he was keeping his good eye on him, Riley was busy using Greenberg's report to substantiate Rick's recommitment to Bridgewater and continued rehab (if you could call it that) treatment. As bad as Bridgewater was, anything was better than a return to Walpole, which, we all knew, would be a death sentence. Her initial strategy paid off within weeks. She received a letter of recommitment. However, the Bridgewater administrators stressed that they had the right to send him back to Walpole if and when they wanted. Still, it was a start.

Gary and I had dinner with Riley to celebrate. She looked great, though when I said so she said, "I was up all night, working." "I was up all night working" was her mantra. She seemed never to sleep. She said the fact that everyone at Bridgewater hated her meant she was winning. She had put a team together, Goodman here in Massachusetts, and also a woman named Lily who was a death row lawyer back in southwest, and some paralegals. She said that Lily wanted $60,000 to work on the case, and to date Riley had paid her $20,000. Gary and I exchanged a look. This woman really was some kind of angel.

She was excited that evening, and very chatty. Apropos of nothing, she said that Kate, Rick's postcard friend, had an issue with her husband over her writing to Rick about a year ago, but now he no longer considered Rick a threat. She'd ordered a steak and shrimp combo dish, and when it came she covered the steak with A1 and submerged her poor baked potato in twice its volume of sour cream and butter. Then she took a taste of everything and pushed her plate aside. She had her third glass of wine while Gary and I were having dessert. She said to Gary, "Does it bother you the relationship that Linda has with Rick?" Gary answered, "He can be very demanding with her." She said, "My husband isn't too happy about it either."

Riley was on the warpath now. Armed with Greenberg's report, she was ready to march. For one thing, she wanted Dr. Jamelli, the prison psychiatrist who oversaw Rick's treatments, to stay away from him for good. She'd learned through her various sources that another inmate, a guy who killed his baby son, had killed himself as a result of his treatment with Jamelli. He'd used a paperclip to rip his wrists open and bled to death. Riley wanted me to have Lucy contact that inmate's family and get more details. She thought there might be enough information out there about Jamelli to get a class action malpractice suit going.

Even though Lola and Rick didn't communicate the way they once had, Riley learned that the occasional letter that Lola wrote him continued to be laced with endearments, and thus she had Lily, her colleague back in the southwest, call Lola and tell her that she was not to communicate with him anymore AT ALL. Lola of course went ballistic. She decided then and there that she would write to Rick even more, get back on his call list, love him until the end of time. When Lily called again a week later, Lola, who was no more prone to cursing that I was, called her a bitch and a fuck head. Riley said this confirmed that Lola was dangerous. She had Lily call her once more and tell her that if she didn't let up, Rick would wind up back in Walpole and he would commit suicide. Riley insisted that I talk to Lola too, as back up. She told me what to say: "Look Lola, in his mind you guys broke up; now he's thinking only about his appeal. You can't help him." Funny, but I thought I'd said that to her a hundred times already, and without anyone's coaching. Lily, in the meantime, made the mistake of saying offhandedly to Riley that maybe it was better if Rick *did* commit suicide, because he was so much trouble. Riley dumped her from the team immediately.

In the end, Riley called Lola ("the weird child" was how she referred to her) herself and told her that Rick was interested in someone else. She must have been believable, because Lola bought it and burst into tears. "But the last time I talked to him, he said 'I love you,'" she sobbed. When I spoke to Riley, she was bristling. She said, "He'd better have an explanation for this, because if he lied to me…." She said she couldn't stand lying, that she'd fired a million-dollar-a-year general manager from the car dealership business because she'd caught him in a lie. She was only giving Rick one chance. Oh dear, I thought to myself.

As for Naomi, Riley had one of the paralegals call and tell her she could still visit, but less frequently, and never was there to be any touching, any reaching for his hand, and no more poems. (I hadn't even known about the poems; apparently they were about going to bed with Rick!) Naomi left messages for me, asking if I knew what was going on. So did Kate and Gloria. Riley told me that my friendship with Rick was important, but that I needed to include Gary in it; it would be better if we visited together.

Riley eventually spoke to Gloria. Gloria had called her to complain about a $600 phone bill. Riley said she'd send her the money, but that she had to leave him alone. To me she said, "I don't want any freaks calling him or him calling them." She said that Gloria had known all about the law firm, all about Lily, the woman Riley had kicked off the team, all of Rick's business. She couldn't believe it. After they'd hung up, she decided not to send Gloria the $600 after all, because if Gloria went to the media, as Nadine had, it could be construed as a payoff. Riley said, "Rick's not guilty, I have evidence to prove it. I just need to be able to get through my agenda with him without all these distractions." Then she burst into tears.

I went to visit Rick during a week when Riley was back home. Gary didn't come with me; there were times when he just couldn't deal with the fact that I was giving Rick so much of my time and emotional energy, and this was one of them. When I arrived at the facility at 9:15 a.m., there was a note saying that a maintenance issue was being addressed and all visitors would have to wait until ten to be let in. The visit would be very short as a result.

When Rick saw me in the visitors room, he almost ran to me, the way a little kid might run to a doting grandparent. His eyes filled up with tears. He apologized for smelling badly. There'd been no hot water for the last three days. I asked him about lying to Riley, and he swore he hadn't said I love you to Lola, that Lola must have made that up. I said, "You know how you always talk about the ABCs of dermatology? How everyone needs to wash twice a day with salicylic acid to unclog the pores? Benzoyl peroxide to eliminate bacteria, moisturizers, moisture-wicking clothing, blah blah blah? Well, Riley is trying to give you the ABCs of getting out of jail...alive. If she doesn't want you to say I love you on the phone, then don't say it. To anyone."

He hung his head. When he was ready to talk again, he asked me about the house. It was the end of the summer and I was *still* waiting to close on it. It still needed a new septic system, and now Stephanie and Harrison didn't want to install one because there were rumors that the whole town might have to go on a sewer system, to eliminate some problems arising from the high water tables in the area. I'd told Chase, my realtor, to tell Stephanie and Harrison to just go ahead and install the septic tank anyway so that we could close on the house. Aubrey, my real estate lawyer, had said it could take five years for the new sewer system to come down the street—and I needed the Title 5 Inspection Certificate now. But there was a hearing coming up on the town's sewage problems, and they didn't want to do anything until that transpired. Meantime, my hands were tied. I was forced to get an extension on my mortgage commitment.

We talked about Lola for a while. She was still writing the occasional letter, but Riley had forbidden Rick to write back. He said he'd seen a TV show that suggested women who fell for inmates did it because the inmate was unattainable and the relationship was therefore safe. Nine times out of ten, if the inmate got out, the woman didn't want to be with him anyway, because she'd never wanted a real relationship in the first place. I had to wonder if he really saw this on TV or if it was something Riley had been whispering in his ear. I said, "You and Lola would have lasted a week out in the real world." He nodded. "You're right," he said softly.

Riley was back from the southwest in no time, and bursting with ideas. She was buying an antique Weatherby, just like the one Rick had allegedly stolen from Alan Lepore, so that she could hold it up in front of the jury. She wanted Rick to hold it up too, to show how small he was by comparison. When she was done with it, she planned to give it to her dad, who was a gun collector.

When we met for dinner she announced, "We're going national with this case. I've put in $50,000 of my own money so far, and my father has put in $150,000, and we're just getting started. But I don't care. This is how I want to spend my time, my life." She looked aside, at her plate of uneaten food. Then she leaned in over the table. "You know, Linda," she whispered, "I have two sources at Bridgewater who say Lola is *still* calling Rick." She must have seen the empty look in my expression. It wasn't what I wanted to talk about. She relented and switched to personal matters, mentioning her husband and then telling me that one of their dogs had only three legs, another was epileptic, and the third one, who was fourteen, was on Prozac, old but very happy. Her cat had one eye. No wonder she liked Rick so much. She was one of those people who were inclined toward the offbeat, the overlooked. She stopped talking suddenly. "I never met anyone like you," she said after a moment, "not since my mom died." She was close to tears. I said, "I feel the same, like you're like my sister."

To make up for the women who were no longer calling or visiting with the same frequency as before, Riley arranged it so that the various lawyers she was working with staggered their visits. In this way Rick would have too many people coming and going to get too depressed. Her father, who was already doing better because of Rick's intervention, called Rick every afternoon. Riley told me that during one conversation her father had to correct Rick regarding some medical fact, and Rick had been taken aback. But he hadn't said anything; he'd allowed Nick's reproach. "He's nicer to my dad than he is to me," she announced happily. "Me he just bosses around. I think he wants a father figure."

Gloria went a little crazy when the check for $600 didn't arrive. Somehow she got the number for Riley's legal secretary's mother, a woman in her eighties, and left her threatening messages. Apparently Gloria had been bothering the Greenes too, Carmen's sister and brother-in-law, because Riley learned that they had put a restraining order on her. We couldn't imagine why she would be trying to contact them. Finally Gloria, who was nothing if not persistent, got a hold of Riley herself. Riley explained that she was not going to be able to pay her phone bill after all and Gloria responded that she was going to have to do what Nadine the nurse had done then, and go to the media. Riley said, "Go ahead. You'll be sued the very next day." And she hung up. But these extraneous incidents were taking a toll on her; she had lost more weight, she told me on the phone. The next time when she went to see Rick, she was still cranky. She wanted to talk about the appeal and he wanted to tell her how he had almost been raped back in Walpole. She shouted, "Everyone is raped in prison! People live through it. Don't wear it on your sleeve!"

Per Riley's counsel, I brought Gary with me the next time I went to see Rick. He'd agreed to come because he didn't want to disappoint me—and because I promised we'd go to his favorite restaurant that night, and then to a movie that he was more likely to enjoy than I would. We were always making deals like that. It was the secret to the success of our relationship. He'd take long walks on the beach with me if I'd eat at seafood restaurants where I couldn't stand the smell; he'd cook dinner after a long day of work if I'd play tennis with him over the weekend. But in spite of his allegiance to fair play, he couldn't hide the fact that he was in a funk by the time we arrived. Some people are just not cut out for prison visits. All the time we were walking through the lot, going through processing, unloading at the locker and getting buzzed through the various gates, he was scowling. At the fifth gate the guard said to me, "Haven't seen you in a while. Where you been?"

We walked into the visitors room and were about the find a place to sit and wait for Rick when the fire alarm went off. The guard in the room rushed over and announced to everyone there—seven visitors and three inmates—that it was just a fire drill. During a drill everyone has to freeze in place.

We were both in a mood by the time the drill was over, but the sight of Rick approaching snapped us out of it. He had bruises all over his face and arms. He'd been beaten up again. While he was shaking hands with Gary I asked him if he was okay. He whispered, "Not that good."

We settled into our seats, and when it became clear that he wasn't going to tell us what happened, I began to talk about the Gloucester house, a neutral subject. We were getting close to winter now and we *still* hadn't closed. It was maddening. Not only was the septic still a problem, but recently I had learned that the 1999 taxes had never been paid and there was a lien. It would get straightened out—Stephanie and Harrison would satisfy the lien—but in the meantime, I'd had to ask for yet another extension of my mortgage commitment.

I was bummed out all the rest of the day after the visit. Riley had told me Rick needed to see me, that it was an emergency. I'd given him plenty of opportunities to express himself, but he had hardly said anything. It didn't seem like an emergency to me. The next day I confronted Riley and she apologized for making it sound so serious. She said Rick had wanted badly to talk to me but couldn't because Gary was there. I threw my hands up. There was no point in reminding her that she was the one who insisted he come with me.

Chapter Thirty – Letters & Livers

I STILL HAD THE FAT ENVELOPE THAT CONTAINED ALL THE LETTERS NADINE THE nurse had written to Rick, and I took pride in the fact that I hadn't bothered to look at them. But now Riley wanted copies of all of them, in case she needed them for the appeal.

It's hard not to notice a thing or two when you are standing at the copy machine, holding one sheet of paper at the ready in one hand while you're waiting for its predecessor to finish up inside the copier so you can pull it out with the other. Nadine's writing consisted of big loopy letters like a kid's. Her characters were all very consistent in size and angle, very neat. She appeared to have taken her time with them; she was someone who enjoyed the process of writing by hand. In contrast, Rick's handwriting was awful. He didn't loop anything. Many of his letters looked like dashes at different angles. He was lucky to fit five words on a line. Writing was just a vehicle for him, a thing you had to do to get your thoughts on paper.

I read maybe one paragraph from whatever page happened to be in my hand during the time it took for the beam of light to float over the one in the copier. Because they had been packaged in chronological order, I got some sense of how Rick and Nadine's relationship had come to be. Even though whenever she popped up in my mind, my response was negative, I couldn't help but feel some compassion for her. Her early letters included responses to his requests for the latest information on her various health problems. She lived in a constant state of discomfort—both physical and emotional. She wrote about how terrible it was to lose custody of her daughter, who was twelve or so, to her ex-husband, how much she missed her. She said sometimes she would see a drunk stumbling down the street, singing, obviously pain free, and she would say to God, Why me? But their phone calls must have been on much hotter topics, because even the early letters were signed, Your Someday Wife, in a line so straight it looked like she had used a ruler.

Lots of her letters were written in blank "thinking of you" cards, with pictures of cartoon children or animals on the front. Sometimes she wrote her own rather mediocre poems in them. Often she used the card cover as a starting point for sexual innuendos, saying things like "I'll name your puppy if you name my kitty." Her envelopes were sealed with yellow smiley face stickers, which I favored myself. In one letter she created an acronym out of the letters in his name: Refreshing, Intense, Charming, Horny, Amazing,

Remorseful, Diligent, Sensual, Heartfelt, Aspiring, Ready, Passionate, Enamored.

As their relationship progressed, it moved from innocent endearments to pure fantasy. She wrote about how it would be when they married and spent their first night in a conjugal trailer. She wrote about the oral sex acts she would perform on him. She spent a lot of ink trying to persuade him that no one was as good in bed as she was. In case he didn't believe her, she tallied up the men who had said so over the years.

Some letters got pretty graphic, describing very specific sexual fantasies, such as him coming up behind her and touching her nipples while she was sitting in her writing chair, and her spinning around and pulling down his pants...and, well, etc.

In one rather heartbreaking letter Nadine told Rick about a phone conversation she'd had with her daughter, Jillian. Jillian was upset because she'd come upon a baby bird that had fallen out of its nest and she thought it might die. Nadine had her go out and check to see if it had its flight feathers yet while she held on. Jillian came back to the phone and said it did. Then Nadine told her to go out and watch for the mama bird and see if the baby would try to follow its mama when she appeared. Thirty minutes later Jillian called back to say that the mama hadn't shown up, that the baby bird didn't seem to be moving. Nadine told her to get a heat pad, paper towels and a desk lamp and make it a small aquarium, an incubator. Jillian probably wouldn't be able to save it, but she could at least make it comfortable until it died.

In reading that, I knew that in some sense Nadine saw Rick that way, that in spite of her fits of anger and propensity for revenge, she had come to him with good intentions, to make him a nest from the only materials she had, strings of information about herself, the dry grass of fantasy.

In some letters she mentioned me. She complained that Rick's family, meaning Bruce, and Harry before he'd died, had accepted me, but not her. She said that maybe she should move out of the way so that I could step in. She had planted her own seed and it had grown into a tall green tree of jealously.

By the summer of 2002 she was writing that she wasn't getting much information out of Rick's letters anymore. Her conclusion: that I was trying to end their relationship. "Well, Richard," she said in one letter, "she forgives you and you're a convict and she thinks our relationship is sick." In another letter she said she was shocked to learn how he really felt about her sexual fantasies, that she had no idea, that she thought he enjoyed them, that she'd never write to him about sex again. It was not long after that that she did the interviews.

I finished up with the letters and put the originals in a box, along the same wall where I was saving my prison stories and some of the stuff that Lola had asked me to store. Then I left the room hurriedly, because really it was exhausting being on the fringe of so much drama. The phone rang. It was Riley but I didn't have enough emotional energy to answer it.

ଽଠଔ

For all that Riley was doing everything in her power to keep Rick out of the news, it just wasn't going to happen. Rick was a magnet for drama, and that was all there was to it. In late fall his most loyal media disciple, *Herald* reporter Shane Field, provided the reading public with yet another breaking news story, the title of which was "Slay doc's scam: Sick woman: Killer reneged on liver offer." The article explained that "gender-bending wife-killer Dr. Richard J. Sharpe" had promised to give a woman, identified only as Gloria, part of his liver but instead took her for hundreds of dollars in phone calls and tricked her into sending birthday cards to his estranged minor children. Gloria claimed she was furious when she learned that he was not allowed to have any contact with his kids, that she never would have sent the cards had she known. Gloria told Field that she had written to the Massachusetts Department of Corrections earlier in the year to see if Rick could make the organ donation and she had even considered marrying him to facilitate the process. Then, more recently, she received a letter from Rick saying that out of respect for his children and the memory of his wife he had to decline her offer of what he said would be a "sham marriage." However, Michael Goodman, the lawyer who was answering the allegations on Rick's behalf, said that Rick hadn't backed out of his commitment, that he remained willing to give up half his liver as long as he didn't have to marry Gloria.

Gary and I got a message the night of the day the story broke from a frantic Riley saying she was losing her fucking mind and would we meet her for dinner at the Hilton. Of course we went. She had calmed down some by the time we arrived. She said they could sue Gloria for the story in the *Herald*. She already had someone back home checking to find out her real name. It didn't matter who said what anyway, because Rick was in a mental facility and donating a liver part was prohibited. It was all nonsense. Shane Field should have fact checked. Anything for a story. She would sue him too. Then she switched gears to tell us that she'd had to fire her limo driver. She'd fallen asleep in the back of the limo, and when she woke up she found him leaning over her with his hand in her shirt. Now she was getting around in a Volvo rental.

It occurred to me that she might dump Rick at some point, that she might come to believe, as had so many others, that he was just too much maintenance. But, in fact, once she got over the shock of the Gloria story, she went back about her work with as much energy as ever. She was still sending Dr. Greenberg's report to everyone in charge at the prison and insisting that Rick be transferred to a minimum security area where he would once again have access to library facilities and where he would not be beat up as often. She even claimed she went to see then Governor Romney so that he would know who she was if ever the threat of Walpole should loom again.

Sure enough, Rick was eventually moved to Max 1. The first time I visited him there, with Lucy instead of Gary, I had to go behind the curtain in the security check room for a strip search. This was only the second or third time I had been strip searched in all the time I had been visiting. When I saw the guard putting on her latex gloves, I explained that I was allergic to latex. She said, "Fine, if you don't like it, leave." She patted my breasts, crotch, anus, and my legs right down to my ankles. Then she was silent for twenty seconds, checking off boxes on her pad, before she gave me my paperwork and locker key and let me get dressed. I figured this was one way the guards would get even for the "special" treatment Rick was receiving in being transferred back to minimum security.

Rick came into the visiting room looking surprised and happy. His hair had been cut short and he was clean shaven and looked rested. His gray prison cottons, with DOC stitched over the front top pocket (for Department of Corrections of course, but I liked to think it was because he was a doctor) looked freshly laundered and I didn't see any bruises on him. I still felt like I was breathing latex. I coughed a few times and felt light-headed. The room fan felt good, but Rick asked the CO to turn it off because he was cold.

Now that he was out of Max 2, Rick was ready to talk about the last time he had been beaten up there. An inmate by the name of Victor Ward came up to Rick when he was working in the laundry room and punched him so hard he fell to the floor. He put his hands over his face to protect himself and waited for a guard to notice what was going on. Finally one did and Rick thought the incident was over, but later that day he was called in to see Lance, one of the social workers. Rick had heard the rumor that Lance had a romantic interest in Victor, but rumors like that abound in prisons and he hadn't given it much thought—until Lance accused him of provoking Victor with his "angry eyes." Rick was upset. Not much he could do to change his eyes. "I never hurt anyone," he said to Lance. Lance quickly reminded him that he killed his wife. Rick in turn reminded Lance that Victor had put a knife through his mother's heart and tried to disembowel his father. Victor was into mutilation big time. He entertained the more vulgar inmates with childhood memories about disemboweling neighbors' pets and leaving them on their doorsteps.

Of course the big news at that time, which had taken place not in Bridgewater but in one of the other prisons in the Massachusetts system, was about Joseph Druce, a convicted murderer who had recently killed John Geoghan, the former Roman Catholic priest who had been at the center of the sexual abuse scandal. Geoghan, who was accused of molesting more than one hundred and thirty children over three decades, was repeatedly shuffled from one parish to another by his superiors, and the Archdiocese of Boston paid $10 million to settle the legal claims of the eighty-six plaintiffs who sued the church for his alleged abuse. But in spite of all his church support he still wound up in jail. Druce trapped Geoghan in his cell and jammed the door closed so that the guards couldn't get in while he strangled and stomped Geoghan to death.

The other big news was about John McIntyre, who had been at Bridgewater, though in a halfway house rather than in the prison facility. After nineteen years of incarceration, for raping a couple of little boys, he was just about ready to be released. And what did he do but use an electric cord to lower himself two floors down onto the facility grounds. Somehow he climbed over an eighteen-foot-high razor wire fence and escaped. An alarm was tripped, sure enough, but the guard on duty took it to be some kind of mechanical failure. McIntyre spent a couple of chilly nights hiding in the woods, evading K9 units and search copters, but then a town worker recognized him on a residential street. He was back now, and the guard who had blown off the tripped alarm had been fired. One more example of our tax dollars at work. Both stories had already found their way into my collection.

Also in my collection were stories reporting that Romney was launching a top-to-bottom investigation of the entire Massachusetts prison system— though Rick and I agreed that it wouldn't do much good. When the governor's men came calling, everything would look just fine. There wouldn't be any shit on the floors or any fighting or any of the other stuff that Rick had been describing for some years. There were mysterious deaths all the time, not only murders but prisoners who died of cardiac arrest, probably because their meds hadn't been mixed right, and bed sheet hangings that were regarded as suicides. Those mystery deaths weren't likely to happen when Romney's people were inspecting.

Rick, Lucy and I talked about Stephanie for a while. She had also been in the news. She was still in the process of suing the Greenes for full custody of the younger kids. So much of the money that had been in their trust had been eaten up in legal fees. Rick was sick over the whole thing. Then we talked about Riley, although Rick was mostly tightlipped about the progress they were making toward his appeal.

Lucy and I stopped at Dunkin Donuts afterward. Rick had been so happy to see Lucy, and he had talked so fast, and about so much, that it seemed impossible that we had only been there for two hours. Ours heads were still spinning. Over a cup of coffee Lucy reiterated her distrust of Riley. Now she thought it was possible that Riley had been hired by Carmen's family to determine if Rick had some money hidden away somewhere that no one had come across yet. Given the fact that he still spent a good percentage of his time trying to get his supporters to start businesses that would generate money, I found that highly unlikely, but I didn't say anything. Instead I stared at the couple in their sixties sitting in the booth across from us. They had come from Bridgewater too. I had seen them in the visitors room. Their expressions were identical. Both were totally vacant-eyed, as if they'd just walked out of a horrible disaster. When we got back in the car I said to Lucy, "You see that couple across from us? They didn't even talk to each other." Prison can be a shocking experience if you're not used to it.

Chapter Thirty-One – Closure

AFTER ALL THIS TIME LOLA WAS STILL CALLING ROBARE, THE SUPERINTENDENT AT Bridgewater, to argue that she had a right to visit Rick. But he was scared to death of Riley, apparently, because he continued to find excuses to keep Lola out. Riley asked me, "What, is Lola still in love with him?" I said she wasn't, she just wanted visiting privileges. It was a matter of principal. She hadn't done anything wrong. Riley and I were on the phone. She must have heard the edge in my voice because she changed the subject. "My father loves Rick," she said. "And Rick loves him too. Rick actually cries when he talks to him about his illness." She took a breath. "I'll get him out," she said, "because he can cure so many people once he's on the outside. Carmen never loved him. He realizes that now. He's had some crying and shaking episodes, but he'll be okay. He doesn't trust anyone anymore except me and you. Did you know that Kate and Naomi started a rumor that I'm sleeping with Goodman?" I hadn't heard that. "Rick's upset about it. That's their way of getting even because I had them back off."

Except for my conversations with Riley and occasional calls from Lola, who was for the most part getting on with her life, my focus was on domestic issues. I *still* had not closed on the Gloucester house. The realtors and lawyers had worked out that a septic tank of some sort would have to go in soon, and the sellers had put $15,000 aside in escrow to that purpose. I was willing to close and deal with the septic later, if the City of Gloucester Department of Health would agree to waive the Title 5 for the time being. I just wanted to get in before my latest mortgage commitment expired and interest rates jumped.

Thinking the closing would not be far off, I called one of the Gloucester neighbors, Margaret, a woman I had met at a party when the house belonged to Rick and Carmen. I was hoping she would remember me and give me some indication that I would be welcomed into the neighborhood. But as soon as I identified myself, she turned cold and said that she couldn't talk, that she had someone on the other line. She said to call back some other time.

I called a local heating company to arrange to have the oil tank filled after the closing. The oil man at least seemed happy to know I would be the new owner. In fact, we talked for a while and he told me that his wife once had skin cancer and Rick had treated her on several occasions. "He was an excellent doctor," he said. "If she hadn't found him, I don't know what would have happened."

At the last minute my real estate lawyer, Aubrey, got the word from the Department of Health that the tank had to be installed prior to the closing, even if it meant changing the closing date yet again. This didn't sit well at all with the sellers. Harrison said it made no sense for him to install the tank when I might continue to delay or even walk. If I wanted the septic tank installed before the closing, he said, I should pay for it and then the associated expenses could be deducted at the closing. This would be an incentive for me to follow through. Otherwise, he would remove the cabinets and take back the house and find another buyer. This was upsetting to hear, but on my side was the fact that I knew the family and they knew me, and I had been patient all this time. The truth was that while there had been many lookers, in the end, no one to date—except me—had wanted to own the house that Rick had lived in.

By then the town had perused the plans for the tank we had been considering and had informed Aubrey that our tank of choice was likely to effect the wetlands in a negative way. The whole situation was becoming a nightmare. Harrison's escrow wasn't going to solve the problem. Aubrey let the sellers' team know that she didn't appreciate the drama and threats and their display of obnoxious behavior. She wrote a letter to the sellers' attorney saying that my offer had been accepted over a year ago. To insinuate that I might walk after everything I'd been through was craziness. I lost five pounds that week.

On November 20, 2003 a tight tank system, paid for by the sellers, was installed, finally, and the closing was pending its inspection. This type of tank was more affordable and would make sense until the town got around to creating its sewer system, which I could then hook up to. By then it had been weeks since I'd talked to Rick. I just didn't have the time. But in the middle of December I finally picked up one of his calls. He knew (Riley had surely told him that I was going crazy with the closing) to keep it simple. And I knew, from Riley, that the Latto trial, which had been pending, had been delayed because now another currently unidentified prisoner had come forward to say he had information. The DA Roger Robertson couldn't meet with him until after the new year and so couldn't determine whether or not he was a potentially viable witness.

With the serious stuff understood on both sides, I asked him if he was getting his *Science News* and *Discovery* magazines. I had just renewed both for another year. He said he hadn't received either yet and I told him to check with the mail room. He agreed they were probably there. "No one steals science magazines," he said flatly. Then I asked him if he was eating okay, if he was brushing his teeth, if the temp filling that Joan had put in his molar was holding up. I could have been talking to a child, but as prisoners don't get the same access to healthcare that the rest of us get, there is potential for them to slack off and let their health deteriorate. Even doctors. Rick said he didn't have much of an appetite lately, but he was flossing every day, and his molar was doing fine. We talked for a while about the best kinds of floss to use. I asked him if he knew how many teeth were in the mouth and he said, "Of course I do, Linda. Thirty-two." In the middle of our conversation we were interrupted by a recording saying "this call is being monitored and recorded." We went back to talking about dental hygiene.

The house closed on December 19, 2003. I couldn't believe it had finally happened. Gary and I drove over right after the closing to have a look around. I found one of Rick's business cards on the floor, from back when he was president, CEO and co-founder of Arcturus Pharmaceutical, years ago. He and his partner had raised over $9 million to start Arcturus, which developed all kinds of products for skin disorders. I also found some paperwork for ClickMed, the company that created software for physicians, from back in 1995. And there was a bulletin board in the basement identifying people who had bought various versions of Rick's women's health tracking software program and what each party had paid for them. Once client, identified only by a surname, had paid almost $30,000 back in 1998; several air force bases had paid between $5000 and $12,000; a women's health clinic had paid just over $1000 for what must have been a simplified version of the program, as had several private ob/gyns and a federal prison camp. The list went on and on and included clients across the country and even one in Europe. I found some pictures as well. And his license to practice medicine from 1993.... Funny how life can change in a heartbeat.

Chapter Thirty-Two – The Gloucester House: Dream or Nightmare?

IT WOULD BE AWHILE YET UNTIL GARY AND I WOULD BE ABLE TO MOVE INTO THE house. It needed a lot of work, and since it was my dream house, I wanted it to be perfect. I had gotten it for a good price, or so I thought at the time, and because I had refinanced the Newton house, I had cash for renovations. In the meantime, I planned to concentrate on fixing up the apartment above the garage—where Stephanie had once lived, where Rick had once had his office and lab—so that Gary and I could stay there while we worked on the rest of the property.

As soon as we were able to iron out some of the major problems—an example: the toilet in the apartment began to leak as soon as we had the water turned on—we started going over on weekends, so as to get to know our new neighborhood and work out what exactly had to be done. It was my house now, but it was hard to forget that it had belonged to Rick (and Carmen!). There were traces of Rick's persona everywhere.

His most obvious mark was on what Gary and I called the "electrical command center," a patch panel which serviced and connected 177 phone lines and computer access points, totaling 708 wire connections in his Ethernet system. There was a 200-amp service which fed over 122 plugs and outlets; a typical home this size might have 60 to 65 receptacles. Every phone jack in the house was labeled and numbered. Rick could access the computer wherever he happened to be. This entire electrical command center was located in the basement furnace room, connecting all phones, electrical and Internet lines. Being in that small room was like being in a jungle, full of vines of current, voltaic hissing snakes slithering into other parts of the house. Sometimes it was almost scary to pass the furnace room and think of the power that had been generated there. In many ways, it seemed a metaphor for Rick's mind—brilliant, but utterly excessive.

At Rick's suggestion we had Dexter in, the same telecommunications engineer who had put the electrical command center together in the first place. Now he would have to break it down, simplify it for Gary and me. Dexter was a small, white-haired man with a red face and a pot belly, a cross between a leprechaun and Merlyn the Magician. He was quite chatty, offering as many particulars on his observations of Rick and his family as he did on the underground cables he had installed to animate the command center. Rick had insisted on hard wiring for his computers because he felt it would better protect him from hackers, which was ironic given that, I happened to know, he'd hacked the websites of a few competitors himself.

Although I had not asked, Dexter was adamant that contrary to what others might think, the Sharpe house was "straight": his work had required him to be in and out of every closet in the place, and if there had been wigs or any other cross-dressing items, he insisted, he would have seen them. Rick already had four full-time people working there when Dexter had first gone to make the installations. Dexter described the scene as a madhouse, with cars everywhere and the kids and their friends running around and computers and office equipment all over the place. Carmen was not happy with all the wiring and the phone and computer lines, he assured me. Her house was no longer a home. He could see that it was troubling her, but somehow Rick was unable to figure it out. Rick was bright but preoccupied, and also clumsy, Dexter added. He would run around the house with a laptop in one hand, a cup of coffee in the other, tripping over his shoelaces. I assumed he was speaking metaphorically as Rick's shoes didn't have laces in those days. Dexter related that once he had arrived in the morning to find Rick running around in his skivvies. On and on he rattled, embellishing his stories. Once, he said, he'd come over to find Rick running through the house with the laptop and the coffee and no bottoms at all!

The house had been Rick's hobby as well as his abode. Now it would be my hobby. But I didn't plan to let it take over my life. For one thing, I still needed to find time every few weeks to visit Rick. I hardly spoke to him on the phone anymore—there just weren't enough hours in the day—and I had never written to him much to begin with.

I visited about a month after the closing, but he was too upset to want to share my enthusiasm for my plans for the house. He'd gotten copies of the documents regarding Stephanie's custody battle over his younger kids. She'd won the battle, he said, and he began to cry. He kept his head down for so long I thought he'd gone into a state of shock. I tried to feel compassion, but on that day at that time it only made me angry to have to sit there waiting for him to recover. Fitting him in was a sacrifice—always. I hadn't been strip searched this time, but I'd still had to fill out all the paperwork and go through the metal detectors and all the gates and show the guard that I didn't have any pockets. And Rick wasn't the only one I planned to visit that weekend. My mother was in the hospital again. She'd stopped taking all her pills and had gone into a deep depression. The week before I hadn't heard

from her, and when I went to call her, I learned that the phone was discon-
nected. I knew the signs, and I was planning on taking her to the hospital
anyway, but before I could get over there, she collapsed outside a local convenience store and they called 911. I was relieved—because she would have
fought me tooth and nail about going in voluntarily. Why had she stopped
taking her pills to begin with? She'd been getting them from one pharmacy
and then she'd switched to another pharmacy. The generic brand for her
thyroid pill at the new pharmacy didn't look like the one they'd given her
at the other place. She assumed that meant she was being poisoned. So she
stopped taking everything. On top of that, she was upset because I'd just
bought Rick's house.

When Rick finally came out of his funk, not long before it was time for
visitors to leave, I tried to lighten things up by asking if he'd ever stashed any
money in the house. In fact, he said, he'd squirreled some cash away in the
attic years ago. But Carmen knew about it, had helped him decide where
to hide it, and would have taken it with her when she left. He asked me if
I'd left the propane stove in the kitchen. "Why?" I asked. In fact it had been
one of the first things to go. He said, "In case the power goes out. That way
you'll always be able to cook."

I hadn't thought of that. My concerns had more to do with spiders and
mice. As if reading my thoughts, he switched gears to tell me about a mouse
that he was domesticating. He had six roommates in the dorm he was now
living in. The mouse had been on one of their beds and Rick had managed to
catch it by its tail. He'd made it a nest in his locker. But one roommate didn't
like it and let it get out and Rick had to catch it all over again. He was feeding it well—salami, cheese, water—to keep it happy. He said he got good at
catching them in the old days, when they would use them for experiments
at the various labs where he'd worked. He never thought he would have one
as a pet. His eyes teared up again and he asked if I'd spoken to Bruce and
when he would be visiting. In the state Rick was in I didn't think it would
help to remind him that having the cops show up at his house a few years
back, to ask whether Bruce had agreed to give a hit man money to pop Latto
on Rick's behalf, had sort of jiggled Bruce. The guy had heart problems to
begin with. His visits had been less and less frequent since, and I figured it
wouldn't be long before they faded out altogether.

The highlight of our conversation that day was Riley's dad. Rick was
able to report that his pulmonary fibrosis was in remission now, and he

was feeling better than ever. His renewed health was due to the formula that Rick had worked out for him. Riley had found a cardiologist who was willing to write the prescription for it when her dad's own doctor refused to get involved, because the formula was not FDA approved. Nick inhaled the magic formula—which administered a protein that regenerated lung tissue—through a nebulizer. According to Rick (I hadn't talked to Riley myself in some time, again because of day-to-day busyness), Nick's gray hair had turned blonde again and he now was renting out empty rooms in his house to students and had even gone dancing with a group of them once or twice. Rick wanted the formula published on the Internet—so that other people with the disease could benefit from it. I said I would look into it, but I hoped he was asking other people too, because I couldn't imagine where I would find the time. Little did I know then that in the months to come my "free time" would diminish even further.

ಜಿ೮ಚ

Back when Oscar was still alive, I had contracted with Andy, Oscar's foreman, for the work at the Newton house. And I had started off giving him the Gloucester work too. I should have gotten other estimates, but Oscar had insisted I could trust Andy, so there didn't seem to be much point. Andy had Barry, the owner of the kitchen store (who had been a friend of Oscar's too) do the custom cabinets for the Gloucester kitchen. I gave Barry a check for $15,000 as a down payment for what he said would be a $25,000 job. But I failed to write "for the kitchen cabinets" on the memo line. Once the cabinets were finished, the cabinet designer, Lindsey, told me that she needed to collect $25,000 from me on behalf of Barry. I explained that I had already paid $15,000, so therefore I only owed $10,000. When I confronted Barry, he said that the $15,000 was only a consultation fee, and that I did in fact still owe $25,000 for the work. Lindsey, who had become a friend, and I discussed the matter between ourselves. She happened to know that Andy owed Barry money for another job, and she surmised getting an extra $15,000 out of me was Andy's way of squaring things up with Barry. She was so upset to think this might be the case that she told Barry she wouldn't work with him anymore and she and her dog moved back to Canada.

I took Andy and Barry to court. They showed up, the both of them, with alcohol on their breath. They lied under oath, insisting that it was clear from the get-go that the $15,000 was a consultation fee. Lindsey was nowhere to be found by then, so she couldn't stand up for me. Since there was reasonable doubt, the judge ruled in their favor.

To make matters worse, when the cabinets had first come in, back before I even owned the house, Chase, the realtor, had opened the door for Andy so that he could receive them from the shipping company. Andy signed off on them. But he never checked the actual inventory against the shipping list. When Barry put the kitchen together much later, some cabinet doors were missing. Since everything had been signed for, I had to pay $2000 to have the pieces remade and reshipped from Canada. The manufacturer insisted on sending the pieces to Barry (because of some import issue), which meant that even though I was furious with him for ripping me off and never wanted to see him again, I had to beg him to come by to deliver and install the pieces. In end, he sent two of his workers to do the job.

In hindsight I could see that Andy and the people who worked for and with him had been cheating me from day one. I'd just been too busy with the rest of life to take notice. Or maybe I was in denial because Andy had been Oscar's man. Andy had told me the work at the Newton House would cost $150,000, which I thought was reasonable for renovating the existing structure and adding a large addition that would feature a master suite over a two-car garage. The house was worth about $500,000 in the inflated market of the times, without any renovations whatsoever. The idea Andy (and Oscar) sold me on was that if I put up $150,000 for renovations and the addition, I would increase the value of the house by $250,000 and the house would thus sell for $750,000, adding an additional $100,000 to the profit I would make.

During the course of the work, Andy would ask me for the money in bits and pieces, as he needed it to pay various tradesmen…$5000 for backhoe work, $10,000 for the electrician, etc. I never saw any receipts. I just gave him what he needed. But I wrote everything down. By the time we reached the $150,000 mark, the new addition was structurally complete. From the outside it looked great; but on the inside it still lacked Sheetrock and baseboard and flooring, etc. Since the finishing work had been included in our contract, I assumed Andy would complete the job without asking for more money. But once he found out we'd gone through the $150,000, he said he'd have to talk to his lawyer before he could do any more work. He pretty much disappeared after that.

I had to sell the Newton house, so I had no choice but to oversee the remaining work myself. I had five credit cards, and between them I was able to get everything done. I figured I could pay them off as soon as the house sold. In fact, when all was said and done, the addition cost me another $100,000, for a grand total of $250,000. This meant that if the house sold for the projected $750,000, I would have endured two years of nonstop construction headaches for absolutely nothing.

There had been a smaller incident early on too, a precursor of what was to come. Andy said it would cost me $5000 to have an outside contractor, his guy Hal, come in to do some painting, and that I should pay Hal directly. Hal asked for cash, and against my better judgment, I gave it to him, but I had him write out a receipt for it. Later Hal and Andy tried to tell me that I still owed for the painting. They said it in front of other people. I turned white. I brought the receipt out and that was the end of that. No harm trying, they must have been thinking.

Oscar was still alive when the incident with Hal occurred, but by then he was quite sick and I didn't want to bother him about something I'd managed to settle on my own. Also, a funny thing had happened between Oscar and me, and it kept me from feeling the candidness that had always been the trademark of our relationship. Oscar had come to the Newton house one day to see how the renovations were progressing. We were in the middle of a conversation about ceramic tile when suddenly, out of nowhere, he reached out and grabbed my left breast. I screamed, "What are you doing? I'm never talking to you again! Get out and don't come back!" I felt totally betrayed. It made me think back to a time when I'd gone with my stepfather to MacDonald's, back when I was twelve or thirteen, and he tried to touch me in the car. I'd turned to Al and said, "That's wrong," and he responded quickly, "You're right." I never wanted my sister or mother to disrespect him, so I didn't tell anyone. But I was on guard ever after when I had to be alone with him.

Oscar left that day with his head hanging and his tail between his legs. A few hours later he called and apologized. I said I didn't want to talk to him and hung up. I was very upset. I had loved him like a father for a long time. He had treated me like a daughter up until then. There was virtually nothing he could have done that would have hurt my feelings more. Later that day the phone rang again, a woman who was a close friend to both Oscar and his wife. She said, "Look, Oscar is really, really sorry. He's had so many physiological changes as a result of being sick. He's been obsessing about not being able to have an erection, and he had that on his mind when he did it. He didn't plan it. It was an impulse, an impulse he never would have acted on if not for all the meds he's taking."

An impulse he never would have acted on if not for the meds.... I was stunned when I realized that his misbehavior was a microcosm of the blueprint of Rick's downfall. I forgave Oscar and we never discussed it again. But then I only saw him a few more times before he died.

Luckily, as soon as the Newton house went on the market we had a buyer for it. It sold for $735,000. I made money (basically I got my initial down payment back) in spite of being ripped off by Andy, and thus I was able to settle the credit card debt that I had accrued. In the meantime, Gary and I were not ready to move in full time at the Gloucester house or even into the apartment over the garage. For one thing, the drive would have been too much on days when we had to be at work. So we found ourselves a small studio apartment in the Newton area and went to Gloucester on the weekends.

Once the apartment over the garage was in pretty good shape, I hired a young woman, Nazera, to go through all of Rick's patient folders in the garage and put them in alphabetical order, in case he needed them for his appeal. I had her sign a confidentiality document, just in case she recognized someone's name and felt inclined to take a peek. There were over five thousand folders (some quite thick, indicating patients who'd had ongoing services) in black plastic trash bags spread out over the floor. In fact, the construction people had thought they were trash and wanted to throw them in the dumpster and get them out of the way. Luckily they checked with me first. I bought forty plastic flip-top file boxes for Nazera to transfer the files into. It took several eight-hour days for her to get through all of them. When I could, I worked with her. When we were done, we stacked the boxes to one side of the two-car garage, but they still took up half the garage. Gary and I would never be able to shelter both our cars at the same time—at least as long as I kept the files.

Every weekend, Gary and I would get a visit from Rosemary, one of the neighborhood dogs. We had first encountered her, a beautiful reddish Golden Lab, at a party that Rick and Carmen had thrown in the summer of 1998. She'd been a puppy then, jumping on all the children and running and playing for hours on end. Now she six; she was much calmer but just as sweet. She would come to the sliding glass door at the back of the house and tap with her paw until we heard her. We always let her in. Gary began to buy special biscuits for her visits, as well as toys and balls. They would play for a half an hour or so. She knew a lot of tricks, and sometimes he would make her work, having her roll over and give him her paw before he gave her a treat. When she saw that he was pooping out, she would look over her shoulder at the door and he would open it and off she would go, with her feathery tail wagging behind her.

Her visits became a ray of light in a period of my life that seemed to darken by the day.

Chapter Thirty-Three – Synchronicity

SYNCHRONICITY" IS A FASCINATING CONCEPT. BASICALLY IT MEANS THAT JUST AS events may be grouped together by cause and effect, they may also be grouped by meaning—in other words, by coincidence. I had always thought of myself as my own woman; I was an entrepreneur and, in more recent years, a risk taker. I'd learned not to let anything stand in my way when I wanted something. But then a series of incidents occurred—beginning maybe with Oscar's act of disrespect at the end of his life and Andy's attempts to rip me off—that left me feeling vulnerable. I began to feel again like the little girl who lived daily with the threat of an orphanage hanging over her head, the young woman who was so insecure that she was afraid to go off to college.

As I said, I hadn't had a lot of time to spend with Riley. But I hadn't forgotten about her. I still considered her Rick's angel and my dear friend. I was thrilled when the dust settled enough post closing that I was able to accept an invitation to visit her.

These days when she was in town, which was most of the time, she was living in a remote rental on the South Shore rather than staying in hotels. So I drove out there to see her. I'd been there a few times before, but this was the first time I didn't get lost and was able to appreciate what a beautiful area it was—a resort community with pretty houses all along the bayside beach.

Her "cottage" was spectacular. It was right on the bay and it featured floor-to-ceiling windows along two walls in the living room overlooking the water. I hugged her upon entering and sat in an armchair near the windows while she went into the kitchen to get me a soda. But when she came back, she said I should sit on the sofa. She took my wrist and steered me toward it. At first I didn't think much of it. For whatever reason she wanted me to sit where she wanted me to sit. Sometimes people try to manipulate seating arrangements because they have hearing problems. If they settle you near their good ear, the problem is solved and they don't have to explain their deficiency. But I never thought of Riley as the kind of person who would try to conceal any flaws. I already knew all about her health problems, as well as those of her husband, father, dogs and cat.

But the seating issue was not the only aberration that day. Riley stayed on her feet most of the time I was there. When she did sit, she sat on the edge of the chair. And she kept making excuses to leave the room…to blow her nose, use the bathroom, check that a window was closed in the bedroom….

When she was in the living room, she kept her hands in her pockets, and I began to imagine that she had a tape recorder in one of them. As for our conversation, it began with her reiterating that she didn't want Naomi or Kate or Lola communicating with Rick. She seemed to want my reaction to that. But with all the demons in my head, I was not inclined to give her one. She also asked me a bunch of questions which seemed strange, including how I would describe the room we were sitting in. I shrugged. Then I looked around and described it for her. She stared at me when I was done, as if to say she'd hoped for more from me.

When she started talking about Rick, she seemed to get breathy, as if the thought of him evoked some emotion. I swear she looked like Marilyn Monroe for a moment, standing in front of me, one hand splayed across her chest and the other sweeping her blond locks away from her face and neck. I sat forward. This was interesting to me. She had always shown passion for the case, but now it seemed to me that she was showing passion for the man. I said, "Riley, you're in love with him, aren't you?"

Her expression changed immediately. She looked at me like I was crazy for a long moment, and then she went totally cold. She asked me if I wanted anything else to drink in a snappy way that suggested we were wrapping things up, though I hadn't been there nearly long enough to justify the hour it took to drive there. When I got up to use the bathroom before hitting the road, I passed her bedroom and couldn't help but notice that it was a total wreck, with clothes strewn all over the floor.

After that evening she stopped talking my calls. I would have apologized if she'd picked up, but she didn't, and eventually I stopped trying. When I next saw Rick, I could tell that he was being very careful about what he said to me. No matter what I asked him, if it concerned Riley, or by extension, his appeal, he answered vaguely, without any details. This was very annoying to me. I had been his savior back when he didn't have a legal team, back in the days when I had to pay Lucy, my personal lawyer, to consult with him. I was good enough when he needed a favor, when he wanted canteen money or a magazine subscription renewed. But now, as far as the important stuff was concerned, I was on the sidelines. I felt used and manipulated.

He'd been working out, and that was what he wanted to talk about. He'd run two hours that day, he said. One thousand sit-ups. Two hundred push-ups. "Look at my muscles," he said. "Touch my biceps." I said, "Are you crazy, I'll get banned." "Go ahead," he said. I looked around. Then I quickly poked his upper arm with one fingertip.

At around the same time that Riley got mad at me, I began to have problems with Bruce about the laser. Our deal was that when the three-year lease was up, he would sell me the laser for $1.00. But after only one year, I decided to tell Bruce to find another client, that it would make more sense for me to go out and buy my own laser. At the time he begged me to stick with the contract, and as I didn't want to take the chance that he wouldn't find another client for it and might get stuck with a laser he himself had no use for, I agreed. But now the three-year mark had come and gone, and the paperwork for the sale transaction was not forthcoming. I had paid Bruce $194,708 over the three years. The original price of the laser was $79,500. I learned, from contacting the laser company directly, that there was a payout amount due, for $9,000. Bruce seemed to think that it was my responsibility to satisfy it.

Bruce had backed me into a corner. I could not do without the laser. Those days were over. While the electrolysis part of my business would always be essential for some, I had plenty of clients who had come to depend on the quick efficiency of the laser. About fifty percent of my laser clients wanted Brazilians (completely hairless around their genitals, including around the anus area) or pubic cleanups just below the bathing suit line, or they wanted their triangles downsized, or they wanted what's called a "landing strip." People were getting very creative and very specific. Some were athletes who wanted less friction when running or cycling. Others just wanted to look good. Others did it for hygienic purposes. The other fifty percent needed face work or back or chest, etc. I needed the laser. It wouldn't have made sense to go out and get another one after I had already paid two and a half times the cost to Bruce for the one I was already using. I had no choice but to drain my savings and pay the buyout cost, and still Bruce did not send the paperwork that would have confirmed the laser was finally mine.

Also during this time I took Andy to court. When I was called before the judge, I went up pulling a roller suitcase behind me. It contained Andy's original contract for the Newton house work, copies of all the checks I had given him, documents designating the projects he'd worked on, lists of the ones he'd failed to do, day calendars, credit card statements, and much more. There were a lot of other people in the courtroom waiting for their cases to be heard. I could hear some of them muttering and sighing behind me when they saw me lift the heavy case onto a table in front of the judge and unzip it to display its contents. I guess they thought I'd be there all day. Even the judge looked nervous. He asked me and Lorraine, the lawyer I'd hired, to go out in the waiting area and go through the documents and find the ones that were essential to the case. We did as we were told. I might have gone overboard, but when the judge asked me a question, I had the answer. In the end he was impressed.

The judge determined that Andy owed me $73,000, and he awarded me triple damages. But there was a time gap from when I'd first found Lorraine Littleton and begun the suit and the day we all wound up in the courthouse in Cambridge. And during that gap, crafty Andy had moved his assets around. Now everything he owned was in trusts. He had no money of his own. The only way I would ever be able to recover damages is if I went after his heirs after his death.

Yes, the stars seemed to be aligning, but not in my favor.

ଓଓଔ

One day over the summer I went to visit Rick and learned that Riley was there working with him. I said to the guard, "Can you check if I can visit with both of them?" I was hoping that Riley and I could mend things and get back on track with our friendship. The guard went off and a few minutes later the phone in the waiting room buzzed and I was told to go in.

Rick was coming into the visitors room from one door while I was coming in from another. We met in the middle, embraced and found a place to sit. He said he had a half-hour. Riley was waiting in the client-attorney meeting room for him to get back to work with her on his appeal. He mentioned that he might need some of his medical records soon, and I was happy to be able to inform him that I'd had them alphabetized and placed in boxes in the garage. He asked if I'd heard from Lola. I said we kept in touch. He told me to tell her to get out of the stock market, to sell everything except Microsoft, because the market was going to crash. Then he asked if I'd talked to Gloria. I hadn't. He said, "I can't write or talk to any women." I said, "Well, I guess I'm okay because I'm here." He nodded. "You're the only one."

He asked about the neighbors in Gloucester. I told him that Gary and I had been invited to a party and we'd met lots of people. What I didn't say was that when I said I'd bought the Sharpe house, everyone talked about what a sweetheart Carmen had been; no one mentioned him. It was as if he'd been erased from the collective neighborhood memory, as if he'd never existed. Some people were nervous when they found out where we lived and got away from us quickly. One woman told me she was sure the house was haunted.

I felt anxious knowing that Riley was waiting somewhere in the wings for me to finish up my visit with him. But as Rick seemed unconcerned, I tried to relax and not look at the clock. While he had been discreet the last time I'd seen him, now he said he was very lonely and he wished I would visit more.

He asked me if I'd heard what had happened at Walpole. Who hadn't? It had begun when the doors in the maximum security unit started popping open—due to some mechanical problem—and the state's most dangerous inmates suddenly found themselves free to escape from their cells. According to the papers, they went crazy, stabbing one another, stealing drugs, throwing feces around, ripping toilets off the walls, attacking guards…. One guy smashed windows and another began handing out razor blades that he had somehow stockpiled. The prison had been forced to close down the entire unit until order could be restored.

Rick said he'd seen Dr. Chives, his mentor, a few weeks back, the very same Dr. Chives who had gotten me to write the *Annals of Dermatology* article that had first prompted Rick to call me for an appointment. Were it not for that article, I realized, my life would have gone in an entirely different direction. I would never have met Rick, so I wouldn't be spending half my free time in prisons and I wouldn't have bought the Gloucester house, which means I wouldn't have sold the Newton house, and thus wouldn't have gotten involved with Andy or Barry…or Riley or even Lola for that matter. Nor would I have made the money I did in the stock market or through LaseHair. Talk about one person changing—for better or worse—the path of your life.

Dr. Chives had been at Bridgewater to visit his son David, who was awaiting his trial. David, who was a Harvard graduate like Rick, had been on the fast track to becoming one of Boston's medical elite—he'd been a back surgeon—when he made a series of increasingly moronic mistakes. It began in 2002, when he'd left a patient (who later sued and was awarded over $1 million) on the operating table so that he could run out to cash a paycheck. But that was only the beginning. He faced charges for allegedly drugging some teenage boys so he could have sex with them and also for distributing crystal meth. Rick said, "David was married once, but then he realized he was gay and broke it off and found a lover. When they broke up, he lost his balance." My heart went out to Dr. Chives. He had to be overwhelmed by these tragedies. Rick looked at the clock and I quickly said I had to go and asked him to thank Riley for allowing him to visit with me on her time.

That week I went to visit Lola. She lived in Brookline, in a brick condo. I had been there maybe five or six times before. Her place was neat and clean, but cluttered and heavy on antique Victorian-style furniture. There were embroidered pillows on the brocade sofa, lots of pictures on the walls—many in ornate frames, floor lamps with fringed shades, statues, clocks, knickknacks…. On the windows were shutters, blinds, drapes, swags…. It almost looked like a museum, or a crowded antique shop. I remembered that Lola had taken photos of the various rooms and sent them to Rick, back when their relationship was in its heyday. On the back of a picture of her dining room table, she had written, "This is where we'll dine and drink the finest wine together." On the back of a picture of the sofa she'd written, "This is where I sit when I talk to you."

Lola went into a bit of a panic when I told her Rick wanted her to sell everything but Microsoft. Initially, when he'd told her what to buy, he'd said to hang onto her stocks for at least ten years. "What should I do?" she asked me.

I told her I was no expert adviser and she would have to decide by herself. She asked me if I'd sold mine, and I said I hadn't yet but I planned to and so did Gary. We didn't have that much in the market, so it wasn't as big a deal, but this was Lola's retirement account. She said, "Did he look you in the eye when he said it?" I told her again that I couldn't be responsible for her portfolio.

We'd been talking loud, so we could hear each other over her parrot, who'd been jabbering nonstop since I'd come through the door. When I mentioned that he was driving me crazy, Lola said, "Oh, he just needs a time out," and she got up from the table. She put him in the bathroom, where I could still hear him but not as loud. When she came back to the kitchen, she called Fidelity. When the guy there told her she would have to pay a capital gains tax on anything she sold, she broke down crying. She put the phone down and said, "Linda, what should I do?" I said, "Cover the phone so he won't hear you. Get a hold of yourself." Finally she got back on with the Fidelity guy.

She was trembling and sniffling her way through the transactions. Meanwhile I had to pee. As I approached the bathroom, the parrot stopped blathering. I opened the door, but I didn't see him. I left the door open a crack so that he could fly out if he wanted to. I had to force myself to pull down my pants and pee and flush. I was afraid I would step on him or flush him by accident. Lola would have lost her mind. When I returned to the kitchen, Lola was off the phone. She said, "I did it." She was still wiping tears off her cheeks, but she was smiling. I said, "Look at all the positives. It's yours now. You don't have to worry anymore about what the stock market does." But I was thinking, Dear God, please look over her, because she *is* fragile. Then I thought about how fragile I was feeling lately and I extended the prayer to cover myself too…and then Gary. I said, "I didn't see your bird in there." She said, "Oh, he stays on the floor, right in front of the toilet."

Later, after we'd had some lunch, Lola said, "I want to thank you, and if the market really drops, I'll thank you even more. If you see him, thank him for me." I said, "Don't thank me. I was just delivering the message." She took my hand. She said I was a friend for life. She looked like she was going to start crying again, so I took out some pictures I'd found in the Gloucester house to distract her. Her portfolio had gone from less than $30,000 to well into the six digits.

When I got home, I called my own stock broker. He said, "You have inside information?" I told him no, but I was thinking, Yep, he's on the inside alright.

�

I wasn't the type to sit and cry like Lola, but maybe I would have been better off if I were. Inside I was carrying a lot, everything from contractors' abuses to Bruce's attempt to swindle me to Riley tossing our friendship overboard. My saving grace was weekends with Gary in Gloucester—eating at seaside restaurants and walking along the beach—and besides, I figured I'd reached bottom and that there wasn't much more that *could* go wrong.

But then, in December of 2004, one of my clients decided to sue me.

As I've mentioned, not everyone is a candidate for laser work. Two sisters came in one day, and Angie, one of my employees, worked on them back to back. They were black, and while one was fine, the other, whose name was Rebecca, noticed some facial discoloration in the days following her treatment. She went nuts and had a lawyer send a letter declaring her intention to sue my company, me, Angie, and our medical director, Dr. Jeffries. Rebecca's sister, in the meantime, had a good experience and wanted another appointment. We didn't give her one; we told her it was a conflict of interest.

Candela, the company that makes the lasers, provides an instruction manual with them. In it, the various skin types are associated with a number, with albino skin being a #1 and black being a #5, and everything else falling in between. There was a setting on the laser to coincide with each number, and Angie, who worked on the sisters on a Saturday when I was not around, consulted the manual and used the correct setting. The manual also suggests that for anyone over a #3, a spot test be done two weeks in advance of the treatment. Most people don't want to wait two weeks, and so we have them sign a consent form saying they're aware of the risks. Rebecca and her sister had signed the consent form, but Rebecca decided to sue anyway.

I never met Rebecca, but as she went to the media with her story, I saw her picture in the newspapers and on a segment of *Inside Edition. Inside Edition* came to my office, and when no one answered their knock, they took footage of my office door! When the segment came out, I hired a police officer to stand at the door for a few days, in case there were any problems.

The laser had left Rebecca with brown spots the size of quarters on her face and neck. The chances that the spots would be permanent were slim to non-existent, but it was still one more unresolved conflict hanging over my head. In the meantime, I lost a few clients, and certainly I couldn't expect to attract any new ones until the media hoopla died down. Lucy said, "Just keep working. Don't think about it." Since she wouldn't be around when the case went to court (she was getting ready to move to Florida), I handed the suit over to Sally Jones, a personal injury lawyer who had been recommended by Lorraine Littleton, the lawyer who'd represented me against Barry and Andy. Sally thought the case was laughable. Not only had Rebecca signed the consent form, but as soon as Angie learned there was a problem, she told Rebecca to go right to Dr. Jeffries, that he would have creams that would diminish the brown spots in just a few weeks. But Rebecca never went. She didn't *want* to get rid of her brown spots; she wanted to sue.

If it turned out she *did* have a case, at least I had malpractice insurance— or so we thought. But when Lucy, who was preoccupied with her moving plans, had a minute to call the insurance company to discuss the suit, she learned that my contract with them stipulated that any claims made had to be reported within sixty days, and more than sixty had already expired.

Who reads insurance policies? I'd had the policy for twenty years and never before bothered to read it. The clause about claim time limitations was on the second page. Now the insurance company was saying I had no coverage.

Nor was my business incorporated. Lucy had been intending to incorporate me, but she was waiting until the beginning of the new year, which was only weeks away. Rebecca Williams wanted $5 million. All I could think was, Here I just got my dream house and I'm going to lose it. I'm going to lose the house, my business, everything.

Chapter Thirty-Four – Saving Graces

ONE DAY I WENT TO VISIT RICK AND FOUND HE ALREADY HAD A VISITOR. A woman. I was taken aback. As far as I knew, Riley Carter was still working on his appeal, and while she wasn't spending much time in Massachusetts these days, Michael Goodman, her partner in the appeal effort, was taking up the slack and meeting with Rick on a regular basis. In other words, Rick was still having to abide by Riley's rules, which meant the ban on women was still in effect. Yet there she was, sitting beside him in the visitors room, an attractive brunette in her thirties. At first I thought to turn and leave; after all, I hadn't let Rick know in advance that I planned to visit. But then Rick saw me and stood up and introduced us—me and Clara Martin—and insisted I have a seat. Rick said, "Linda is a good friend." Then he paused and asked, "How long have we known each other?"

I didn't have to think about it. "Almost fifteen years. Since the early nineties." I turned to Clara. "We're like brother and sister, no sex." They both looked at me like I was crazy. I started to laugh. I was nervous, I realized; I've been known to have such outbursts when I'm on edge. I continued in that vein: "Who are you? Where do you live? Are you like a new girlfriend?" I glanced at Rick and it occurred to me that he looked just like Dr. Oz, who I had seen on *Oprah*. Dr. Oz without the smile.

I could tell I was making her uncomfortable. She looked to Rick to see how to answer. But he didn't say anything. Finally Clara said, "I'm from New Jersey," as if that explained everything. Rick added that they'd been writing for a while.

I said to Rick, "You have other friends from New Jersey too." I was thinking of Nadine the nurse. I asked if he'd heard from her lately, and when he said he hadn't, I reminded him of some of the damage she'd done when they were friends. Then Clara piped up to ask if *she* should leave.

I was on a roll and I couldn't seem to stop myself. Part of it might have been that I was mad at Rick, that I'd been mad ever since he'd gone secretive on me regarding his appeal, ever since his brother had tried to cheat me regarding the laser. I didn't know if Rick was behind that or not, probably not, but I had been manipulated by just about everyone in my life over the last several months, and I was in a "guilty until proven innocent" frame of mind. Besides Gary, Lola was my only saving soul; I always knew I could believe what she said.

I changed my seat to the other side of Rick, so that he would be between us. Then I looked Clara over. "You were born between September and October, a Libra, like me," I announced. They both looked at me, astonished. I'm good that way, with astrology. I said, "I think you're thirty-six, even though you don't look that old. You look thirty-four."

She said, "Right again, I am thirty-six."

Rick sat back, so we weren't having to lean so far forward to talk past him. He said, "You two talk, get to know each other."

I said, "Rick, we're not really interested in each other. We came to talk to you. So, how are you feeling lately?"

He mumbled something about how slowly time passed, how it would be nice if I visited more often. I looked at Clara. I said, "See, he needs support." Then I added, "My father says that any woman who visits an inmate she's not related to is probably in love with him."

Clara looked shocked at first. But she got me back, saying, "Are you in love with him then?"

I said, "I told you, I love him to pieces, like a brother. I have a man I'm in love with, for eleven years now."

She stared at me a moment longer, then she started talking to Rick, picking up, apparently, on the conversation they'd been having before I arrived. After a minute I realized they were talking about products he was trying to get patents for, products related to anti-aging, lung expansion for pulmonary fibrosis, lung supplements for pulmonary fibrosis, autoimmune helpers, and more. I recalled that the 1998 newsletter we wrote together mentioned that he had once been co-inventor of six issued and twelve pending patents for medical therapeutic products. Eventually they finished up with the patents and Clara leaned forward and told me how she'd met a woman at a party, someone named Gracie whose daughter Rick had once saved from a rare form of cancer. Then Rick interrupted to say he'd heard from Lola, a couple of letters and a birthday card. Clara said, "Who's Lola?"

"Don't worry, she's no threat," I offered.

Rick said to Clara, "I told you about her. She's the one who was banned for a green pill found in a letter she sent to me. She was set up."

I said, "How long has Clara been coming to see you?"

They looked at each other. "Almost a year," Rick answered.

I said, "Well, she'll have to worry about being set up too then."

All told, the three of us sat together for almost two hours. I probably wouldn't have stayed so long, as it was awkward to sit there with a stranger, but the guards had announced a lockdown right after I arrived; my choices were either leave before it began or stay for the duration. Of course I could have said at any point that I had to use the bathroom, in which case I would not have been allowed back in, but I didn't. I had already timed my liquid consumption so that my bladder would be empty during visiting hours, and I didn't want all my efforts wasted just because it turned out that Rick already had a visitor.

Although I behaved badly and gave her a hard time, Clara remained pleasant. She smiled a lot and encouraged me and Rick to do more of the talking. Before I left she revealed that she planned to buy a URL to post some of Rick's scientific papers. In fact, he'd asked me to buy a URL with his name and set up a website and link it to my website, but I'd declined because I'd already lost enough patients. Of course he had been writing papers all his life, and they had been published in various scientific and medical journals over the years, but now he had some new ones that he wanted up on the Internet.

It became clear as I listened to them that Rick was doing quite a lot of writing these days, that what he and Clara had in common was a love of ideas, that apparently she'd inspired him to start writing again. She was an artist, I learned, and also a writer. She had a blog site on which she posted essays on animals, friends, politics, languages, history, geography, film and book reviews and more. She was also the owner of a photo retouching company. I thought that was interesting. If we three had anything in common it was that we all worked (or in Rick's case, *had* worked) to remove flaws from people's faces. I could tell just by talking to Clara that she wasn't a troublemaker, the way some of Rick's previous female friends had been. She was just a nice calm person who lived in her head and wanted to get inside Rick's head too. You could see that she had a calming effect on him. Maybe Riley Carter had met her too and had seen what I saw and had given their friendship the green light.

৪৩৪৪

During this period of time, the avian flu scare was in full force all around the world and everyone everywhere seemed to be bracing for disaster. Domestic poultry in Thailand, Vietnam, Japan, South Korea, Pakistan, Cambodia, Indonesia, South China, and Malaysia had become infected and had been slaughtered. Then a new strain of the flu was discovered in the U.S., and nearly 100,000 birds were thought to be affected as a result. Counties across the country set up hotlines so that people could call in and report dead bird sightings. The fear was that the virus would continue to mutate; accordingly, the World Health Organization had begun warning of a pandemic.

Like many people in the medical field, Rick became obsessed with the bird flu and his letters to me began to include his thoughts on it and on flu viruses generally. If I were to string those letters together chronologically, there would be an encyclopedic history of the flu, as well as an extensive and highly detailed list of ways to protect against it, and how to treat it if you got it. These letters were tedious to read, especially as they contained information about specific doses of specific medicines. But he was sincere in his concern, and at the end of every letter he advised me to share the information with friends and loved ones. In retrospect I could see that he was building a theory, working out the details in his letters, and I wasn't surprised when I learned that the avian flu was the topic of one of the scientific papers he was so busy working on. When he was ready, he sent a copy—hand-written, twenty-eight pages—of the completed manuscript to Michael Goodman, who in turn sent it to me for safekeeping.

Rick believed, like the officials at the WHO, that the avian flu had the potential to do us in once and for all. With doomsday front of mind, he began his paper with a foreword that included a quote from the Bible, from Isaiah 46:8 – 46:11:

> *Remember this, and show yourselves men: bring it again to mind, O ye transgressors.*
> *Remember the former things of old: for I am God and there is none else; I am God and there is none like me, Declaring the end from the beginning, And from ancient times the things that are not yet done, saying My counsel shall stand, and I will do all my pleasure:*
> *Calling a ravenous bird from the east, the man that executeth my counsel from a far country: yea, I have spoken it, I will also bring it to pass; I have purposed it, I will do it.*

The work, which he'd dedicated to his wife, children and family, pro-claimed that the coming influenza pandemic was the greatest threat facing humanity. Governments worldwide were stockpiling one kind of vaccine, which almost guaranteed that the flu would become resistant to it very quickly. So, assuming there would be no adequate vaccine available long term, Rick proposed a series of treatments, just as he had in his letters to me, that might save at least some individuals. He made distinctions between what would work best for adults and what was best for children, and he even included a list of alternative medications in case some of the principal meds didn't work on people with existing ailments. He also included information on vitamins to take, temperatures to keep the body at (even if it meant taking cool baths all day long), and what to do if seizures occurred. Since the pandemic was coming but hadn't yet arrived, he suggested that people begin to stockpile drugs now, because once the pandemic hit, the healthcare infrastructure, he predicted, would fail. He included notes on cleanliness measurements that would help to keep the flu from spreading from one family member to another—wearing latex gloves, washing and bleaching clothing, washing steering wheels, doorknobs, keys, wallets, etc.

Could his paper have been a work of genius? Possibly. The pandemic never happened, so it's impossible to know for sure. But I suspect it would have saved a few lives at the very least—if you could get anyone to read a paper written by Dr. Richard J. Sharpe—and in the end and in spite of all the mistakes the man had made, saving lives was his main purpose.

Chapter Thirty-Five — The Beginning of the End

WHILE RICK WAS STRUGGLING TO FIND WAYS TO SAVE HUMANITY FROM THE bird flu, nothing much changed in Gloucester. The neighbors I encountered continued to speak of the Sharpes as though the family had consisted only of Carmen and the kids. At a local convenience store that I liked to visit on the weekends, I got to know a woman named Eleanor, who worked at the deli counter. For a long time we only made small talk, but then one morning just after *Dateline* had run yet another rerun of the Sharpe story, I asked her if she'd seen it and she admitted that she watched it every time it came on, that she was still very upset over losing Carmen. Carmen used to shop there, she said; she'd bring the kids in—hers as well as their little friends from the neighborhood—and let them have whatever they wanted, candy, gum, baseball cards, and she would stop and pick up coffee and pastries for the crew when they were working on the Wenham house. Sometimes she would spend more than $100.

I learned from Eleanor that Stephanie had been in town recently for a wedding. She'd brought Leo and Judy with her, but she'd left her own baby—a boy, Eleanor said—at home. In fact, Stephanie had had a girl; Eleanor either had the information wrong or she felt somehow that she was protecting Stephanie by deceiving me. I assumed the latter and was hurt—because I had always loved Stephanie. I had known her even longer than I'd know her father; I had always hoped that she would have a happy life. Then Eleanor started to rant, about how crazy Rick was, how she'd heard that he'd abused Carmen for years and years. I could see I wasn't going to be able to pay for my order until she finished. When she took a breath I asked her if she'd ever seen a bruise on Carmen, and she said she hadn't. I wasn't trying to make a point. There was no point to be made. Rick killed his wife and that was the bottom line. I was just asking a question. Eleanor was quiet for a few seconds. Then another customer appeared and she finished ringing me up and I hurried outside with my order. I had my father waiting in the car. Both he and my mother liked to come out and visit Gary and me on the weekends, though not necessarily together or at the same time. In fact, between friends and family, we had visitors frequently. And of course every weekend there was Rosemary—who we loved so much we sometimes forgot she wasn't ours—scratching on the sliding glass doors and begging to be let in so she could see what new treats Gary had brought for her.

Riley Carter and I began speaking again, albeit infrequently, but there was nothing left of our friendship in our brief conversations. Basically she called now and then to suggest that I visit Rick more often. It was clear that she was worried about him. The first time she called she admitted that it had been some eight months since she'd been to see him herself. She had so many other things going on. I didn't ask her what they were. But I did try to make the effort to get to Bridgewater even more often.

On one occasion, I got to the visitors room and was waiting for Rick when one of the other inmates, a man named José, started a conversation with me. He said that Rick was so neat about his clothes, that he would lay them out on his bed before he went into the shower in the exact order that he would be putting them on. But his papers, José exclaimed, were all over the floor—documents, medical books, law books, magazines, newspapers... a real mess.

When Rick came in I asked him about his projects, and he turned to the side a bit, so that he wouldn't be facing the security camera, and said that in addition to the papers he was writing, he was working with Riley Carter and Michael Goodman to sue several attorneys, including Ben Jr. and Joan Falcon and Wyler Grange. He and his legal team had determined that his sixth amendment rights had been threatened because Carmen's divorce affidavits were made public by Grange and handed over to the newspapers. Rather, they should have been impounded until the trial was over. The documents contained inadmissible hearsay, conjecture and accusations. Not only had this impeded his chances for a fair trial, but it was an assault on the privacy of his minor children. He lamented anew that so much money had been signed over to various lawyers that should have gone to his kids. I covered my mouth when I responded to him, in case the security cameras were rolling.

While we were having this discussion we were distracted by a young boy, maybe seven, who came into the visiting room crying, "Daddy, Daddy, Daddy," and flung himself into the arms of one of Rick's fellow inmates. Rick stopped talking to watch their embrace, and when he turned back to me, he burst into tears—which caused me to do the same. We sat there with our heads bent, saying nothing, crying silently over everything that Rick had lost.

By the middle of 2005 Rick was writing to ask for canteen money again, which, along with the fact that he seemed so open with me these days regarding his trial plans, made me wonder if Riley Carter was gradually weaning herself from him. God knows how much money she had already spent, having paid fees to all the lawyers who were now part of the legal machine that she had constructed and set in motion for him. And as he still had his appeal—not to mention the prosecutor (Latto) trial—ahead of him, she had to still be dishing it out. In any case, he didn't mention her at all when he asked me for the canteen money, so I concluded that he was okay with her detachment. I paid for his canteen for the month and I renewed all his magazine subscriptions.

In return, he offered me the only thing he could, stock tips. I didn't tell him that I had pretty much depleted my savings account and that with the prospect of being sued by Rebecca Williams still looming over me, I wasn't in the right frame of mind to buy any stocks anymore anyway. So the tips kept coming, along with medical advice.

Around this time there was an article in the *Gloucester Daily Times* saying that Rick was one of eight prisoners in the Massachusetts prison system asserting that they suffered from Gender Identity Disorder and petitioning for a sex change operation. Three of them, the article stated, including Rick, had gone to court to plead that the state fund the operation, which, the reporter noted, the Senate would most likely vote against.

I had a hard time believing this was true. I had known Rick for a lot of years, and while it might have been a fact that he felt an occasional need to express his feminine side, and maybe had even taken birth control pills to calm himself at times, I didn't think he believed that he suffered from full blown Gender Identity Disorder. I of all people knew what true GIDs were like. I'd just had one in my office the day before: Georgette, who looked like a librarian with her conservative haircut and her straight skirt and cardigan sweater, had been living as a woman for five years and was scheduled to have her sexual reassignment surgery in the very near future. In preparation for the surgery, she wanted some "bikini" laser work done, above her pubic line and at the top of her thighs. During our session I said to her, "Can you hold your testicles and the rest of it off to the side so I can get in there?" She sighed loudly and a clouded look crossed her face. She said, "I can't bear to touch it. I can't stand it." I said, "Well, you'll have to touch it, because I'm not going to." Now that is Gender Identity Disorder.

When I went to visit Rick a day or two later, he looked five years older than the last time I'd seen him, only three weeks before, and I assumed that the sex change incident was the reason. But the first thing he said to me was, "Did you know I almost died?"

I sat down and he told me the story. Whether or not it is true I can't say. But what he said was that two weeks earlier, on Friday the 13th, he was at work—his most recent job was cleaning inmates' razors—when he began to feel dizzy and asked the guard to excuse him so he could lie down. He couldn't believe I didn't know about this. Apparently he'd called Bruce and asked him to call me. But Bruce and I were still not speaking because of the issue with the laser payoff. Anyway, a nurse came in to check on Rick in his cell and found his blood pressure to be extremely low and called an ambulance. When the paramedics arrived, the nurse suggested that maybe Rick had swallowed a razor, not a blade, which he wouldn't have had access to, but an entire razor, in another suicide attempt. When they reached the hospital, Rick told the attending physician that he thought he might have an ulcer or a clot and he asked for platelets (the part of the blood that generates clotting). The doctor insisted that Rick needed a blood transfusion, and when Rick said he wanted to have the platelets first, the doctor wanted him to sign a document saying that he had in fact refused blood. Rick countered that he was not refusing blood, that the doctor was incompetent, that he just needed the platelets first. The doctor responded, "I'm a board certified ER doctor; you're a dermatologist." Rick said, "I worked as an internal medical doctor for five years; I'm a scientist and chemist and an engineer." The doctor said, "You're an arrogant man."

The confrontation continued. Rick argued that if he accepted blood and it was too much, the clot could burst and he would die. "Then you'll have to explain," he added, "and there are three nurses here as witnesses. One of them will break down in court and tell the truth. I'm not refusing blood. I want platelets first." Finally the doctor relented and got a hematologist in and Rick got his platelets.

Afterwards he was transferred to another hospital for an MRI and a colonoscopy. He had to yell at the correction officers who accompanied him to take off his shackles before he went into the MRI. Just the year before, there had been a horrible accident when a metal oxygen tank was whipped across the room by the electromagnetic waves from an MRI and the kid who was having the testing got slammed in the head by the flying tank and died. Rick's correction officers left the area too as they had metal on. The MRI found a clot in his stomach and an ulcer, just as he'd said.

When he was all done with his story, I told him about the newspaper article saying that he suffered from Gender Identity Disorder and had asked the state for a sex change operation. He became furious all over again. He had nothing to do with that, he said, hadn't even known about the inmates who were involved. It was another setup. When would it end? It took awhile for him to calm down. He made me promise to call Michael Goodman as soon as I got home and get him to get the newspaper to retract the part of the story referring to him. He asked me to check to see if the story had appeared elsewhere.

I contacted Goodman later that day, and just a few days later the same newspaper reported that in fact Rick was *not* one of the inmates seeking a sex change. Michael Goodman was quoted in the article as saying that the whole cross-dressing thing had been overstated during Rick's trial, that Rick did not have a Gender Identity Disorder.

A few days later I bit the bullet and called Bruce to find out why he hadn't told me that Rick almost died. He said he was unable to get the details, that he and Glenn weren't even able to find out what hospital Rick was in at first. Then I switched the conversation to the laser. He said I could have it, it was mine, but when I reminded him that I'd had to pay the payout that he was supposed to pay, and on top of that, that he'd never even bothered to send over the paperwork acknowledging my ownership, he said he'd look into it, that he'd been sick himself and had to get off the phone. He'd just gotten out of the hospital, for his heart again, and he couldn't get stressed. Then his wife got on the phone to say I was stressing him out and to leave him alone.

Hurricane Katrina happened, and Rick wrote me a letter telling me how upset he was and that he was praying for the victims, those who had died and those who were still suffering. I wondered what the victims would think about that. But his letter was so touching that I made a point of visiting him some days later. Again I didn't tell him I was coming, and I wound up sitting for twenty minutes waiting for him in the visiting room. To pass the time, I counted the chairs, sixty, plus two picnic tables, so total seating for maybe sixty-eight. There were two vending machines in the room, both empty.

Finally he came in. I said, "What took you so long?" He said he'd been exercising and had to shower. He said his cholesterol was good because he'd been doing sit-ups, push-ups, and running track. All this exercise required him to take four showers a day. He was working in the laundry now, but he said he didn't mix his own laundry in with the rest of it. He washed his stuff in the shower by hand and hung it to dry in his cell and used a fan to puff up the material to get the wrinkles out.

I asked him about Riley Carter. It had been a long time since he'd given me more than a one word response when I mentioned her name. But on this occasion he said that she was upset about the cottage by the bay, the one where I'd gone to visit her, because the owners were spending a lot of time there. They'd told her previously that they'd only want the place for a month and then she could have it again, but they'd been there much longer. I didn't say so, but I wondered if she was making excuses so as to stay at home in the southwest.

At 5:00 p.m. the countdown bell rang, and all the inmates in the visitors room went to line up and be counted. Rick went to the far end of the line, nearest the corner, as usual. In a few minutes he was back again. We talked about his appeal, which he thought would take place in the not-too-distant future. He went on about how Falcon had turned out to be his worst enemy, making him say things that were exaggerated and even getting him to look insane. I wondered if Rick was the one who was exaggerating. Then he talked again about how his children's trust funds had been used to pay legal fees, and even for the Gloucester house upkeep bills, until I bought it, including the new septic tank. If only Stephanie had stayed in contact, he lamented, he could have helped her with investments and their money would have tripled by now. Then he switched gears to tell me about a patient whose life he once saved, maybe ten years ago. She was only twenty years old and she had basal cell carcinoma, which is the most common type of skin cancer. Rick looked me right in the eye. "I need her file, but I can't remember her name."

I could only stare at him. In my mind's eye I could see the boxes, all forty something of them, in the Gloucester garage, piled up to the ceiling, one on top of the other. I had mentioned to Riley awhile back that I'd sorted and boxed the files and either she or Michael Goodman could take them, but no one wanted them. I waited for Rick to laugh and say he was only joking but he didn't. Instead he said, "Riley really wants me to find this one particular file," and all of a sudden it made sense to me why she'd started calling me again. Since I couldn't think of a response, I asked him if he'd ever taken Carmen's birth control pills. He said, "No, I didn't. If I wanted birth control pills I could get them myself. I'm a doctor."

In fact, I did eventually hunt down a few particular folders for Rick and Riley, but the ones they sent me looking for turned out to be empty—folders with no files left inside. Someone had beaten me to it.

Chapter Thirty-Six – The Calm Before...

DISASTER, DISASTER, DISASTER. IF SOMEONE FROM ANOTHER PLANET WERE TO beam down and sit in front of the TV during the news hour, they'd be convinced that it was only a matter of time until everything came to an end for Earthlings everywhere. So much hardship in New Orleans on the heels of Katrina. So much talk about the super-cell storms that would be coming in the future. As for the bird flu, things were only getting scarier. The U.S. bought $100 million of vaccine, but scientists were saying, as Rick had, that the virus would mutate regularly anyway and no vaccine could catch up with it fast enough to prevent a worldwide outbreak. Some estimates put the American death toll potential at 1.9 million. And then of course there was still terrorism to think about, and the wars in Iraq and Afghanistan.

Time passed and I didn't hear from Riley about the basal cell carcinoma patient. In fact, I didn't hear from her about anything. Rick went back to monosyllables when I brought up either her name or the work being done on the appeal. I had to read between the lines to guess where they were with things. I noticed that while the body of Rick's letters remained the same (which is to say that they still offered stock tips and medical advice), the closing had changed, from "Love, Rick," to "Very Truly Yours." The holidays came and went, and Rick seemed to get through them with more ease than in previous years.

Despite my best efforts, I still didn't get over to Bridgewater as often as I thought I should. I'd refinanced the house and used part of the money to pay off some of the debt I'd incurred over the last few years and the rest to make upgrades. Everyone seemed to agree that I would get it all back if and when I sold the house. I loved the house and so did Gary, but we still kept the apartment in Newton so that we wouldn't have to make the drive out to Gloucester on work nights. When I finally got around to visiting with Rick again, Gary came with me. He looked shocked to see us, as if he'd given up the hope of seeing us—or me at least—ever again, and I felt bad that I'd stayed away for so long. The first words out of his mouth were, "Where have you been?"

I explained that I'd been busy, not only with the house but also with my family, a disaster in their own right. My mother had had a small tumor removed from her lung and was having chemo treatments. My dad's old car had been repossessed a year earlier, and so he got a loan and bought another one, but that one was repossessed too. He was not only neglecting to pay his bills but also not shaving himself or keeping himself clean. He was beginning to show signs of dementia. In fact, he drove off the road one day and the new car had to be pulled out of a ditch. After the second repossession, Gary and I made the decision—not an easy one—to get the car back and give it to my brother, who needed a car. We got my father to agree to hand over his driver's license to us. But then my brother needed car insurance. I felt compelled to explain to Rick that as my brother was having financial problems, it had fallen to me to pay his insurance premiums. I was justifying why I hadn't sent canteen money in a while, though I still kept up with all the magazine and newspaper subscriptions. Rick didn't seem to be listening. "I thought you were mad at me," he said when I was done.

I had to think about this. Yes, I had been busy, but to be honest, I had continued to feel some low-level resentment towards Rick too, mostly still about the laser buyout. Rick was the one who'd come up with the idea that Bruce should buy the laser and I should lease it from him. He thought it would be a win-win for both of us...for all three of us actually, because he hoped that if Bruce had a little extra money, some of it could be used to pay for his appeal. Another one of Rick's schemes. The man was incarcerated. I had to remind myself that he had no control over his brother. It wasn't his fault that Bruce had failed to live up to his end of the bargain. Nor was it his fault that at the time I didn't have the chutzpah to purchase a laser on my own.

I said I wasn't mad at him about anything and asked how he was. The last time I'd seen him he'd been running three miles a day; now he was up to eight miles, he said. He drank green tea all day long. He said you could reduce your risk of heart attack by thirty percent if you drank enough of it. He had three cups each morning, each cup made with four teabags. Then he had three or four more cups during the day and one or two more after dinner.

He was still writing papers, and Clara Martin was still posting them for him. In addition to the scientific stuff, he had also written a document about how to generate software that solves Sudoku puzzles. And he was working with other inmates now, tutoring them in math and science and economics.

Listening to him it occurred to me that he was actually adjusting. After all this time in prison he seemed to be content. I asked him if he'd had his teeth cleaned lately and he said no, that he chose not to because the guy who did it scraped his gums with the tools and treated him roughly the last time. He used floss instead, and he picked up his lip to show me his gums.

His mouth looked immaculately clean. Knowing I would want to know about tooth number thirty-one, the one Joan had put the temp filling in, he stretched his mouth further. It looked good. I made a mental note to let Joan know. Rick was taking good care of himself. His breath was good too—a further indication that that he was really doing okay.

His cellmate Salvatore was there in the visiting room. His wife was visiting him with their baby daughter. At some point they came over to show us the baby. After they walked away I said to Rick, "Do you remember when your kids were that small?" He continued to stand, so that he could still see Salvatore's daughter even when the couple were back in their seats again. He had his hands entwined behind his back. Then he remembered that he had visitors and sat down again. "Have you seen Stephanie?" he asked me. I shook my head. "Where would I see Stephanie? Just because I spoke to her the one time when she passed me the 800 number, right after everything happened, you think I talk to her on a regular basis!"

Gary had been good to accompany me, but he didn't have much to say to Rick. It wasn't that he didn't like him; he just didn't have a relationship with him; he didn't understand our pattern of communication.

We talked for a bit about Dana Reeve, who had died recently from lung cancer. Rick so admired the great work that Christopher and Dana had done in advocating for stem cell research. Christopher had put himself smack in the middle of the debate, a fixture on Capitol Hill in hearings regarding the stem cell controversy, and together they had set up their charitable organization to find treatments for paralysis caused by spinal cord injuries. Rick loved the idea that Christopher Reeve had used his personal catastrophe as an opportunity to create something spectacular—real heroism, far beyond what he had portrayed when he had been Superman. And he loved Dana because she had been such an incredible caregiver. I think he saw in their story what he and Carmen might have been if they had followed a smoother path.

After we had both shed a few tears over the death of Dana Reeve, I told Rick about one of my clients, a woman who started changing over to become a man at the age of twenty-two. "Ray" got tattoos, took testosterone, grew a beard, and developed muscles. He had plastic surgery to remove beautiful breasts that anyone else would die for. Now he was twenty-eight, and he regretted the changes. He was one of the few I had ever encountered who'd made the changeover and wasn't happy with the results. He was still living as a man but he was miserable and wanted to be a woman again. He had deformed-looking nipples and discolored surgical scars under the breast where the wire of a bra would sit. He had been too young, he said, when he'd made the decision. He said if he could do it all over again, he would wait until he was thirty, and then he would see shrinks and doctors and get adequate information about what he was getting into—because at twenty-two you think you're invincible. He was off hormones now. I'd been working to help him get rid of his beard. He hated all the hair on his body. He hated not having breasts. The last time I saw him I said, "Well, at least you won't have much of a chance of breast cancer."

I mentioned another client of mine, a sweet transgender who had battled issues of severe anxiety, bi-polar disorder, obsessive compulsive disorder and tendencies toward suicide from childhood. When she was twelve, her mother recognized that her "son" was unbalanced and was suffering greatly. As a healthcare worker, the mother sought out help from three sources: her primary care doctor, a psychiatrist, and an endocrinologist. After concluding that they were dealing with a transgender issue, the doctors worked together to stop the natural puberty process. Instead they used hormone therapy, along with medications, to help combat the various psychological disorders. The mother, in the meantime, worked to get her "daughter" sexual re-assignment surgery—though no one in the U.S. would perform it due to her age. Finally they flew to Thailand, and after much consultation, doctors there agreed to do the surgery. By then my client was almost eighteen. She remained under the care of all her doctors, but she felt great. Besides "paying it back" by volunteering at a hospital, she was studying healthcare and languages as a full-time female college student.

I mentioned that I'd refinanced the house and that the banks pulled out most of the equity. Rick grew very concerned. He didn't think it was a good decision. "I believe it's a mistake," he said. I told him not to worry, that all the work I'd done had raised the value significantly.

Rick told me there were six sinks in his unit's bathroom, and there was a crazy inmate with a bad stomach who had to puke all the time, and when he did, he would run over to Rick's sink and puke there. He did it a few times while Rick was brushing his teeth.

The one thing Rick and I shared was a fascination with the great diversity in human nature. I decided I wasn't angry with him anymore after all.

ဆာ

In August of 2007 the alleged Latto murder plot finally went to trial, in Dedham. I attended both days, and I brought my father with me. Not only was he interested in the subject matter, but he wanted to see Roger Robertson, the Norfolk County assistant DA, in action. He didn't like Robertson because Robertson had been his defense attorney years earlier for one of his capers, and my father had wound up behind bars. But I'd read the transcripts from that trial, and I thought Robertson had done as much as anyone could.

The Latto trial gave the media yet another opportunity to recount the details of Rick's allegedly sordid history. Reporters all over the state dug out their favorite picture of Rick in fishnet stockings and a wig and splashed it throughout newspapers and on TV. In spite of their efforts, the trial itself, which began on Rick's 53rd birthday, went well. Michael Goodman's partner, Charlotte Brown—a middle-aged woman with curly reddish hair and a serious demeanor—did a great job representing Rick.

According to fellow inmate Norman Watne, during Rick's very first night in Walpole he asked Watne what effect the death of the prosecutor in his trial, Ronald Latto, would have on his appeal. Watne testified that during the next several weeks he and Rick discussed killing Latto on several occasions.

Brown pointed out that Rick was terrified of Watne, a lifelong carnival worker who was a convicted kidnapper and rapist and who boasted to anyone who would listen about his long history of assaulting prison guards and throwing feces and urine on them. When Rick had first arrived in his unit, Watne threatened to beat him up, and there was evidence to support that fact. So once Watne started acting chummy—inviting Rick to share coffee made with a piece of wire stuck into an electrical outlet in Watne's cell— Rick was willing to go wherever Watne led him in order to keep from being the victim of harassment.

And Watne had motivation for provoking Rick to talk about his careless fantasy. Watne had had all of his entitlements—phone, TV, radio and visitation rights—revoked for a period of three years because of his terrible behavior. He was in a corner, and he desperately needed to find a way to regain his privileges. Rick, who came into Cedar Junction paranoid and anxiety ridden, was the perfect target. In fact, it was the day after Watne learned about his loss of privileges that he went to the guards with his story about Rick's conspiracy efforts.

When Watne was ready, he invited a security guard to hide in a duct shaft behind his cell and hear for himself. Then he lured Rick into his cell. The guard heard some discussion about Latto, but, as Brown argued, it amounted to no more than a fearful Richard Sharpe going along with Watne's leading questions.

Watne made a lot of mistakes on the stand, and it was evident to me from the get-go that he was extremely manipulative and ready to do whatever was necessary to get what he wanted. For one thing, he told the jury that Rick wanted him to get someone on the outside to go to Lawrence to murder Latto on his behalf. Everyone, including Rick, knew that Latto's office was in Salem, not Lawrence. For another, he told the jury that he and Rick had first become friends because Rick wanted to talk football with him. That was actually laughable. Rick had zero interest in football. He wouldn't have known an intercepted pass from a blocked punt if he tripped over it. In fact, he had zero interest in spectator sports, period. I can still remember the blank expression on his face when I told him, during a visit in late October of 2004, that the Boston Red Sox had just won the world series. Now it was looking like the Sox might be in a position to pull off yet another championship, and I was willing to bet Rick didn't know a thing about it.

In return for Rick's head on a silver platter, Watne hoped to get a transfer to a New Hampshire prison as well as the reinstallation of his privileges. He even threatened on the stand not to tell his story unless he could first be assured that his demands would be met. In the end, as Brown stated, "Watne was inherently unbelievable." Brown called him a "crazy, violent, predatory sort of prisoner." Besides, there was just no logic to his story. Rick knew that Latto was about to retire from the DA's office and would have nothing to do with his appeal. Brown said that Watne was just rigging the game, just like in the days when he worked in the carny.

The case was a waste of resources and money, Brown concluded. The jury, which deliberated for a little more than two hours, agreed with her. Brown congratulated them on their verdict, saying, "I am really impressed that the jury could set aside the fact that the defendant had already been convicted of first degree murder and still give him a fair shake." Robertson, the DA, declined to comment on the verdict. As for Latto, his comment in the papers the next day was "the case really rested on the credibility of Norman Watne, and obviously he had some major credibility issues."

I left the courthouse relieved. This case had been a major hurdle. If Rick had been convicted, he would have been sent to a super max facility and his chances for an appeal would have diminished significantly, if not altogether. He needed to stay in Bridgewater, where he had come to feel safe, relatively, where he could eat his oranges and drink his green tea and exercise and read and write scientific papers. Now with this behind him, he and his lawyers could really concentrate on his appeal. Everything, I believed, would be okay after all.

So much for my gift of prophecy.

Chapter Thirty-Seven – The Storm

Rick asked me to send him a photo of myself. I ignored his request at first but he kept asking. He said he wanted to do a pencil sketch. I didn't even know he could draw, but so many prisoners spent time drawing, and I guess he was picking it up from watching. Or maybe he planned to have someone else do the sketch. I finally gave in and sent a picture, but a very small one, maybe an inch square, cut out from one of my business brochures. You never know in whose hands something is going to wind up. I pasted it into a blank greeting card. I laughed when I pictured his expression when he saw it.

Rick's letters to me continued to consist primarily of health advice. He could have had his own newspaper column, *Advice from the D.O.C. (Department of Corrections) Doc*.... He wanted me and Gary drinking green tea and taking vitamin D3 in large doses. He said that people who took 2400 units of D3 daily for a period of seven years had a seventy-seven percent less chance of getting cancer. How did he come up with this stuff? He wanted my mother to see a lung cancer expert in Maryland to reduce the risk of her cancer coming back now that her tumor had been removed. A friend of mine had melanoma, and Rick had very specific advice for him as well.

He was giving and giving, in the only way he knew how. He professed to be praying all the time too, for everyone's good health. Lately his letter closings had gone from "Yours Truly" to "God Bless You." The only thing he asked in return was that I continue to renew his newspapers and magazines. He didn't even ask for canteen money anymore. The prison was paying him $6.00 a day to wash floors, so he had what he needed. His stock tips continued too. He wanted me to invest in uranium stocks, which he said would go up as a result of global warming and the worldwide outcry for limitation of greenhouse emissions plus the non-viability of options such as ethanol. He told me exactly what stocks to buy and what percentage of my savings to use on them. I'd mentioned offhandedly a few times that I had no savings to speak of anymore, but either he didn't believe me or it didn't sink in—or he thought I might have just enough to invest and then I'd get on my feet again.

In April of 2008 he wrote to ask me for Skye's phone number, which indicated that he hadn't been in touch with her for a very long time. I didn't have her number anymore, but I had an email address for Patricia, her daughter, so I was able to pass along the message. When I visited him not long after, he seemed very calm. Again I found myself thinking that he had finally adjusted to the prison life. Or maybe his contentment stemmed from knowing that his appeal was on the horizon.

In September of 2008 Rick was transferred from Bridgewater to MCI-Norfolk. This was shocking news. As soon as I found out I called Lola. Though the romance had long been over, Lola continued to advocate for Rick's wellbeing. She in turn called the superintendent at Bridgewater, insisting on knowing what was going on. The superintendent said there was nothing more they could do for him at Bridgewater. Did that mean that he seemed normal to them at that point? I wondered. Or did they know that his appeal was around the corner and thus were hoping to make his life as miserable as possible in the meantime? As for Riley Carter, the word was that her father was very sick. It appeared that he had gotten an extra two years of life out of Rick's medical advice, but now he had other health issues to contend with. Riley was preoccupied with that, and there was nothing she could do to help Rick avoid the transfer anyway.

When I talked to him, a few weeks after the transfer, he said he was okay with it, that the new facility, though home to prisoners of a more violent nature, was set up like a college campus. There was a jogging track and a basketball court, and a general recreation area. The grounds were well kept and there were flower gardens. But when I asked him if he felt as safe there as he had come to feel at Bridgewater, he didn't answer me.

I went to visit him to check the place out for myself. I'd been there before, to visit my father when I was a little girl, and I had forgotten how high the walls were surrounding the facility. From the parking lot you entered into the main reception building, and when you came out the other end, you found yourself in the tower, with a guard on top looking down. Once the guard buzzed open the doors, you exited out onto a narrow concrete path surrounded by a green lawn and flower gardens. The actual visitors area was now housed in a building that hadn't been there before, an attractive-looking octagon-shaped building.

The visitors room consisted of a large cafeteria-style space with air-conditioning and windows which, while too small to allow anyone to escape, actually opened to let in the fresh air. There was even an area where visitors could take pictures with their inmates against a dark blue folding screen set up in the corner. There were vending machines for sandwiches and salads, and they were full. You could get a pre-paid canteen card ahead of time and use it to buy food. There were rows of comfortable chairs, set up in two semi-circles to fit the shape of the room, with the semi-circles facing each other. The guards could walk down middle from one side to the other and see everybody. The lighting in the room was good.

I went in determined to find out if Rick was really okay with the place. I couldn't help but remember how, in the beginning of his incarceration, he'd attempted suicide when he'd been moved out of Bridgewater. My fear was that if he felt unsafe, he might try it again. But the visitors room at MCI-Norfolk gave me a good feeling. And when he appeared he seemed to be okay.

Or at least the transition from one facility to another hadn't caused him to lose a beat with his writing. He told me he'd written a paper on the dangers of Tylenol and got it published, with the help of Clara Martin, online. As promised, she'd set up a webpage just for him, with his name in the URL. Next came a paper on organ regeneration, and this one caught the eye of the public. One critic called the paper bizarre. Another, a professor of cell biology from the University of California, conceded that the paper might be a work of genius—or, on the other hand, it might be the work of a bored inmate.

In the paper Rick stated that the salamander was the only vertebrate that has a substantial capacity to regenerate severed limbs and damaged organs. A condition for this response was lack of scar formation, known as fibrosis, at the site of the injury. He postulated that supra-pharmacologic doses of gamma interferon administered locally to the site of an injury or diseased organ could unlock regenerative capabilities in humans. His "preliminary data involving advanced pulmonary fibrosis" was of course based on his work with Riley Carter's father, though he never named him. In the paper he said that his anonymous patient had gray hair for twenty-five years, and about five months into his treatments, the roots turned blond again. His hair got thicker. His activities increased, and he was able to work longer hours. His critical thinking skills sharpened too. Treatment was discontinued after fourteen months with no recurrence at the two-year point.

While no one was about to come out and give Rick any credit (in his text Rick identified himself as a doctor even though the medical world knew he'd lost his license to practice years ago), research related to the reprogramming of cells was dubbed the scientific breakthrough of the year in *Science* magazine. Christopher Reeve had put the issue of regeneration into the spotlight through his foundations, which supported regeneration of spinal cord cells.

We talked about the *New England Journal of Medicine*, his subscription for which needed to be renewed. We talked about *Inventors Business News*, which he said I could stop sending because the administrators didn't want him to have it. I asked him again if he felt safe, and he nodded, but not in a decisive way. Then he stared at me like he had more to say but wasn't sure whether he should say it.

The last thing we talked about that day was Dirk Greineder, who was also incarcerated at Norfolk. Rick said that Greineder was trying to become his friend, but Rick didn't want any part of him. I asked him why not. In my mind, the two had quite a lot in common. For one, Greineder had been a doctor, an allergist who was a nationally-known authority on childhood asthma. He'd attended Harvard and, like Rick, had also taught there. His wife had even been a nurse, up until they had kids. Once the kids were born, they'd both agreed that in order to ensure the wellbeing of the family, Mabel would quit nursing and become a stay-at-home mom. I didn't remind Rick about the other thing they had in common—that they had both killed their wives and were serving life without parole.

But after I got home that day I got out my newspaper clippings and re-read the articles about Greineder, and I began to surmise why Rick didn't like him. Greineder's three grown kids had stood behind him from the get-go. "We love you, Dad!" they cried out at his trial in March of 2000, and even after his DNA samples had linked him to the bloodied knife and hammer that were the murder weapons, and after his stories about what happened in the park where he and Mabel had been walking had been shown to be wildly inconsistent, and after a neighbor had testified to seeing him emerge from the place in the woods where the weapons were later found...even after all that, his kids insisted he was one hundred percent innocent, that he couldn't have killed their mother because he was not that kind of a man. In interviews they refused to even discuss the fact that their father had had a secret life, visiting prostitutes and spending time on Internet porn sites and running up phone-sex charges.

At least no one could say that Rick had a secret life at the time of Carmen's death. If he was doing any cross-dressing at all then, Carmen surely knew about it. After his incarceration the police had devoured all his many computers looking for porn or other indications of a kinky alter ego. But the only porn to be found was associated with the email program that had been used by the liposuction assistant who had pocketed office cash and brought some of Rick's stuff to her doctor friend setting up in the Midwest.

My hunch was right. The next time I talked to Rick he admitted that seeing Greineder only made him feel worse about the fact that his kids weren't part of his life.

ℰℭ

In November of that year Rick was still going strong. He was drinking seven glasses of milk a day, his newest obsession. In spite of the fact that the stock market was dropping, Rick had helped his cellmate, whose wife had a Charles Schwab account, to increase their portfolio by eight percent. He wanted me to buy Genetech, which he said would soon be sold and would go up. Of course I couldn't. I had just paid Rebecca Williams $8000 to put an end to her lawsuit. The marks on her face had faded out long ago. She had never been able to find a doctor to stand up in court and say that she'd been wronged, and in the end she went from insisting that my company pay her five million to asking for $8000 to cover her legal expenses. I consented for the same reason I'd paid the buyout fee for my laser. Sometimes it just takes too much energy to fight. Rick asked me if I thought Stephanie would ever visit, but he asked this all the time, and I didn't think of it as an indication that anything was wrong. As always, I said, "You never know what's going to happen in the future." A lot of the prisoners attended classes at MCI-Norfolk, but Rick was not allowed to sign up for any of them because, the administrators said, classes were crowded and he already had too many degrees. Still, he was hoping to take music lessons and maybe learn to play the guitar. In the meantime he was tutoring inmates on math and economics, as he had in Bridgewater.

December was always a bad time for Rick, because of the holidays. I didn't usually visit with him during the Christmas season because more often than not Gary and I flew out to the Midwest to be with his parents. So I visited him early in December, my last chance to see him before Gary and I left for our vacation.

He was subdued during the visit, but I asked some questions and managed to get an update on some of the things going on in his life. For one, Clara Martin was working to get a new paper of his published in *Bioscience Hypotheses*. The paper was concerned with how "the honey bee colony collapse disorder is possibly caused by a dietary pyrethrum deficiency." I asked about his appeal and he said it was looking like it would happen in June or July of 2010. I asked how his tutoring was going and he said he'd written a letter to prison officials about extending his outreach to more inmates and in a more formal setting. I asked what he thought about us having our first black president in just a few weeks, and he looked up at me. "I lost my vote a long time ago, didn't I?" he said.

It was cold that day, but beautiful and sunny. The windows were opened a crack and the fresh air felt good. Since Rick didn't seem to want to talk after he'd answered my questions, I spent most of what was left of my two hours there chatting about my own life. I talked about Gary and the house and my family—small talk, just filling the vacuum. At some point, when I didn't have much more to say either, he asked again if I thought Stephanie would ever visit, and I whispered, "Come on, Rick. Wake up. I don't know if she'll ever visit. I don't have a crystal ball. What do you think?" After all this time the question was wearing me down. Then visiting time was over and I stood up to hug him goodbye—and he wouldn't let me go. I tried to break free. I was afraid one of the guards would see us and they would punish him, or tell me to never come back, but he just held on to me so tightly that I could actually feel his heart beating between us. I said, "Richard, let me go."

He did finally. He whispered, "I just want to thank you for everything you've done for me."

I wished him a good holiday. I told him I'd be back on January 6th, because I had off from work on Tuesdays and that was the first Tuesday that I would be back in town after my trip to the Midwest. He just stared at me, without any expression. I said, "Don't worry, the time will go quickly and I'll see you in January." But he still just stared, and looking back at him over my shoulder as I was exiting the room, I could feel a tightness in my head, as if there was too much blood in there all of a sudden.

I left the octagon visiting building through two guarded glass doors and started along the concrete path toward the lookout tower. I was almost to the tower when all of a sudden it hit me. On an almost subconscious level I had been asking myself if I was ever going to see him again, and the answer broke the surface to reach me on the conscious level, but it seemed to come not from me but from somewhere else, from God maybe, and the answer was no. I was surrounded by people, other visitors taking their leave, so when I stopped short along the path, I was jostled by a few of them who couldn't help but bump into me. "NO," I screamed. The woman behind me dashed to my side and asked if I was alright. I came back to my senses then. I told her I'd tripped and I began moving along with the crowd again.

Once I was in my car I began to cry. But then I stopped crying and started the car and continued on with my plans for the day. A few days later, Gary and I packed up for our trip, and I didn't hear any bad news, and we got back from our trip, and everything was still good, and I chided myself for having an overactive imagination.

I was working late the night of January 5, 2009. When the call came from Lucas, a police officer who was married to my friend Beth, Gary got it. When I walked in the door he broke the news to me. I immediately called Lucas back. Lucas said, "Yeah, they found him hanging from the upper bunk in his cell."

Chapter Thirty-Eight – The Aftermath

THE STORY HIT THE NEWS LATER THAT NIGHT. RICK WAS FOUND HANGED IN HIS cell, tied with a bed sheet to the upper bunk of the bed. It was his cellmate who discovered him. Rick was taken to a hospital and pronounced dead at 8:11 p.m. According to a prison source, a correction officer had just made the rounds past his cell and had delivered mail to him about an hour earlier.

Clara Martin made herself available to the media in the next few days and she did a few interviews. She said that she knew he had committed a terrible crime, but that she'd befriended him in spite of that, because of the positive things about him. She also wrote about him on her blog site. Her essay began: "My friend, Richard Sharpe, was found dead last night in his cell at MCI-Norfolk where he was an inmate. I found out about my friend's death this morning via Internet news reports. No one is likely to give Richard much of an obituary. He is known for having killed his wife in July of 2000. That's very hard to defend. I have my own views as to how Richard came to do this and maybe at a future date I will write about it. For now, though, I can say from my own experience that this is NOT all there was to Richard. Despite his flaws, he was a good friend to me."

I was ashamed when I read her beautiful tribute. She was not the least bit uncomfortable about admitting that she had been Rick's friend. I had known him longer, had stood by him longer, but I had been embarrassed about our friendship at times, and even though I tried very hard to see the man first and then the crime, there were times when I could only see the crime, especially in the beginning.

Clara Martin and Lola, who had never talked to each other before, had a long conversation over the phone the day after Rick's death, and Clara followed it up by sending Lola a hard copy of Rick's honey bee paper, which *Bioscience Hypotheses* had indeed agreed to publish, as long as Clara would do some editing on it now that Rick was gone. Lola was happy to receive it, but she was preoccupied with trying to get information from the medical examiner. I called the medical examiner too. They said the final report wasn't ready, and when it was it would go to Stephanie. There was nothing they could ever tell me; the information was only for next of kin.

Lola also received a letter from Griffin, the inmate who'd found Rick. She'd written to him right after Rick's death in her effort to find out exactly what had happened. He said he'd been Rick's friend, that they'd shared a love of business, stocks, and flying, that they were studying music together and working on a program to help other inmates. He lamented that he hadn't been able to offer Rick better protection, which suggested that Griffin thought he'd been murdered.

Michael Goodman was quoted in the papers as saying he'd been in touch with Rick only two weeks earlier and Rick had been in good spirits. Just the week before, he'd received a letter from Rick talking about how he was looking forward to tutoring more inmates. Also, Rick knew that Goodman was preparing a motion for his appeal with the Supreme Judicial Court. I spoke to Michael Goodman myself, over the phone. I suggested that maybe Riley Carter was running out of money to support the appeal, that maybe that was what caused Rick to lose hope. He said no, because he would have gone through with the appeal anyway, pro bono, if he had to—and Rick knew that. Goodman called for a thorough investigation of Rick's death. He didn't seem to believe it was a suicide either.

Glenn, Rick's lifelong friend, learned of Rick's death from Riley Carter. They'd become friends over the years. By the time I talked to Glenn he was able to tell me that Stephanie had signed papers agreeing that Bruce be the one to cremate him; she wanted nothing to do with it. Glenn said that the last five times he talked to him, Rick thanked him for everything he had done for him. But Glenn never put it together. He said he should have, that he'd asked Rick long ago to let him know if he was ever going to do anything like that, and in retrospect he could see that was exactly what Rick was doing.

I told him what Rick had said to me during our last visit, that I *had* put it together, but then I kind of went into denial. While Glenn was reassuring me that it wasn't my fault, I thought about the last time Rick had asked me if Stephanie would ever visit. He had asked the question so often over the years that it had become highly irritating. Maybe if I'd answered, "You never know, maybe she'll show up at the next trial...," maybe that would have been enough to keep him going. But I quickly reconsidered. No one could have given him enough encouragement to hang on. His despair was not based on any one person. He had managed to sever his relationships with all the people he had loved most in the world. How ironic for a man who was so afraid of abandonment all his life. Do we all do that? I wondered. Provoke the very thing we are most afraid of?

Looking back, I wondered if it would have done any good if I'd told someone at MCI-Norfolk about Rick's despair, if they would have sent him back to Bridgewater where he would have been more closely observed. But then again, who in the prison system cared that much about Richard Sharpe's wellbeing?

Rick was cremated on the 15th of January. Only Bruce and Glenn were in attendance. They had both agreed it should be a quiet, private affair. I would have been there too, and probably others would have, but we were not told the date of the event until after the fact. I talked to Glenn again afterwards. He said that Rick looked good, but that he was thin, and of course his head was at a funny angle.

On the same day as the cremation, a Letter to the Editor in the *Gloucester Daily Times* caught my attention. It was from a Gloucester-area psychiatrist who'd never met Rick, but who seemed to know a lot about him. He said that while it was horrifying that Rick had killed his wife, the tragedy of the story was lost to the titillating details that the national media picked up on. He said that Rick should have been sent to a secure psychiatric hospital for treatment and possible rehab instead of being dumped into a maximum security prison, that the problem was with our judicial system, which was committed to revenge rather than rehab, and which often "refuses to recognize the role of mental illness in a capital crime unless it is clear that the defendant could not distinguish between right and wrong at the time the crime was committed." He ended by saying that while he was pleased there is no death penalty in Massachusetts, in Rick's case a speedy trial and painless execution might have been a more humane sentence.

Another Letter to the Editor in the same paper admonished the *Times* for using a photo of Rick in a dress to "feed prejudices." The writer stated, "The prominent placement of a photo of Dr. Sharpe dressed as a woman gives the casual reader the harmful impression that there is a connection between transvestism or transexuality and violent crime. The fact is that the vast majority of men who identify with women, dress as women, and even change their bodies accordingly do so without harm to another human being. Conversely, the sort of 'news' displayed on your front page does feed prejudices that lead to violence against transvestites and transsexuals." The writer identified herself as a Revered from the Unitarian Universalist Church.

Finally, some months later, there was an interview in the *MetroWest Daily News* conducted with none other than Dirk Greineder, Rick's fellow Harvard graduate super physician. Greineder said that he'd given a eulogy for Rick at one of his Lifers meetings, the "Lifers" being a group of inmates who had in common that they were all in for life. Rick wouldn't have liked that at all. Greineder said that Rick was a bright man who had tried to help other inmates. He said that he and his fellow lifers had tried to draw Rick in and befriend him, but he was so vulnerable and so often harassed, and in the end no one was able to get close to him. "His suicide touched me personally," Greineder said. "It was a shock to me. It disturbed me."

Epilogue

IN OCTOBER OF 2010 I CALLED AN ON-SITE PAPER SHREDDING SERVICE AND SCHED-uled an appointment for them to come to Gloucester and destroy all forty boxes of Rick's five thousand patient files. I probably would have kept them forever...if I planned on keeping the house. But in the months following Rick's death it became increasingly clear that I would not be able to go on making the mortgage payments.

In the state of Massachusetts, and probably countrywide, there is a "HOPE" line that you can call when you can't make your payments. When I first realized that I was in a bind, I called them to see if I could have my interest rate adjusted to a lower rate. The person I spoke to took down all my information and said they would talk to my bank and get back to me. They suggested I keep making the mortgage payments, at the higher interest rate of course, in the meantime. Although it was a struggle, I did as they asked, draining my 401K—and thereby incurring tax penalties—in the process, but no one got back to me. I called again a few months later and got someone else and they told me the same thing—keep paying the mortgage and we'll see if we can work something out with the bank. Again I did not get a response. This went on for several months. So much for the "HOPE-less" line.

If the house had really gone up in value like everyone had said back when I bought it, then I could have refinanced for a lower rate. But of course that is not what happened. Like the homes of so many other people, the value went down instead of up, and because I had refinanced already (the bank was only too happy to give me money in 2005 when the house was worth between $800,000 and a million) in order to pay for upgrades, my beautiful home was well "under water." I had expected to spend about $200,000 to get the house the way I wanted it, but in the end, partly because I could not be there all the time to oversee the workers, the upgrades had cost almost twice that. I learned that my house was under water not from the bank but on my own, by contacting local realtors and hiring an appraiser. At first I had thought to sell it, but it soon became clear that no one would buy it for what I needed to clear the first and second mortgages. In fact, one realtor refused to even put it on the market.

Finally I got wise and figured out that the only way the bank was going to talk to me was if I stopped making my payments (I couldn't possibly continue to pluck enough hair to pay a mortgage of $5000 ad infinitum), and sure enough, that is what came to pass. But they were still not going to change my interest rate, and I was not going to be able to keep the house the way things were. I had no choice but to try a short sale. It was either that or foreclose.

The bank for the first mortgage decided that the house would be a candidate for a short sale and we were able to settle. The bank for the smaller second mortgage wouldn't work with us. They wanted all their money. Finally a foreclosure prevention specialist got involved so the would-be buyer, a realtor, could make things work...just weeks before the scheduled foreclosure. The second mortgage bank settled for about half the mortgage amount after all. An investor, who was represented by the realtor, was able to buy both mortgages, post settlement. Two weeks after the investor sold the house to a couple for $475,000. The couple made out because the house was valued at $550,000—just what I'd bought it for in 2003. In fact, everyone made out on the deal. I came out empty-handed but with my credit rating intact. I was back to where I had been before I met Rick, which is to say broke. Gary and I started looking for a rental. The plan was to give up the Newton apartment, which was too small, and find a place that would be close to where we worked.

I already had Rick's death certificate by then. I'd gotten it back in July of 2010. I would have had it sooner, but I had trouble getting the right information and vital statistics are not available online in Massachusetts. First I thought to call the town in Connecticut where he was born. Then I called Bridgewater. It never occurred to me that it would be in Norfolk, as he'd spent such a small part of his life there. But that was where he died.

I drove over to Norfolk, to the Public Records Department, with my Dad. The building was right near the prison, and when my father saw MCI-Norfolk, he said, "Look at that; I used to live there!" He said it dreamily, and it made me feel sad to think that he would have nostalgia for a prison. He would probably never see it again.

I went inside Vital Statistics and paid the clerk $10 and came back out with Rick's death certificate. Dad was convinced Rick had been murdered. The death certificate indicated that his death was a suicide, "asphyxia by hanging." I tried to explain to my father that there had been clues, that Rick was showing signs of despair. But my father still insisted he'd been murdered.

To change the subject, I asked him if he thought they'd ever catch Whitey, meaning Whitey Bulger. He liked to talk about Whitey now and then. He'd known him back in the day, or at least they'd been acquaintances. My mother had known Stephen "The Rifleman" Flemmi, an associate of Whitey's; she'd danced with him once when she was sixteen. My father said, "I don't think they'll ever get Whitey. He's too smart to get caught. I think he's living a good life in Ireland." (Little did we know at the time that the fifteen-year international manhunt for Whitey was nearly at its end, that, to my father's amazement, by June of the following year, Whitey's capture—in Santa Monica, California—would be followed by a trial that would draw more attention to the Boston area than even that of Dr. Richard Sharpe.)

Later, Dad and I reminisced about the time Al, my stepdad, had worked for the Castucci family, doing handyman jobs, Richie Castucci being another player in the Boston-area crime scene. Al always wondered if he might find money while working in the house. Sure enough one day when he was making a repair to an overhead light fixture, money fell out of the ceiling. I have no idea how much or whether or not Al returned it. Probably he did, because when they found Castucci dead in the trunk of his own Cadillac Deville in an abandoned parking lot in Sommerville in 1976, my stepfather was devastated. It wasn't until 2006 that the world learned for certain that Castucci, an FBI informant, had been killed at the behest of Whitey and Flemmi.

I'd thought getting the death certificate would bring me some kind of closure, but it was actually on October 31, the day the shredder came, that I got the closure I was craving. To me it was a big thing to get rid of Rick's patient records. Richard Sharpe the man had been depressed, needy, morbid, probably mentally ill. But Richard Sharpe the doctor had been sincere and tenacious. In shredding his patient records, I would be destroying that which represented the best part of him, though of course I had no choice.

But it wasn't just that. While I'd had conflicting feelings about my relationship with Rick Sharpe through all the years I'd befriended him, I could not deny that there was some bitter-sweet relief in knowing that this very needy person wouldn't need me anymore. I imagined I felt the way parents do when their kids finally move out of the house to go off to college or start their lives away from home. But I was also experiencing a sense of something bigger coming to an end, a sense of loss for the circle I had been a part of: Glenn, Lola, Lucy, Riley Carter, Clara Martin, Skye and Patricia, Gloria, Naomi, Bruce, Harry, Nadine the nurse, and so many others. Whether we liked one another or not, whether we remained friends or not, we had all come to know one another, and to find ourselves impacting one another's lives, because of Rick, because we had all sought, to various degrees and for various reasons, to form a protective ring around him. We were the people who supported him. We were the people who found a corner for him to live in our hearts.

For all these reasons, the prospect of shredding Rick's patient records felt ceremonious to me, and it was a ceremony I didn't wish to attend alone. But Gary had a lot going on at work that week, and he couldn't take a day off to wait with me for the shredding truck to arrive.

I called Lola, but she was feeling really tired that week and unwell. (Later she would tell me that I hadn't made it clear how badly I needed her company; in tears, she would say that if I'd only communicated my urgency, she would have come no matter what.)

I happened to run into Caroline, one of my neighbors and also one of the realtors who had helped me to understand that my house was under water. She and a child were up on her horse, trotting down the road. Caroline was the one whose house had been struck by lightning years before, the one for whom Rick and Carmen had thrown a party so that all the household items she'd lost in the fire could be replaced. I asked her if she would be around that Friday. I didn't really know her well, and I didn't tell her what I wanted her for, but she seemed like a compassionate person and I needed someone familiar with the Sharpe history. She informed me that she was now going back to school, to become a nurse, as had been her dear friend Carmen. She had classes on Friday.

I had other friends I could have called, but I didn't want the company of anyone who hadn't known Rick or who wouldn't get that this was an official ending for me. As it was, most of my friends didn't understand why I'd bought the house—the house of a man who'd committed a terrible crime—in the first place. What they didn't know, what was nearly impossible for me to explain, was that I had been in the house back when it was a hub of joy, on a few perfect days when a then-perfect family lived there: a perfect hostess and her successful husband, people everywhere, adults and kids, and pets, all of them exuberant. Those moments got burned in, like the painting on the urn in the Keats' poem; don't ask me how or why. All I know is that I wanted *that*. I wanted to be part of that tableau.

Ultimately I had no choice but to surrender to the fact that I would have to say my farewells—to Rick and to the impact he'd had on my life—alone.

The truck, which was the size of a furniture mover, arrived that Friday right on time. The driver got out and removed a large green plastic tote from a side panel and tipped it onto its two back wheels and wheeled it into the garage. One by one he emptied six or seven boxes of files into the tote and took it back to the truck, where the tote was hoisted onto an electronic lift so that the contents could be dumped into the shredder. There was a small video camera attached to the side of the truck, so that anyone really worried about the integrity of the shredding operation could actually watch it.

Earlier that morning before Gary went off to work we had gone out into the garage so that he could take a picture of the wall of boxes. While we were standing there, I opened one box randomly and removed one patient file from it. I read enough to know that the one I'd grabbed represented a success story. It indicated the dates of the patient's various appointments and the date of the surgery and a final lab report in which "all margins" had been declared "cleaned." I burst into tears. Poor Gary hurried into the house to put the camera away and get to work.

While I had been waiting for the shredder to come, I'd gone through additional files in a few other boxes, being careful not to look at the patient names. Many of the files were handwritten. Rick was a voracious note taker, at least in the beginning, and he had scribbled notes on top of notes. Sometimes there were two or three different colors of ink on one chart page, indicating that he had taken the page out after he'd had time to consider and added insights to his original conjectures. "SPF" (sun protection factor) was scribbled in large letters on nearly all of them, no doubt a reminder to warn his patients to watch out for the sun. If not for the thing that betrayed him—whether it was mental illness or abuse as a child or simply severe personality flaws—he could have been a famous doctor, a heroic doctor, a cure-finding doctor who saves thousands of lives.

The great machine inside the truck ate the first tote-load of files and the driver went back into the garage for more. He worked quickly and quietly, dumping the contents of another several boxes into the receptacle. If he noticed that I was trembling with suppressed sobs beneath my wide-rimmed hat and sunglasses, he didn't say anything. I couldn't blame him. I'm sure he had other clients to get to that day. I was paying him by the tote-load, not by the hour.

While he worked, I looked back in time and calculated that this would be my seventeenth move. That seemed amazing to me. I wondered if the trauma of moving so often was taking its toll on me without me realizing it. My mother had a sister who still lived in the same house she'd been born in.

My aunt was a very positive person. She giggled a lot. Did her good humor come from a stability I would never know?

The driver was just finishing up the second load, and I was just dealing with a fresh wave of self-pity, when I saw her lumbering in my direction: Rosemary, the neighborhood dog, the very same dog that Rick and Carmen and their kids had entertained (or had she entertained them?) back when I had first come to the house—the house that I could never have guessed then would one day be mine and then one day later no longer be mine. Gary and I hadn't seen her in a couple of weeks, and we had discussed the possibility that the neighbors who owned her might have put her down. She had a huge tumor on her shoulder, and something was wrong with one of her back legs too, because she was limping. Her once-beautiful red gold hair was dull and matted, and she stunk the way old dogs often do. But there she was, there for me, a creature who had known Rick not as a criminal but as a man who loved kids and animals and was even capable, at times, of loving life. I fell to my knees to welcome her and I burst into the tears that I had been holding in since the shredding truck arrived.

It went much easier after that. On the third load, the shredding apparatus jammed up and the guy had to climb into the truck and free up some of the half-eaten folders before he could go on. Rosemary sat on the lawn beside me and we watched together.

It took six loads to empty all of the boxes. I paid the driver $300 and he left. Rosemary stayed by my side to watch the truck move noisily down to the corner of the street and then turn and disappear. And it felt good to have her there with me, because she was loyal if nothing else. And it felt good to be me at that moment too, because I could say the same thing of myself. I had been a loyal friend.

About the Author

Linda DeFruscio is the founder and president of A & A Laser, Electrolysis & Skin Care Associates in the Boston area. Her articles on skincare, hair removal and other esthetic concerns have been published in many journals over the course of her 35-year-long career. *Cornered: Dr. Richard J. Sharpe As I Knew Him* is her first book. She is currently completing a second book, which will feature profiles of some of the many transgender people she has come to know through her work. Linda lives with her husband and is surrounded by extended family, including children and grandchildren.

Author web site: http://www.thecorneredbook.com/

If you enjoyed this book, please post a review
at your favorite online bookstore.

Twilight Times Books
P O Box 3340
Kingsport, TN 37664
Phone/Fax: 423-323-0183
www.twilighttimesbooks.com/